Scotland Saw His Glory

Acknowledgements

The editor exercised no originality in the volume before you. It is a compilation of materials gathered principally from the very scarce work by W. J. Couper of Glasgow entitled *Scottish Revivals* which was published in a limited edition of only thirty-seven copies in Dundee in 1918. This has been supplemented by materials from *The History of Revivals of Religion in the British Isles, Especially in Scotland* by Mary Lundie Duncan, published in Edinburgh in 1836, and *Narratives of Revivals of Religion in Scotland, Ireland, and Wales published under the Auspices of the Glasgow Revival Tract Society* in 1839 (the volumes from which Couper drew much of his material originally). Additional material has been added from *Narratives of Revivals of Religion in Scotland, Ireland, Wales, and America*, published in Philadelphia by the Presbyterian Board of Publication in 1855; *The Fulfilling of the Scriptures Or an Essay Shewing the Exact Accomplishment of the Word of God in His Works, Performed and to Be Performed, For Confirming of Believers and Convincing of Atheists of the Present Time: Containing Some Rare Histories of the Works and the Servants of God in the Church of Scotland* by Robert Fleming, Boston, 1743; and *Outpourings of the Spirit; or, a Narrative of Spiritual Awakenings in Different Ages and Countries*, Philadelphia, 1841.

Chapter two on *John Knox and the Reformation* has been edited from James Burns' volume *Revivals: Their Laws and Leaders,* the 1909 London edition.

Scotland Saw His Glory

A History of Revivals In Scotland

By
W. J. Couper, James Burns,
Mary Duncan, etc.

Edited by
Richard Owen Roberts

Wheaton, Illinois
1995

Published By
INTERNATIONAL AWAKENING PRESS
P. O. Box 232
Wheaton, Illinois 60189 U.S.A.
A Division Of
International Awakening Ministries, Inc.

Copyright 1995
by
Richard Owen Roberts
All Rights Reserved

Printed in the United States of America

ISBN 0-926474-16-2

Library of Congress
Catalog Card Number 95-078264

Contents

Acknowledgements	ii
Foreword	vii
Introductory Survey	9
1. John Knox & the Reformation	29
2. Sixteenth Century Men of Revival	63
3. The General Assembly of 1596	83
4. Stewarton, 1625	99
5. Kirk of Shotts, 1630	111
6. Cambuslang, 1742	125
7. Kilsyth, 1742	145
8. Beyond Cambuslang and Kilsyth, 1742	165
9. The Cambuslang Controversy	185
10. Moulin, 1799	197
11. Arran, 1812	215
12. Skye, 1812	225
13. Breadalbane	237
14. Lewis, 1824-1833	255
15. Kilsyth, 1830	269
16. 1859-1860	289
17. Moody and Sankey	307
18. Summary and Conclusion	325
Bibliography	337
Index	341

John Knox
From the original in possession of Lord Torphichen, at Calder House.

Foreword

As will be quickly evident, the period of history covered in this volume is only from the time of the Reformation thru the nineteenth century. There are two reasons for this: first, the long out-of-print sources used in this volume were all published prior to any revivals of this century, and second, at least abbreviated accounts of recent movements, especially in the Hebrides Islands, are still in print. It is to be hoped, however, that someone will provide us with a more definitive account of twentieth century movements than we now have.

Those with a scholarly bent will be particularly pained at the absence of documentation for so many of the quotations. While the general sources are cited in the acknowledgements and in the bibliography, the authors used in this volume felt no compulsion to conform to our more modern approaches to scholarship.

A volume on the history of revivals has the potential of instructing and inspiring. Every effort has been made to accomplish both in this book. Instruction is greatly needed in this day of confusion and uncertainty. I draw two particular themes to your attention:

First, note the frequency with which the Holy Spirit came to Scotland at Communion occasions. Without question, revival comes when God sends it, but there is some relationship between what His people do or don't do and His coming. One of the most treasured questions which has ever been asked me was this: "Having prayed for revival, is there anything else that it is legitimate to do?" The answer that I gave to that question is one I wish I could give to the entire interceding Church:

FOREWORD

"Having prayed for revival, we must now make the fullest possible use of the means of grace." If today's churches were to make the fullest possible use of all the means of grace—prayer, preaching, ordinances, fellowship, discipline—but especially that ordinance of the Lord's table, the prospects of revival would be richly enhanced. Just imagine what would happen if our celebration of the Lord's supper were extended to seven serious, heart-searching, God-honoring days!

Second, the immensely helpful details provided on the role of physical phenomena in the revivals should be given very careful consideration. In a day in which few believers seem able to distinguish between the work of Satan on the flesh and the work of God in the soul of man, there is an urgent need to weigh carefully the attitude toward prostrations and other physical phenomena which the wise leaders of Scottish revivals held. Several things seem very clear. When phenomena did appear, it tended to be early in the work of grace. As the movement deepened and extended, the phenomena lessened or ceased altogether. The most likely subjects of phenomena, especially prostrations, were those persons who resisted the Holy Spirit and would not immediately yield to Him. The occurrences of phenomena among believers was uncommon. The subjects of phenomena tended to be less stable converts than those that came to faith apart from it, the fall-away rate among them being higher than among those persons who yielded quickly to the Spirit's convicting power.

But inspiration is also a concern. The very title itself is stirring—***Scotland Saw His Glory!*** No people on earth ever see more of the glory of God than during seasons of revival, and no people ever needed to see His glory more than the people of our day. Hopefully, this volume will encourage you to cry, "Do it again, LORD! Do it again!"

Introductory Survey

The use of the word "revival," to describe such religious movements as are chronicled in the following pages is of comparatively recent origin. Its earliest appearance in this sense, according to the editors of the Oxford English Dictionary, is to be found in the "Magnalia Christi Americana" of Cotton Mather, published in 1702—a fact not without interest when it is remembered that America has been described as the "Land of Revivals."[1] It was not, however, until the second half of the same century that the word came into popular use. The writers on the phenomena at Cambuslang in 1742 were forced to employ such circumlocutions as "the great success of the gospel," "the present progress of the gospel," or "the wonderful conversion." It is true that after the movement had reached the disagreeable region of controversy, it came to be called, both by detractors and by supporters, the "Cambuslang Wark"—a name that had some sanction in former usage—but the title did

---

[1] It is important to note that although we are not aware of any writers using the word "revival" before Cotton Mather, the blessing itself was much in the minds of American writers prior to him. They were greatly concerned about the condition of the church in their day and frequently used such expressions as "That the Lord's gracious presence may be continued with posterity," Eleazer Mather, 1672; "The prolonging of our prosperous days in the land," Thomas Shepard, 1673; "The former spirit of New England revived in this generation," Peter Folger, 1676; "The effusions of the Spirit," Samuel Hooker, 1677; "Prayer for a Spirit of converting grace to be poured out," Increase Mather, 1678; "The necessity of reformation," Synod of Boston, 1679; "The necessity of the pouring out of the Spirit on high upon a sinning apostate people set under judgment," William Adams, 1679; "Returning unto God," Increase Mather, 1680; and "The wonderful works of God," Cotton Mather, 1690.

not become a general one for such movements. The widespread effects of the religious awakenings in the middle of the century, both in England and in Scotland, seemed to demand a more technical term. The most suitable was found in the word "revival," which, for at least a century previously, had been employed to describe an awakening interest in other departments of life. In addition to its inherent appropriateness, the designation had the advantage of being Scriptural. It suggested such texts as that of the psalmist—"Wilt Thou not revive us again: that Thy people may rejoice in Thee?" (Psalm 85:6).

Some of the contemporary descriptions of the earlier works of grace are interesting. Fleming, for example, speaks of the Stewarton Revival as an "extraordinary outletting of the Spirit," and the phrase is something more than the author's acknowledgment of the origin of the movement: it is his name for it. Similarly, he calls the events at Shotts "a convincing appearance of God and downpouring of the Spirit," while like experiences in Ireland are named "a solemn and great work of God." A fine phrase was sometimes used in speaking of American revivals: it describes them as "a general attention to religion." The impressive work done under the ministry of Jonathan Edwards in New England became known as the "Great Awakening," a name which is still used side by side with that of "revival."

But while it took a long time to settle upon a definite name for the phenomena, the phenomena themselves were age-long. Records of them are to be found in the Old Testament, and they abound in the history of the Church since the time of Christ. "They have not been confined to one generation," says Principal Lindsay. "Every age and every century of the Christian Church has experienced them, has seen them come unexpectedly, unobtrusively, almost imperceptibly in their first beginnings, has watched them grow in intensity and spread out on all sides,

Introductory Survey

no one knows how; has noted them die down and pass away." But though their active features have been temporary, revivals have not been evanescent in their effects. Long after their activities had disappeared, the impetus derived from them lived on. As the same scholar says in another place: "From one point of view, and that not the least important, the history of the Church flows on from one time of revival to another." Revivals have in fact made for the preservation of the Faith and the continuance of the Church.

The isolation of Scotland, both geographically and, with the exception of its intimacy with France, politically, may be sufficient explanation why it seems to have had little or no share in the great revival movements that now and again swept over parts of Europe during the Middle Ages. "Scotland," says Dr. Lindsay, "never seems to have been visited by those revivals of religion which from time to time awakened the medieval Church to its Christian duties; the force of these great movements always seems to have spent itself before they reached Scotland." Prior to the Reformation, the turbulence of the nobility and, later, the evil lives of the priesthood made the soil of Scotland a difficult ground for the growth of religious enthusiasm and reality. Lollardism did, indeed, secure a foothold for a time, chiefly in the southwest, but it seems to have been the only protest against the prevailing deadness. That it made some progress and gave some concern to the authorities is acknowledged.

"The schip of faith, tempestuous wind and rane,
 Dryvis in the see of Lollerdy that blaws."

But evangelical truth was not yet strong enough to prevail against the reign of error.

The Reformation was Scotland's first great religious awakening—an awakening all the more thorough because of the people's deep sleep throughout the preceding centuries. That the

Scotland Saw His Glory

movement was a spiritual revival has been obscured by the fact that it was political and ecclesiastical in its outward aspect. Its historians have laid almost exclusive stress upon what can be found in State documents and in the papers and letters of politicians and churchmen. No doubt the movement did consist largely of conferences and negotiations between parties, of the passage of armies, of legislation proposed or actual, and of the devices of statesmen. Discussions about forms of church government and discipline were required for a new ecclesiastical establishment had to be created. But, important as these things are, they did not after all constitute the whole of the Scottish Reformation. Its real history lay deeper.

From one point of view, the Reformation was merely part of the intellectual renaissance that was visiting western Europe. It was the outcome of the fresh breathings of intellectual and political liberty that was calling into new life the long dormant faculties and energies of the nation. For Scotland, the Reformation was not, as Professor Hume Brown points out, merely "the substitution of one religion for another: it was the highest consciousness of the nation deliberately choosing between authority on the one hand and individualism on the other." In another aspect, it was the birth time of a nation. As becomes such an occasion, the throes and pangs were oftentimes violent. "It was not a smooth business," says Carlyle, "but it was welcome surely, and cheap at that price, had it been rougher. On the whole, cheap at any price, as life is. The people began to live; they needed first of all to do that, at what cost and costs soever."

In still another view of it, the Scottish Reformation was a triumph for democracy. It has been asserted that it was mainly the work of the nobility and the upper classes. They may have been the leaders in the cause, but there can be no doubt as to those whom the Reformers had always in mind when arrange-

Introductory Survey

ments were being made for the future. They never forgot that it was the common people who were chiefly interested. The Scottish Reformation, however, being all these things was yet more than them all. It was in reality a deep moving of the heart of the nation towards God. The argument might take the form of debates on doctrines, church government, and the method of public worship: the real question at issue was how each human soul could best find God through Jesus Christ.

That this side of the movement was widespread and embraced all classes is evident. As early as 1547 an English Admiral wrote from Dundee to Protector Somerset that in his neighborhood "the most part of the town favors the Word of God and loveth not the priests and bishops very well," and he adds: "They are much desirous here in the country of Angus and Fife to have a good preacher and Bibles and Testaments and other good English books of Tyndale and Frith's translation, which I promised them." This could no doubt be written of other districts both then and afterwards.

Perhaps it will be enough, in this rapid sketch, to point to two circumstances as showing how the Scottish Reformation was a real religious revival among the people.

Song is acknowledged to be a most powerful influence in spreading doctrines of all kinds among people for it has a peculiar appeal to the multitude. What Luther's hymns did for the propagation of the reformed faith in Germany is well known. Scotland had the same experience. "Indeed," says Professor Mitchell, "after the prayerful study of the Scriptures . . . there was not, during the twenty years of struggles and suffering which preceded the full establishment of the Reformed Church, any instrumentality that contributed so much to keep alive the faith of the sufferers, to spread their doctrine among their countrymen, and to bring their opponents and their teaching into discredit as the godly and spiritual songs, the tragedies and ballads of those whose hearts He had touched with the love of His truth." We can still read how the Wedderburns' *Dundee Psalms* entered into the life of the people and how naturally they became the expression of certain experiences. "Probably the range of their circulation was much more among the middle than among the higher classes of our countrymen, and especially among the substantial burghers of the cities and trading communities; but among these classes their influence was confessedly great." The connection of sacred song with religious revival is too marked to be accidental and there is no reason to suppose that in Scotland at the Reformation they were separated. Perhaps no one now would be inclined to defend the destruction of sacred buildings that took place, but the record concerning the iconoclasts of Perth is surely not without significance. It is said of them "so praising God continually in singing of psalms and spiritual songs, they rejoiced that the Lord wrought thus happily with them."

The other point is the kind of preaching that was welcomed by the people. We read of secret gatherings where the newly-found gospel was heard with joy. Small congregations met here and there, not to discuss the political situation created by the advance of Protestant opinions, but to hear the Word expounded and applied. Evangelical preachers could obtain an audience almost anywhere. When no authorized minister was available, the people met and mutually exhorted and instructed one another.

It is probably not unfair to take John Knox himself as an example of the preachers of the time. He was a man of genius, eloquence, and power, as a subsequent chapter will show, and no doubt stood head and shoulders above them all; he was, nevertheless, one of them in his contentions and doctrine. Their message was his, even if sometimes they took their cue from him. He was but the chief of a company upon all of whom was

Introductory Survey

laid the necessity to preach the gospel.

When Knox returned to Scotland in 1555, the government was still hostile to the Reformed Faith, but the people eagerly received both the man and his message. "The trumpet," he wrote his mother-in-law, "blew the ald sound thrie dayis together till privat housses of indifferent largenes culd not containe the voice of it. . . . O! sueit war the death that suld follow sic fortie dayis in Edinbrugh, as heir I have had thrie. Rejoise, Mother, the time of our delyverance approaches: for as Sathan rageth, sa dois the grace of the Halie Spreit abound, and daylie giveth new testimonyis of the everlasting love of oure mercifull Father." What the message he delivered was is apparent from the letter he sent his "brethren in Scotland," when again driven into exile. "Nothing," he said, "is mair dispytfull to Satan than Chryst Jesus exaltit, trewlie preached and constantlie affirmit to be the onlie Saviour of the warld." What searching effect Knox's preaching had upon the souls and consciences of his hearers is evident from the tale James Melville has to tell. He describes how Knox came to St. Andrews in 1571 and expounded the prophecies of Daniel. "I haid my pen and my little book," he says, "and took away sic things as I could comprehend. In the opening upe of his text, he was moderate the space of an halff houre: bot when he enterit to application, he maid me sa grew and tremble, that I could nocht hald a pen to wryt." It was preaching of this kind and with such a message that made the word of Reformation so triumphant in Scotland. While its effects were partial elsewhere, "in Scotland the whole nation was converted by lump. . . . Lo! here a nation born in one day; yea, molded into one congregation, and sealed as a fountain with a solemn oath and covenant."

Knox died in 1572, and by that time the Reformation was in a measure consolidated. As was almost inevitable, a certain

Scotland Saw His Glory

reaction in public manners and morals took place after the stress of conflict and uncertainty had been long enough removed. There is ample testimony in contemporary legislation and in the proceedings of the General Assembly, as well as in those of the inferior church courts, to prove that a grave state of affairs prevailed morally. A recent writer does not hesitate to say that "thirty years of the gospel had done nothing more than illuminate the borders of the darkest places." Hill Burton speaks strongly of "the spirit of ferocity, rapacity, and sensuality that was spreading moral desolation over the land." But the country was not left to its own devices. There was a sufficiency of spiritual leaders among the people who were alive to the growing evils of the time. The persistent attempts of John Davidson to create an adequate sense of the dangers that abounded and the success his efforts achieved in the Assembly of 1596 will be narrated in due course. Hill Burton is not likely to be accused of partiality towards religious movements of the kind that would be favored by Davidson, yet he is constrained to call the results that followed the work of these devoted men "a great religious revival" and to say it was so slightly connected with current political events "as to have a separate history of its own." It was the time of the first National Covenant when many took an oath of fidelity to the gospel and when an exiled minister could be received home again to Edinburgh by an entire population, who, "with bear heads and loud voices, sang to the praise of God, and testifeing of grait joy and consolation, the 124th Psalm. 'Now Israel may say and that trewlie, 'till heavin and erthe resoundid.'" Though many deplorable things prevailed, there was thus always a seed to serve Him.

Some corners of the land, indeed, were visited with special blessing. The reputation of William Cowper suffered greatly in the eyes of his countrymen because in 1612 he accepted a bishopric, but he was nevertheless a pious and earnest man, and

Introductory Survey

he exercised a fruitful ministry with significant revival benefits.

About the same time, a work of grace was done in Ayr under the ministry of John Welsh, Knox's son-in-law. Few particulars are available, but the tradition of the greatness of the work accomplished has remained until this day. "If his diligence was great," says Wodrow, "so it is doubted whether his sowing in painfulness or his harvest in success, was greater: for if either his spiritual exercises in seeking the Lord, or his fruitfulness in converting souls, be considered, they will be found unparalleled in Scotland. And many years after Mr. Welsh's death, Mr. David Dickson, at that time a flourishing minister at Irvine, was frequently heard to say, when people talked to him of the success of his ministry, that the grape gleanings in Ayr in Mr. Welsh's time were far above the vintage of Irvine in his own."

The opening years of the seventeenth century brought struggle and darkness for the Scottish Church. Her liberties were crushed and alien forms of worship forced upon her. But the period was not altogether fruitless of religious impression and spiritual results. One of the most famous preachers of the age was Robert Bruce, and his ministry covered almost the whole time. Calderwood testifies of him that he "won many thousands of souls to Christ." In addition to the work of separate ministers, there were the remarkable outpourings of the Spirit at Stewarton and Shotts, "a dispensation," says Kirkton, "both strange and new amongst the people of Scotland." These gracious movements are treated at length in the chapters that follow. Meantime it may be enough to say that they had at least these effects: they impressed the truth that, after all, personal piety is better than the mere exaltation of ecclesiastical authority, and they prepared the way for the national outburst of religious enthusiasm that marked the signing of the National Covenant.

Scotland Saw His Glory

The Covenant was signed February 28th, 1638, and was the outward indication of perhaps the most extraordinary revival of religion that Scotland has ever seen. The whole country was moved by a religious fervor as even the Reformation had not moved it. The subscription by the people over all the land, gentle and simple alike, was not a formality connected with a political or patriotic device. Many signed it with their blood. All signed it in the fear of the Lord and to the glory of His kingdom. Preaching at St. Andrews a month after the notable scene in Greyfriars Churchyard, Alexander Henderson declared: "This is a note of the power of God that He has touched the hearts of the people, that there was never such a howling and a weeping heard amongst them this long time as there is now; and yet it is not a weeping for sorrow, but a weeping for joy. How oft has there been preachings in the most part of the congregations of this land this long time past, and yet people have never found the power of it in working upon their hearts." But all was now changed. The people gathered in the churches to hear the Word with gladness and take the Covenant with tears in their eyes.

Livingston's experience in this respect was probably not unique. He tells how "I was present at Lanark and at severall other parishes, when on ane Sabbath after the afternoon sermon, the Covenant was read and sworn, and may truly say that in all my life, except one day in the church of Shotts, I never saw such motions from the Spirit of God: all the people generally and most willingly concurring, where I have seen above 1000 persons all at once lifting up their hands, and the tears dropping down from their eyes." Fleming's summing up of the situation was—"Must we not say that since the land was engaged by Covenant to the Lord in these late times, what a solemn outletting of the Spirit hath been seen: a large harvest, with much of the fruit of the gospel discernable? which we may say,

Introductory Survey

with a warrant, hath been proven in the inbringing of thousands to Christ."

When the horrors of the "Killing Times" were abroad in the land, the poor, driven, and harried people looked back with longing to the peace and privilege they had enjoyed from these days of the Covenant to the close of the Commonwealth. Naphtali spoke of them as the time when the land was "holiness unto the Lord." Kirkton's estimate has been called in question, but there seems to be no good reason for rejecting his testimony. He speaks of "the great success the Word preached had in sanctifying the people of the nation. And I verily believe there were more souls converted to Christ in that short period of time than in any season since the Reformation, though of treeple its duration. Nor was there ever greater purity and plenty of the means of grace than was in their time. Ministers were painfull; people were diligent; and if a man had seen one of their solemn communions where many congregations met in great multitudes, some dozen of ministers used to preach, and the people continued, as it were, in a sort of trance (so serious were they in spiritual exercises) for three days at least, he would have thought it a solemnity unknown to the rest of the world."

The outstanding ministry of the time was that of William Guthrie of Fenwick. Livingston calls him "a great light in the west of Scotland," and there can be no doubt as to the wonderful results of his preaching. Crowds journeyed to hear him from all quarters—Glasgow, Paisley, Hamilton, Lanark, and places even more remote. "It was their usual practice to come to Fenwick upon Saturday, spend the greater part of that night in prayer to God, and conversation about the great concerns of their souls, attend on public worship on the Sabbath, dedicate the remainder of that holy day to religious exercise, and then, on the Monday, go home ten, twelve, or twenty miles, without grudging the fatigue of so long a way and the want of sleep and other refreshments." Kirkton tells us the country people "turned the corn field of his glieb into a town, every one building a house for his family upon it; only that they might live under the drop of his ordinances and ministry." The secret of this attractive ministry is probably to be found in the fact that Guthrie is said to have had "a strange way of persuading sinners to close with Christ, and answering all objections that might be proposed."

The name of John Carstares is not so widely known as that of Guthrie, but he seems to have been a man of the same stamp. He was the father of the famous Principal Carstares and, until cast out at the Restoration, minister of the High Church of Glasgow. One or two stories are told of his power as a preacher which recall the famous Monday at Kirk of Shotts. Once he assisted at a communion at Kirkintilloch, and the evening proving very stormy, the people lingered in the church. He addressed the waiting congregation "upon believing in Christ; and there was such a mighty power came along with it that either two or three hundred dated their conversion from that discourse." Upon another occasion about the same time, he was helping at a sacrament at Cadder. "Upon the Sabbath he was wonderfully assisted in his first prayer, and had a strange gale throu all the sermon; and there was a strange motion upon all the hearers." When he came to serve the table, "all in the house were strangely affected, and glory seemed to fill that house!" Such incidents were not isolated. Oliver Cromwell's rule may have been of iron but the people at least had a measure of the outpouring of the Spirit of God.

Although the plans of Charles II and James II and their advisers were designed to destroy evangelical truth throughout the land, the period covered by their reigns was nevertheless in many respects a time of extraordinary fidelity to the interests of vital religion. The numerous martyrdoms are sufficient proof

Introductory Survey

that the gospel had free course in many lives. The persistency with which clandestine meetings were held and evangelical preachers heard at them, in spite of manifest danger, shows that it was not a mere stubborn defiance of the authorities which caused these meetings, but a real hunger for the living Word of God. Many examples could be given, but perhaps the following may be enough. Hugh Miller says that a hollow is still shown among the hills on the east of Ross-shire where a notable communion was held in September 1675. The minister of the parish had been driven from his congregation in 1662, but he contrived to continue his ministrations to an attached people. "Many serious people," says Wodrow, who tells the story, "were longing much to partake of the sacrament of the Lord's Supper, and having been at much pains in public preaching and from house to house to prepare them for it . . . he administered that holy ordinance at Obsdale in the house of the lady dowager of Fowlis." Two ministers assisted, for which one of them had to pay dearly. At the last sermon "there was a great many present, and the eldest Christians there declared they had not been witnesses to the like. In short, there were so sensible and glorious discoveries made of the Son of Man, and such evident presence of the Master of assemblies this day and the preceding, that the people seemed to be in a transport, and their souls filled with heaven and breathing thither while their bodies were upon the earth; and some were almost at that, whether in the body or out of the body I cannot tell. Even some drops fell on strangers."

Praying societies had existed since the earlier days of the century; they became exceeding precious when fiery persecution was rolling over the land. The whole time, however, was not propitious for an open movement of religious revival, but whenever the pressure of persecution was removed, the life that was in the people showed itself in the usual way. "I have heard old Christians," says one of Gillies's informants, "speak of a remarkable reviving and uncommon power attending the Word immediately after the Revolution, in the West and South of Scotland, Fife, Lothian, etc. Particularly I have heard of a remarkable communion at Stow, near Galashiels, just about the time of the Revolution."

The Church as it was constituted at the "glorious Revolution" did not satisfy everyone, but the arrangement came to do this at least—it gave a distracted, tortured country rest, and that in itself was cause for gratitude. Men had time to possess their souls. It would be easy to paint a somewhat sad picture of the state of religion throughout the country in the years that succeeded the enthronement of William and Mary, but the story has another side. Daniel Defoe may not be an impartial observer for his affections were quite pointedly drawn out towards Scotland. His verdict, however, is extremely favorable. Contrasting England with Scotland, he emphasized the enthusiastic and laborious efforts of the latter's ministers on behalf of the people and extols the attention which the people themselves gave to divine things. It was amazing, he exclaims, "To see a congregation sit with looks so eager, as if they were to eat the words as they came out of the mouth of the preacher; to see the affection with which they hear, that there shall be a general sound of a mourning through the whole church upon the extraordinary warmth of expression in the minister, and this not affected and designed, but casual and undissembled." Long afterwards Whitefield was struck with the sound of turning pages when he gave out his text for the first time before a Scottish audience. Defoe had noticed the same thing: "In a church in Scotland, if you shut your eyes when the minister names any text of Scripture, you shall hear a little rustling noise over the whole place, made by turning the leaves of the Bible." There may have been indifference in some quarters, but there

Introductory Survey

seems no good ground for doubting the general earnestness of the people.

There is a consensus of opinion that when we advance into the eighteenth century we proceed deeper and deeper into the most lifeless section of Scottish religious history. Even those who have loved the Church best have been constrained sorrowfully to admit that she fell from her high estate. "There was a lack of open vision in the Church of Scotland during the eighteenth century," says Principal Tulloch. "She failed to realize the greatness of Her mission as a National Church. She failed to witness as she ought to have done to the living love of a Divine Saviour." But the land was not altogether in darkness. Between 1730 and 1740, there were some remarkable outbreaks of religious awakening on the continent of Europe and in America. Away in the far north of Scotland, in Sutherland and Ross, similar occasions of merciful visitation took place about the same time.

The "Marrow Controversy" and the "Secessions" had their ecclesiastical aspect, but they also showed that in the hearts of many there was a deep-rooted love of Evangelical truth. When Whitefield came to Scotland in 1741, he found the common people eager to hear him. "Every morning," he wrote from Edinburgh on August 15, "I have a levee of wounded souls. At seven in the morning we have a lecture in the fields attended not only by the common people, but persons of great rank. I have reason to think several of the latter sort are coming to Jesus. Little children are also much wrought upon. Congregations consist of many thousands. I preach twice daily, and expound in private houses at night, and am employed in speaking to souls under distress a great part of the day." The description can truthfully be applied to many a scene which Whitefield saw in Scotland during the next few years. The movement, comprehensively known as the "Cambuslang

Scotland Saw His Glory

Revival," which broke like glad sunshine over large tracts of the country in 1742, needs only to be referred to here. It may be regarded as part of the work done by Whitefield: it is best looked upon as a separate awakening having affinities with similar events then going on in various parts of the world.

At least one historian believed that the reign of "Moderatism" did not begin officially until 1752. It is certainly true that the second half of the eighteenth century was the most barren evangelically. The whole land lay in a kind of religious stupor, with only slight stirrings at long intervals here and there. When revival outpourings fell on Moulin in 1800, they were noted as the first drops after the long drought. However, the Spirit of God had not wholly deserted the land. Dr. Kennedy wrote of the favored district of Easter Ross: "There met at Kiltearn, on a Communion occasion in 1782, under the preaching of Dr. Fraser of Kirkhill, perhaps as blessed a congregation as ever assembled in Scotland. Hundreds of God's people from the surrounding district were there, and all of them had as much of the comforting presence of the Lord as they were able to endure. It was then the culminating point of spiritual prosperity of Ross-shire was reached."

An interesting story, too, comes from the northern parish of Tongue. After being settled there for four years, Pastor William McKenzie came to the conclusion that his work was a failure, worldliness having taken the people for its own. Accordingly, in 1773 he told his parishioners he hoped God would soon remove him to a more suitable sphere. His address proved the turning-point in the history of the parish. "From that day forward," says the Rev. A. MacGillivray, "there was a blessed outpouring of the Spirit of God. He told me himself (and he was a man incapable of vain boasting) that for years afterwards he never preached on the Lord's Day but some of his people on the ensuing week, at times as many as six or eight, came to him

Introductory Survey

under conviction of sin, asking the way to Jesus. . . . I remember asking him what were the truths in his preaching which seemed to have been specially blessed for producing the awakening, and I could never forget his answer. . . . He told me that the truth which seemed above all others to impress and awaken his people was the dying love of Christ."

Before the nineteenth century actually dawned, there was evidence that the worst time for Scottish religion had passed. A more evangelical ministry had been slowly scattered over the land. It had come to be felt that necessity lay upon believers actively to propagate the faith both within their own borders and beyond them. Missionary societies, home and foreign, were being formed. Accounts of the moral and educational neglect in which large tracts of the Highlands lay, aroused the conscience of the country and set it to work to carry out needed reforms in the remoter districts. Not only were many parishes furnished with educational equipment that was distinctly religious, but preaching tours were carried through on behalf of the Churches in the south. For almost the first time in Scottish history, lay evangelists undertook the duty of preaching, and men like the Haldanes and their followers carried the gospel over the whole land.

The first place to feel the awakening impulse was the parish of Moulin in the Perthshire Highlands—and it is notable that the districts where evangelical religion made the greatest advances during the next thirty years were all beyond the Highland line. The gospel seems to have come to them with all the freshness of a new discovery.

The part the Haldanes played in this general revival of religion was undoubtedly great. Their energy in penetrating to remote places produced spiritual movements where they had never appeared before. The tour of 1797 extended to Caithness and the Orkneys, whose religious records were barren of revival

Scotland Saw His Glory

history. Everywhere, the people flocked in thousands to hear the missionaries. "Multitudes," says the biographer of the brothers, "dated their turning to God from the period of this awakening. Several years later," he adds, "the Rev. John Cleghorn publicly named, as within his own knowledge in the little town of Wick alone, forty cases in which there had been a solid work of conversion by the preaching of James Haldane, which he compares to an 'electric shock.'" The same was so, with perhaps less conspicuous results, on subsequent tours elsewhere.

It is somewhat curious, however, that although the Haldanes did memorable work in stirring up the Scottish dry bones, their names are not associated with any of the historic revivals of the time. Their followers had indeed to do with some of the awakening impulses felt in Perthshire, and Robert Haldane appeared as an interested spectator at Breadalbane and Dundee. But the function of the evangelist brothers seems rather to have been to aid in creating throughout Scotland the conditions necessary for the coming of revival blessing.

If one name more than another is attached to these special outpourings of grace, it is that of the famous Dr. MacDonald of Ferintosh, whom men called the "Apostle of the North" from the multitude of his journeys and the magnitude of his labors. For many years he moved over the Highlands, and it was seldom that he preached without conversions following. Peculiar interest surrounds what may not inaccurately be described as the beginning of these special labors. He had been transferred to Urquhart in 1813, and a few days before his first communion there, his wife died. His Session tried to persuade him to forego the trial of preaching so soon after the distressing event but he refused to be guided by them. On the Sabbath, ten thousand, it is said, gathered to the ordinance. MacDonald's text was: "I will betroth thee unto me forever." "Few eyes were

Introductory Survey

tearless in that vast assembly," says his biographer, "and when, in the evening, he appealed to the unconverted, commending to them the love of Jesus, urging on their acceptance His offer of marriage, and warning them of the danger of refusing His advances, the hearts of many sinners were pierced. The excitement at last was very great, the groans and outcries of the stricken ones sometimes drowning the voice of the preacher. During the closing service on Monday the same scene was repeated. The awakening, then begun, continued for some time." The news of these events spread and was the indirect occasion of the revival in Breadalbane.

Though the Highlands were thus being blessed, it was not until 1839 that a marked movement took place in the Lowlands. As will subsequently be narrated, this revival originated at Kilsyth and spread over a large part of the country. The Disruption came almost immediately after it. Though outwardly a conflict which had the appearance of an ecclesiastical struggle, the Disruption was nevertheless a real spiritual movement among the people. There is abundant testimony that this was the case. It is perhaps needless to elaborate the point, but the following may be taken as typical evidence of the fact: "I have now lived," said the Rev. William Grant of Ayr, "to see the Revival of 1859 and the religious movement of 1874. I cannot, and therefore do not, speak of other localities, but I may safely say that in Ayr the earnestness was deeper and the fruit more abundant in the summer and autumn of 1843 than during any time of my ministry. . . . As I gazed on the upturned countenances of the assembled people, they always seemed to me to say: 'Sir, we would see Jesus.'"

From 1843 to the end of the nineteenth century, Scotland was seldom without the Spirit's working in some part of the country. In 1846 the fishermen of Ferryden were deeply moved, just as the farmers of Forfarshire had a special visitation of

Scotland Saw His Glory

grace in 1868. The whole land was drenched with heavenly showers in 1859-60. The coming of Moody and Sankey in 1873 brought salvation to thousands of souls. Other evangelists, lay and ordained, carried on the good work in divers places and in divers manners. Professor Henry Drummond opened up a new field when he touched the educated youth of the land in the remarkable work he accomplished among the students of Edinburgh University in the "Eighties." As Dr. N. L. Walker has said: "It is no longer an uncommon thing to hear of a work of grace going on in this part of the country and the other. Scotland in that respect has come to resemble America, where revivals are incidents of constant experience."

To those who long for the full light of the gospel day, the present hour may be dark enough in Scotland. There is no open vision and the love of many waxeth cold. But it seems ordained in the economy of grace that there should be such occasions. "Christianity," says Dr. Lindsay, "has flowed like a stream of clear fresh water over the arid soul of mankind. It is too often forgotten that the stream, like an Arabian river, seems frequently to lose itself in the soil it was meant to fertilize. There must be explosive outbursts every now and then from the fountainhead, and revivals are manifestations of this volcanic force which is latent in Christianity." The river at present runs underground, but still—it runs.

Chapter 1

John Knox and the Reformation

Four hundred years ago, Scotland was one of the most benighted countries in Europe. The towns were few, thinly populated, and wretchedly built, while the people were sunk in a degrading poverty and in the grossest ignorance. The feudal system which elsewhere, with the growth of the population and the increase of trade was broken down, was still supreme in Scotland at the beginning of the sixteenth century. That source of a nation's wealth and stability which we call the middle class did not then exist. The state was composed of three orders—the clergy, the nobility, and the people. The people existed merely as the vassals of the baron. He was their protector, and in return they tilled his land, fought his battles, and in all the other relations of life were acknowledged as his serfs.

A like condition prevailed in spiritual affairs. The people were the serfs of their ecclesiastical superiors. They were sunk in the grossest superstitions and in the most slavish obedience. Independence, as we know the term, had no real existence. The people were enslaved in body and mind.

Three influences were at work, silently converging and uniting to break up this condition. By destroying the old they cleared the way for reformation. The first of these was intellectual, the second political, and the third religious.

The intellectual factor was the renaissance of learning. For centuries the minds of men had been imprisoned and held in servitude to the church. Art, science, and even literature were subordinated to theology. Freedom of thought, the rights of private judgement, liberty of investigation, and the opportunity of public criticism were all alike denied. Wherever an attempt

Scotland Saw His Glory

was made to break the shackles, it encountered an instant and implacable opposition. The hand of the ecclesiastic darted out to seize the victim who was given the choice of recantation or the stake.

Slowly, as the world rolled out of those dark centuries, this bondage was broken. The mind of man cannot be permanently imprisoned. The Middle Ages were but the slumbering wintertime preparing for the festal joy and radiance of the spring. The birth of learning was awakening a new hope and preparing the way for a revived spiritual life. That great wave, which spread across the greater part of the continent of Europe, sent a tiny ripple which broke against the shores of Britain and awoke a response even in the north. The connection between France and Scotland had long been close, and this was not without its compensations. Scottish noblemen who fought in the French army brought back with them into their rude homes something of the polish, courtesy, and the outward show, if not the inner refinements, of learning. The awakening of the intellect, though confined to the narrowest limits, was sufficient to inspire a certain number of youthful enthusiasts to leave their own shores and, repairing to the Continent, to imbibe something of the new learning. When they returned they quickly infected others with a like enthusiasm. This was one of the factors preparing the way, but there was a second and more important one.

For more than a century, Scotland had been rent by internal dissension. On the one side were the powerful nobles. On the other side were the king and the clergy. Each was fighting for supremacy. At the beginning of the sixteenth century, victory seemed to rest with the nobility. Constant wars with England had depleted the country. By weakening the central power, they had added to the security of the nobles, who, aided by the physical structure of the country, shut themselves up in their fortresses and bade defiance to all authority. On the death of

John Knox and the Reformation

James IV in 1513 and during the minority of his son, the control of the State passed entirely into their hands. They held the king a prisoner, and the clergy, who were the natural allies of the crown, were powerless to help. However, in 1528 there occurred an event which altered the whole situation and which was destined to profoundly affect the history of Scotland. A conspiracy, organized by Cardinal Beaton, was set afoot. It aimed at the release of the king and the subjugation of the nobles. The plot was successfully carried through, and the king took refuge in Stirling Castle.

Once more the reins of government changed hands through this daring act. The Church was now supreme and the nobles were ruthlessly persecuted and driven from the land. The struggle, however, was not over. It broke out again and again with increased fury. On the one side was the Church, seeking to guard its authority and its riches. On the other side was the nobility, embittered by persecution, caring nothing for the Church, but thirsting for revenge and looking with a greedy eye toward the Church's wealth. Between the two, the chief pawn in the game was the king, who was working for his own interests and leaning naturally toward the side most likely to further those interests. With this in view, he increased the power of the clergy, nominated them for every important position under the crown, and by such acts, so alienated and exasperated the nobles that their acceptance of Protestant principles, whether they believed them or not, gave them their one hope of revenge.

The corrupt state of the church and clergy, which existed everywhere at the beginning of the sixteenth century, found no exception in Scotland. Nowhere was the prevailing corruption more apparent. While the people were held down in a debasing poverty, the clergy were everywhere bent on amassing wealth. Half of the wealth of the country was in their hands. Bishops and abbots rivalled the nobles in the magnificence of their retinues while they scandalously neglected their spiritual office. They never condescended to preach and were too ignorant to have done so if they had chosen. The Bishop of Dunkeld, who "thanked God that he knew neither the Old nor the New Testament," was typical of his class. Benefices were openly bought and sold, and whole parishes were left without incumbents in order that the Bishop might enjoy their emoluments.

Quentin Kennedy, the Catholic apologist, describes with frankest candor the system by which benefices were filled: "And when they have gotten a benefice, if they have a brother or son who can neither sing nor say, nourished in vice all his days, he shall be immediately mounted on a mule with a sidegown and a round bonnet, and then it is a question whether he or his mule know best to do his office." The lives of the clergy were scandalously corrupt. Many of them lived in open immorality, and the people perished through lack of knowledge. Such services as occurred were conducted in a dead language of which the people were entirely ignorant and which many of the priests could not even correctly read. The country swarmed with ignorant and idle monks who, both by menace and force, robbed the poor of the very necessities of life and, not content with this, forced themselves into the very chambers of the dying to extort bequests, disturbing their last moments by their rapacity.

Prayer, as an act of communion of the soul with God and as a means of consolation in times of distress, was practically unknown. To the people enslaved in superstition, a paternoster acted like a spell. If it was repeated forward, it brought blessings from heaven; if it was repeated backward, it thwarted the designs of hell. The turbulent state of the country, its poverty owing to the absence of manufactures and large industries, and its sanguinary and incessant wars added enor-

John Knox and the Reformation

mously to the influence and numbers of the clergy. The timid sought the Church for its protection, the ambitious for its influence, and the avaricious for its wealth. Exceptions, of course, there must have been. Did not Thomas a' Kempis live in encloistered retreat through all the corrupt period preceding the Reformation, directing the gaze of his soul exclusively on Christ and living unspotted by the world?

There must have been in Scotland, as well, many who had not bowed the knee to Baal and who, amid terrible temptations, kept the flame of spiritual love alight in their souls. But these were the exceptions. The light was dying out of the souls of men. Darkness had covered the earth, and gross darkness the people. It was one of these crises in a nation's life when, if the race were not to sink back into a worse state than barbarism and lose all that the centuries had toiled for, some sudden and dramatic act was required. The nation, like Israel of old, waited for the fulfillment of the prophecy that when darkness covered the earth, and gross darkness the people, the Lord would arise, and His glory be seen, so that all those in darkness might come to the light, and to the brightness of His rising.[1] The great and comforting truth of history is that God is ever preparing new epiphanies, that man cannot "reel back into the beast" and lose all that mankind has won. The powers of evil and corruption can flourish for a while, but a limit is put to their empire. When that limit is reached, the gathering waters are already heaped up, the avalanche is already preparing, and the dislodgement of a single stone is sufficient to set its mighty forces in movement. Such was the case in Scotland, for God had prepared a man.

John Knox was born at Gifford Gate in the town of Haddington in the year 1505. This little town, nestled in the

---

[1] Isaiah 60:1,2.

Scotland Saw His Glory

heart of the richest agricultural district in Scotland, is of ancient fame. It became a royal burgh in the early part of the twelfth century and in the ruthless wars of those days was several times burned to the ground. A bridge which crosses the river Tyne leads to a suburb known as the Nungate, and the place where Knox's house stood is marked by an oak tree surrounded by a wall and railing. This tree was planted by Thomas Carlyle. Across the river, only a stone's throw away, in the beautiful parish church, Carlyle's wife, who claimed descent from the great Reformer, is laid to rest. Nestling in a green valley, amid fields of rich cultivation and beautiful in situation, the old town lies. It was once the scene of many bloody fights but is now steeped in peace and sleepy with age.

Of Knox's parentage, of his early life and associates, little is known. Haddington possessed one of the few schools in Scotland which could offer to its scholars anything approaching what might be called a liberal education. In early annuals this school is one of six mentioned as giving, in addition to the ordinary subjects of instruction, Latin and, in rare instances, Greek. To this school Knox was sent. In Haddington he remained until, at the age of seventeen, he entered the University of Glasgow. How long he remained there is uncertain. His name appears among the Incorporati in the annals of Glasgow college of the year 1522, but it is not found in those of subsequent years or indeed in those of any other Scottish university. This leads to the supposition that he may have remained a student without matriculating. He made no claims to scholarship although he was well acquainted with Latin. In Geneva, at middle age, he acquired proficiency in both Greek and Hebrew. Somewhere about the year 1530, he was ordained to the priesthood, though of his early life little is known until he embraced the Reformed Faith. He seems to have been

John Knox and the Reformation

occupied with tutorial rather than parochial duties, being mentioned as tutor in different houses in East Lothian.

Unlike the other Reformers, Knox had grown to middle age before he embraced the Protestant Faith. With him it was not the rash exuberance of youth, with its love of change and adventure, which led him to attach himself to a new cause. It was the matured reflections of middle age, of a time when prudence takes the place of recklessness and when the habits are so formed that change can only be effected with pain and difficulty. Doubtless, for a long time, his mind had been moving toward change, but he was forty years of age before he definitely detached himself from the existing church. Beza declares that his change of opinions came largely through his study of the writings of Augustine, that early father from whom all the Reformers drew inspiration and from whom they gained their most distinctive tenets.

But it was more the influence exerted upon him by George Wishart than anything else which gave to his mind the final coup de grace. This learned and amiable youth who, after a period of banishment, had returned to his native land was one of the forerunners and first martyrs of Protestantism in Scotland. Having imbibed the Reformed doctrine, he spent his time going from place to place instructing the people. Among other places, he visited East Lothian and met with Knox. Immediately Wishart's message found an echo in Knox's heart. A warm affection sprang up between the two men. Knox followed him everywhere, bearing before him, it is said, a huge double-edged sword which he was prepared to use in defense of his friend. Wishart, however, was not destined to see the harvest of his labors. The emissaries of the wily Cardinal Beaton were dogging his footsteps. Being apprehended, he was tried, condemned, and burned at the stake. Knox was eager to accompany him but the remonstrance of Wishart is well known.

Scotland Saw His Glory

"Nay, return to your bairns. One is sufficient for a sacrifice." Wishart died with heroic fortitude, but did not remain unavenged for long. On the twenty-ninth of May, 1546, a body of men broke into the castle of St. Andrews and, dragging the Cardinal from his bed, put him to death. The assignation was partly political, for the cruel prelate had many enemies. But it was also a deed of vengeance by lawless men stung to madness through the death of one whom they regarded as a saint.

The heroic character of Knox soon declared itself in the turbulent days which now ensued. In the sea-girt castle, filled with desperate outlaws, ardent Reformers, and young lads who had followed Knox for the purpose of instruction, a man was wanted to cheer the garrison and to publicly defend the stand many of them were making for freedom. They had listened to Knox as he instructed his pupils, and being struck with his intense earnestness and with his knowledge of Scripture, they formed the resolution of appointing him as their minister. The call itself came with dramatic suddenness and was totally unexpected by Knox. Sitting one day in the public preaching place, listening to a discourse on the ministerial office, he was startled by the preacher turning and directing his address to him personally. He pointed out the needs of the times, the call for service, and Knox's own qualifications for the office. Then, turning to the congregation, he asked them to ratify what he had said. This they solemnly did, with one voice calling Knox to exercise the office of minister in their midst. The effect upon Knox himself was overwhelming. He could not shake off the call and treat it lightly. He heard in it the voice of God, but his spirit, which knew no other fear, quailed under the weight of the responsibility. Bursting into tears, he rushed from the place, and only after prolonged struggle did he accept the heavy task.

Once accepted, however, there was for him no turning back. With his usual intrepidity and vehemence of character, he flung

John Knox and the Reformation

himself into the fight. His first sermon, preached in the parish church, drew a great crowd, among which were not only the chief men of the city but also many monks and priests who watched over the perishing interests of their church. Knox's sermon, which exhibits even at that early date his vast powers of vituperation, caused an immediate sensation. "Some hew at the branches of the Papacy," men said, "but this man strikes at the root." Quickly, under Knox's ministrations, the Reformed Faith began to grow, the first visible signs being a communion service after the Reformed manner, presided over by Knox and held in the parish church. At this service, the first of its kind ever held in Scotland, Knox dispensed the sacrament to over two hundred people. It was a small number, but it revealed better than anything else the change that was coming over Scotland.

The garrison at this time, which was practically in a stage of siege, was expecting help from England when there appeared a new source of anxiety on the horizon in the shape of a French fleet. Knox at once prophesied disaster. "Your corrupt life," he told them, "could not escape the judgement of God." For a while the garrison held out, but the forces of the enemy and the deadly precision of their artillery proved too much for them. On the last day of July 1547, the garrison capitulated to the French admiral, trusting in his promise that they should be taken to France and allowed their liberty. But a promise to heretics imposed no burden upon the conscience, according to the French code of honor. While the chief prisoners were cast into French dungeons, the rest, with Knox among them, were sent to the galleys.

For nineteen months Knox was chained to the oar. His sufferings were so great that he never afterwards cared to recall them. His health was permanently damaged, and he contracted a painful disease which never afterwards left him without

Scotland Saw His Glory

suffering. "How long I continued prisoner," he once said in a sermon at St. Andrews in 1569, "what torments I sustained in the galleys, and what were the sobs of my heart, is now no time to recite." During this terrible time, his hope still survived and his courage remained undaunted. On one occasion, lying between Dundee and St. Andrews the second time that the galley returned to Scotland, the said John Knox being so sick that few hoped for his life, James Balfour willed him to look to the land and asked if he knew it. He answered, "Yes, I know it well, for I see the steeple of that place where God first in public opened my mouth to His glory, and I am fully persuaded, however weak I now appear, that I shall not depart this life until my tongue shall glorify His godly name in the same place."

As terrible as his sufferings were on board the galley, neither these nor the threats of his captors could quench his spirit. One day, it is related, a picture of the Virgin, a "painted brod," was brought on deck, and the officers thrust it into Knox's hands telling him to kiss it. Knox, looking advisedly around, took the image and flung it into the river saying, "Let our Lady now save herself, she is light enough. Let her learn to swim." This merry fact was dangerous jesting, and it was strange that Knox should have escaped with his life. "After that," he says, "there was no Scottish man urged with that idolatry." Knox was not released until early in 1549, at the instigation, as supposed, of Edward VI. Scotland was then in so disturbed a state that nothing could be gained by his returning to it.

For the next ten years we find him submitting to exile. The first part of this time was spent in England as a minister of the English Church. The ecclesiastical affairs of England at this time were passing through a transition stage. Episcopal government was acknowledged, but the use of the Prayer Book was

John Knox and the Reformation

not obligatory nor was kneeling at the communion. The Prayer Book has a note appended to the Communion office explaining that the attitude of kneeling is "well meant for a signification of the benefits of Christ therein given . . . but therein no adoration is intended either unto the Sacramental bread and wine . . . or unto any corporal presence of Christ's natural flesh and blood." This is known as the *Black Rubric* and is from the hand of Knox.

Knox was first called to labor in Berwick. In early 1551 he went to Newcastle where it is said, "Many Scots resorted to enjoy his fellowship." In 1552 he was summoned to London as King's Chaplain. There he was one of the six who revised and sanctioned the Articles concerning a uniformity of religion which became the basis of the Thirty-Nine Articles of the Church of England. The bishopric of Rochester, falling vacant, was offered to Knox, who declined it. A year later, when in exile on the Continent, he explained his reason for refusing all such appointments. "What moved me to refuse, with the displeasure of all men, those high promotions? Assuredly, the foresight of troubles to come. How often have I said that the time would not be long that England would give me bread."

The troubles predicted by Knox were not long in arriving. Edward VI, long in feeble health, was removed to Greenwich in April 1553 and died there on the 6th of July. The country was immediately plunged into confusion. Mary began her reign ostensibly with toleration, but it was not long before her real character was disclosed. Knox was reduced almost to beggary and, with others, fled the country.

After many wanderings Knox arrived at Geneva. There he came under the powerful personality of John Calvin. Deeply conscious of his lack of scholarship, he hoped in this city of freedom to find opportunity for study. However, he was not settled there long before he was called to minister to an English

Scotland Saw His Glory

church at Frankfort. Once more he returned to Geneva where he was appointed to minister again to an English congregation. Here he remained for three years until 1559.

Meanwhile the seeds of the Reformation were beginning to grow up in Scotland and to bring forth fruit. A great awakening was taking place among the people who were beginning to shake off their lethargy and to awake to a sense of their wrongs. The priesthood still hurled their anathemas at them but they fell now on skeptical ears. "They so lightlied the Mass," the priests complained, "that there was no longer a living to be made out of it."

The Queen Regent at this time was Mary of Guise, an implacable enemy of the Reformers. A proclamation forbidding any Reformed minister to preach or administer the sacraments was issued, and it seemed as if the whole movement was on the point of collapse. There was only one man who could save the situation, and urgent messages were sent to Knox, then in Geneva, to return and assist the cause in his native land. Knox immediately complied and on May 2, 1559, arrived in Edinburgh. From there he set out for Perth, the chosen meeting place of the Reformers. Entering the Parish church, he preached an impassioned sermon to a huge congregation. His eloquence was so tempestuous that the whole congregation was roused to action. Before the night fell, the churches were stormed and every vestige of popery was destroyed.

News of these and similar events was conveyed to the Queen Regent at Stirling and caused the greatest indignation. The Queen threatened to visit this contempt of her authority and this violence done to her faith with extreme penalties. With her French troops she marched towards Perth. It would have gone ill with the Protestants at this time had it not been for Knox. Danger was the atmosphere which called forth his highest qualities. Instead of weakening before the perils con-

John Knox and the Reformation

fronting them, he adopted the most imperious tone. Though the Protestant cause could then number but few preachers and though men of influence were sorely lacking, Knox bowed down to none. Writing to the nobles of Scotland at a time when smooth words were needed if safety was to be considered, he adopted instead a tone of menace. "Unless you join yourselves with us," he declares, "as of God you are reputed traitors, so shall you be excommunicated from our society. The glory of the victory, which God shall give to His Church, yes, even in the eyes of men, shall not appertain unto you." Such was the spirit of the times that, instead of alienating those to whom it was addressed, it brought over large numbers of waverers to the side of the Reformers.

A new spirit was breathing over Scotland. Beneath all the political unrest, the clash of faction and the bitterness of sect, a reviving breath of spiritual life was animating men's hearts. Serious men and those inclined to better things felt the glow of living conviction in the words of these new preachers. They spoke with that unmistakable accent of authority which so deeply impresses the human heart and which is ever present in times of spiritual awakening. Even the Church fell to setting its house in order, and with furious energy, it sought to introduce reforms. But the people were too much exasperated to view these with favor. They grasped with sufficient clearness the message of the new preachers to know that they had been wronged, and the attempt at the last hour to set these wrongs right only inflamed them by its tacit acknowledgements.

The Protestant cause thus gained ground every day, and when Mary arrived before Perth, its leaders were able to make terms with her. They agreed to disperse on condition that no one should suffer on account of the past and that all questions of religion should be considered by the next Parliament.

Scotland Saw His Glory

Meanwhile, Knox was going from place to place, carrying the fiery cross, preaching the new evangel, and calling his countrymen to free themselves from the bondage imposed upon them by the priesthood. At length he reached St. Andrews, whose towers he had seen when tossing with pain in the galleys and where he longed again to lift up his voice. Archbishop Hamilton had entered the city the previous evening with a retinue of armed men. He forbid Knox to preach, warning him that if he did, "twelve hackbuts would light upon his nose at once." Vainly his friends entreated him not to make the attempt, but Knox refused to listen to them. Entering the pulpit of the Parish church, he proceeded to address the people. Neither Archbishop nor military appeared, and so overwhelming was Knox's appeal that the people rose in mass and, before night had fallen, had destroyed every vestige of the old faith. The violence with which this was done aroused neither misgivings nor regrets in the heart of Knox. "Pull down the nests, and the rocks will fly away," he believed. "The long thirst of my wretched heart is now satisfied in abundance . . . for now, forty days or more, has God used my tongue in my native country to the manifestation of His glory. . . . The thirst of the poor people, as well as of the nobility here, is wondrous great, which putteth me in comfort, that Christ Jesus shall triumph for a space here in the North, and in the extreme parts of the earth."

Following their successes at St. Andrews, the Reformers next turned their eyes towards the Capital. As they entered, the Queen Regent retired to Dunbar with her troops. In Edinburgh, however, the Reformers found little left for them to do, as the burghers had already demolished the religious houses, leaving nothing but the walls standing.

The Protestant cause in Scotland was now taking definite shape, and the country was drifting into civil war. The Reformers were trusting in support from England. Mary of Guise and

John Knox and the Reformation

the Catholics looked for their support from France. For a long time the results hung in the balances, but the appearance of an English fleet finally weighed the scales in favor of Knox and his followers. In the midst of these events, the Queen Regent died, and the French allies, after agreeing to a treaty which conceded to the government the power to settle the ecclesiastical affairs of the country, embarked with what remained of their army for France.

In August of the same year, 1560, Parliament met in Edinburgh and was found to be overwhelmingly Protestant. With almost incredible swiftness and unanimity, it declared for the Protestant faith, abolished Roman Catholicism, and called for a form of confession. This was drawn up and presented in four days and was accepted almost without a dissentient voice. There were bishops present, but they remained silent while every vestige of their old authority was being wrested from them. Certain of the temporal lords, without combating the new doctrines, declared their adhesion to the old faith, but these only numbered three. "The rest of the lords," wrote Randolph, "with common consent, and as glad a will as I ever heard men speak, allowed the same." The scene was profoundly affecting. Men were moved out of their habitual reticence to declare their profound gratitude to God. It was not political passions which thus moved them, but deep, spiritual earnestness. "I am the oldest in this company," said Lord Lindsay, "but now that it has pleased God to let me see this day, where so many nobles and others have allowed so worthy a work, I will say with Simeon, Nunc Dimittis."

Thus the old faith fell almost without striking a blow in its defence, a startling indication of how slight a hold it had obtained over the affections of the people, how unworthily it had maintained its high traditions and had used its power. On the 20th of December of that same year, the first General

Scotland Saw His Glory

Assembly of the Church of Scotland was held, and the first chapter of the movement in Scotland was closed. Throughout it all, one man soared high above all others. Through the stormy days, it was Knox's voice that was heard, ever claimant and insistent, often strident, always intolerant, but ever dauntless. From the pulpit of St. Giles, he thundered forth his appeals, warnings, and threats, and such was the force of his personality that he may be regarded at this time as being the real ruler of Scotland. His convictions were maintained at white heat. His speech, which was rugged, impassioned, and majestic, especially when he assumed the role of the prophet, swept away the timid opposition of other men. His sincerity, which none doubted, the transparent honesty of his motives, and his utter fearlessness of consequences appealed even to his enemies. His outstanding ability and his knowledge of affairs made him an ally which no party in the state could afford to disdain.

The complete triumph of the Reformed opinions, the acquiescence of the nation as a whole in them, the tranquility which everywhere abounded, all seemed to promise times of peace and prosperity both for the nation and for the church. But then there entered upon the pages of Scotland's stormy history one whose beauty and sufferings have strangely affected the human heart and who, notwithstanding the crimes which stain her name, remains one of its most romantic and pathetic figures.

When James V died of a broken heart after the battle of Solway Moss, he left behind him, as heir to the throne, a little daughter who afterwards gained fame as Mary Queen of Scots.

Being connected from her mother's side with the powerful Guise family, she was brought up in France. As heir to the throne of Scotland and next in succession to the throne of England, she became one of the chief pawns in the game of conquest then going on in Europe. When little more than a

John Knox and the Reformation

child, she was married to the Dauphin of France. He died two years later in 1560, the year which saw the triumph of the Reformed opinions in Scotland.

Left this early a widow, proud, ambitious, beautiful, unprotected in the midst of cruel and ambitious men, herself the object of ambition because of her hopes, the center of attraction because of her beauty, and being called to govern a lawless people at a time of danger and revolution, it is no wonder that her way was beset with pitfalls and that pity for her sufferings has blotted out the remembrance of her misdeeds.

During her sojourn in France she had not been kept ignorant of the affairs in her native land. In determining to return to Scotland and assume the throne, she had already determined her policy. As a devout Catholic, she viewed with intense indignation the ecclesiastical changes which had taken place, and her intention from the first was to restore the old religion. She had heard of Knox, too, and vowed that she would either banish him from her kingdom or be banished herself. With these intentions fully established in her mind, she set out for her native shores. She landed at Leith on August 19, 1561. The day was chilly with fog. Knox records that "the very face of heaven, at the time of her arrival, did manifestly speak what comfort was brought into this country with her—sorrow, dolour, darkness, and all impiety."

Mary had not been in her kingdom for a week before she was to taste something of the character of its people. On the first Sunday after her arrival, she ordered Mass to be celebrated in the Abbey of Holyrood. Instantly, the fiercest indignation was aroused and the worst fears of Knox were realized. Thundering daily from the pulpit of St. Giles, he declared that "one Mass was more fearful to him than if a thousand armed men were landed in any part of the realm to suppress the whole religion." On her part, Mary exercised successfully those gifts of attraction which she so supremely possessed. Even the most confirmed of the nobles who had embraced the new faith felt himself weakening in her presence. She seemed to possess some enchantment whereby men were bewitched. Mary was not long in her realm, however, before she realized that her one obstacle was the preacher of St. Giles. To silence him would be better than to win over an army. She determined, therefore, to confront him without delay. He was summoned to Holyrood. They met in the council chamber and the meeting was historic. "She was at the height of her glorious beauty, the fine outlines of her features softened and rounded by youth and health, while strong vitality and a sense of power gave the sparkle and fascination that no painter could reproduce. She saw before her a man already old, below middle height, but broad and well made. A long, black beard, already grizzled, shaded the lower part of his face, while deep-set grey eyes looked out keenly from under the narrow, prominent brow. Both were accustomed to read the characters of men quickly and keenly. In the beautiful girl opposite him, Knox recognized the power of a practiced diplomatist. . . . In the grave, worn preacher, Mary found an unhesitating authority and a disregard alike of her womanly charms and her royal prerogative that, for the moment, almost disconcerted her."

    The encounter from Mary's side failed. Neither on this occasion nor on any subsequent one could she overawe him by her authority or move him by her charms. Vainly she tried flattery and power, but Knox had suffered too deeply to become a gallant of the court. "If there be not in her a proud mind, a crafty wit, and an indurate heart against God and His truth, my judgement faileth me." However this judgement may be viewed, there is no doubt that it saved Scotland from a grave political danger and from its relapse back into the conditions from which it had emerged. Knox's attitude may have been uncompromis-

John Knox and the Reformation

ing, as he certainly had little of the spirit of compromise; but compromise on vital issues is betrayal, and in great crises, it is ruin. Bitter, implacable, intolerant, no doubt he was, but what the history of Scotland might have been had he been found at this time plastic and open to corruption is not pleasant to imagine.

Mary's subsequent history, the crimes of her court, the mistakes of her government, the failure of her rule, and the pathos of her death, do not concern us here. Throughout all the trouble, sin, and the terror of the times, Knox remained the same. These were years of anxiety and of strenuous toil, years when, but for Knox's intrepid character, the wheels might again and again have rolled backward and the work of the Reformers have been undone.

At length, broken down with the labors of his stormy life, the great Reformer felt that death was drawing nigh. On the 9th of November, 1572, Knox preached for the last time in St. Giles. So feeble was he that he had to be helped into the pulpit, but once there, the old fire which had set Scotland in a glow broke out once more. The cathedral rang with his trumpet notes. So vehemently did he preach that "he was like to rend the pulpit in pieces." When the sermon had ended, however, it was seen that his strength was spent and the end near.

His closing days were days of peace. The stormy spirit, so long intent on public affairs, withdrew itself into the inner chamber where peace abides and where vision takes the place of sight. Once, when repeating the Lord's Prayer, he was heard to stop and to add with awe-struck whisper, "Who can pronounce such holy words?" His friends gathered around him. All the great men of the kingdom visited him as he lay weak and helpless, and he bade them a kindly farewell. A little after noon on Monday, November twenty-fourth, he asked his wife to read to him part of the fifteenth chapter of First Corinthians which

Scotland Saw His Glory

he pronounced "a comfortable chapter." Later on he requested the fourteenth chapter of John "where I first cast my anchor." Being asked if he heard, he answered, "I hear, and understand far better, I praise God." Soon after, the end came, and he "slept away at even, without any pain." On the Wednesday following, amid the grief of the whole population, he was laid to rest in the shadow of that old cathedral which had so often rung with his eloquence and which had been the scene of his greatest efforts. From the greatest to the lowest in the land, it was recognized that there had passed away a great man, a true lover of his country, and a faithful follower of Jesus Christ.

The Reform movement in Scotland has frequently been dismissed as a mere political upheaval, agitated by political intriguers and consummated with only the minimum of religious feeling. This is to invert the facts. That political considerations entered in, contributing their own influence to the movement, is undoubted. It could not be otherwise. In every great spiritual movement which profoundly affects a nation's life, political and social conditions are bound to enter. They are bound to enter because no part of a nation's life can be isolated from the whole. Each part acts and reacts upon the others, and no part can be affected without the whole being stimulated or depressed. The Reformation in Scotland, just because it so profoundly challenged the whole existing order, produced an agitation which left no part of the nation's life untouched. It both affected the political conditions and was affected by them. In some ways, these promoted the Reformation; in other ways, they retarded it. But in no sense did they create it.

The dominant impulse was not political. The movement did not begin by a social or political revolution. It was not initiated by men who sought to change conditions in social or political life which had become intolerable. It was a religious movement set in motion by men who profoundly realized the corruption

John Knox and the Reformation

around them and who, having received light to their own souls, were willing to lay down their lives to hand on that light to others.

The "reek which blew from the fire which burned Patrick Hamilton" and which affected so many did not arouse bitterness at existing political conditions. It aroused men who were weary of the empty seeking in empty cisterns for water which would quench their thirst and who, with eager desire, turned to the new and found it. It is true that many nobles attached themselves to the movement on unworthy grounds and that the sin of covetousness had much to do with their decision. But this is only a part and is not the greatest part or the best part. Even then all that can be said is that they took advantage of its existence. They did not bring it into life nor did they maintain its life. Owing to the conditions then existing, the Reformation had to run alongside a political revolution, which largely it created and shaped. Yet beneath this, as the supreme fact, was the new spiritual life which had been awakened. To neglect this is to fatally misinterpret the whole spirit of the times.

The movement in Scotland, however, has marked characteristics of its own.

First, it was a popular movement, "broad based upon the people's will." It did not filter downwards from above, reaching first the well-to-do and intelligent parts of the community and then slowly move the masses. On the contrary, it began among the people. Nothing in our history is more remarkable than the change which came over the poorer classes when the first breath of the Reformation reached them. It seemed to call into instantaneous and active life elements of national character long slumbering. It seemed to call into being in a moment that intelligence, firmness, and independence so characteristic of the Scottish race. "A poor, barren country," says Carlyle, "full of continual broils, dissensions, massacres; a people in the last

Scotland Saw His Glory

stage of destitution. It is a country as yet without a soul, nothing developed in it but what is rude, external, and semi-animal. And now at the Reformation, the internal life is kindled, as it were, under the ribs of this outward material death. A cause, the noblest of causes, kindles itself, like a beacon set on high, high as heaven, yet attainable from earth, whereby the lowest man becomes, not a citizen only, but a member of Christ's visible church, a veritable hero, if he proves a true man."

Thus, what the Reformation did in Scotland was to call into being a nation. It awoke among the people a national consciousness. Before they were serfs. Suddenly, at the first breath of the Reformation, they became citizens. "You would be astonished to see how men are changed here," one writes to Lord Burleigh. "There is little of that submission to those above them which there used to be. The poor think and act for themselves. They are growing strong, confident, and independent."

This new awakening startlingly revealed itself in the stormy days which followed. The nobles, who had adopted the Protestant faith for political reasons, found no difficulty in changing their faith when the same motives prompted a change of front. When, therefore, they turned to the people to carry their schemes into effect, they were astounded to find that their power was gone. They realized, to their amazement, that they could no longer use them as their tools for revenge and aggrandizement. A new order of things had arisen of which they had never dreamed. The old order of peasantry had silently passed away, leaving scarcely any trace of its existence behind it. A new peasantry had arisen whose independence, tenacity of purpose, and sincerity of conviction were not to be surpassed by any other peasantry in the world. "I know nothing finer in Scottish history," says Froude, "than the way in which the

John Knox and the Reformation

commons of the Lowlands took their places by the side of Knox in the great convulsions which followed. If all others forsook him, they at least would not forsake him while tongue remained to speak and hand remained to strike."

We are here, then, at the resurrection of a nation. In no other country was the influence of the Reformation so immediate. In Scotland, it seemed like a call to arms to men lying half asleep, yet expectant and eager for the call. When it came, they leaped into life.

The second characteristic was the birth of a living national church.

Scenes of violent spiritual emotion, outbursts of intense joy, exhibitions of uncontrolled anguish for past transgression are not the predominant characteristics of the wave of spiritual revival which passed over Scotland through the middle of the sixteenth century. But one would sadly err who, from the absence of report of these things, would deny the depth of the movement. In no place in the world, perhaps, was the effect more deep, and in none more lasting. The deplorable condition of the Church of Scotland before the Reformation we have seen, but the difference discernible among the Scottish peasantry as compared with the peasantry of other nations is that, while they were not less ignorant of spiritual things, they were much less superstitious regarding the Church and much more contemptuous of the priesthood. In the *Complaynt of Scotland,* the peasant laments that the priest and the noble "lives by me, and I die by them."

"Our parson here, he takes no other pyne (pain),
But to receive his teind and spend it syne,
Though they should want preaching seventeen year,
Our parson will not want one sheaf of bear (barley)."

Scotland Saw His Glory

The threats of the Church fell on indifferent ears and became a subject of laughter and mockery. Suddenly, all this changed. Religion became not only a factor, but the dominant factor of the nation's life. Already, in 1551, John ab Ulmis, a foreign divine visiting the Scottish border, was struck with the religious character of the people. "There appears to be great firmness and no little religion among the people of Scotland," he says, "but the chiefs of the nation resist and oppose truth in every possible way." The movement seems to have spread at first largely of itself. No one could say of it, "Lo, here!" or "Lo, there!"—silently and unseen, it did its work of regenerating and blessing. Even Knox, with all his intensity of character, was amazed when, returning from Geneva, he came into contact with the deep spiritual life which had sprung up during his absence. "If I had not seen it," he says, "with my own eyes, in my own country, I could not have believed it. . . . The fervency here doth far exceed all others I have seen. . . . Depart I cannot until such time as God quench their thirst a little. . . . Their fervency doth so ravish me, that I cannot but accuse and condemn my slothful coldness. God grant them their heart's desire." "Night and day," he says, he found them "sobbing and groaning for the bread of life." They had practically no teachers, but meeting together in *assemblies,* they read the Scriptures, confessed their sins, and united in earnest prayer. In the homes, not only of the humble, but in the castles of the highest in the land, these *assemblies* were held, and over the lowlands of Scotland, the breath of the Spirit of God passed, awakening a nation to newness of life. When Knox returned from Geneva and traversed the lowlands, he found everywhere the fuel gathered, needing only a spark to set it ablaze.

The effect of the Reformation upon Scotland was thus to create a church in which the poorest was made to recognize his responsibility as a member to maintain its purity, to promote its

John Knox and the Reformation

interests, and to share in its government, while the weekly expounding of Scripture became a great educational asset in the national life, giving to a people, naturally shrewd and intelligent, those intellectual and theological interests which they have never since completely lost.

But it did more than this. It brought religion to bear upon the common life. It made the awful verities of the Christian faith the supreme facts of existence. Its evangel, as Knox loved to call it, was wholly Calvinistic. The awfulness of sin, the recoil of infinite holiness from the sinner, the comfort of the elect, the doom of the reprobate, the sole efficacy of Christ's atoning sacrifice—these were the doctrines vehemently declared and passionately accepted, which entered into the very fiber of the nation's life. Stern, illiberal, intolerant though its theology was, it turned out strong men who, amid their daily toil, kept before them the awful fact that the Judge of all the earth did right, that His eyes were constantly upon them, and that at His stern judgement seat, they all alike must stand and give their account. "So far," says Lecky, "as one can look into that commonplace round of things which historians never tell us about, there has rarely been seen in this world a set of people who have thought more about right and wrong, and the judgement about them of the Upper Powers."

A still more intimate picture of the religious life as it concerns the peasantry of Scotland is found in Burn's immortal poem, *The Cotter's Saturday Night*. Here, as nowhere else, we are made to realize how religion became bound up with the common life of the people, as we see this humble family kneel together in worship. This practice, which was begun at the insistence of Knox, became one of the most beautiful characteristics of Scottish piety. "Within their homes," he says, "they were bishops and kings, and their wives, children, and families were their bishopric and charge." So in his poem Burns

Scotland Saw His Glory

introduces us to the humble cottage of the Cotter, to its simple joys and homefulness. Then, at the hour of rest, the father becomes the priest:

> "The cheerfu' supper done, wi' serious face,
> They, round the ingle, form a circle wide;
> The sire turns o'er, wi' patriarchal grace,
> The big ha'-Bible, ance his father's pride.
> His bonnet reverently is laid aside,
> His lyart haffets wearing thin and bare,
> Those strains that once did sweet in Zion glide,
> He wales a portion with judicious care,
> And 'Let us worship God!' he says, with solemn air.
> Then kneeling down to Heaven's eternal King,
> The saint, the father, and the husband prays. . . .
> From scenes like these, old Scotia's grandeur springs,
> That makes her lov'd at home, rever'd abroad:
> Princes and lords are but the breath of kings;
> An honest man's the noblest work of God."

The third characteristic of the movement in Scotland was its awakening in the people the sense of individual freedom.

This characteristic of the awakening in Scotland was shared with the awakenings which took place elsewhere, but in Scotland it found a race of men who, though long depressed by their masters, were by instinct freedom-loving and independent. The reform movement broke the stupor which so long had lain upon men's minds and energies, and the call to freedom, to liberty of conscience, to the rights of private judgement in the realm of religion, awoke the slumbering energies of the race and created a new era of civil and religious liberty. It cannot be said, however, that these great benefits were gained without corresponding loss. Freedom is ever in danger of running into license. The effect of the Reformation was to rend western Christianity in half and further, to break up one of the halves

John Knox and the Reformation

into numberless and warring sects. Yet even this, no doubt, is better than slumbering uniformity. Though the Reformers very imperfectly learned the lesson of tolerance, it may still be admitted that the new-found sense of freedom was a gain of the most momentous character and that, while its first effects produced outstanding evils, its ultimate effects were for the good of humanity and for the progress of the race.

This love of freedom, which the Reformers awoke in the people's hearts, the Scottish Church has preserved. No one will readily quote Buckle as an historian prejudiced in favor of the clergy, especially of the Scottish clergy, but even Buckle is roused to enthusiasm as he relates the struggles and sacrifices made by the Scottish clergy in the age succeeding Knox: "Much they did," he says, "which excites our strongest aversion. But one thing they achieved which should make us honour their memory and repute them benefactors of mankind. At a most hazardous moment, they kept alive the spirit of national liberty. What the nobles and the crown put in peril, that did the clergy save. By their care, the dying spark was kindled into a blaze. When the light grew dim and flickered on the altar, their hands trimmed the lamp and fed the sacred flame. This is their real glory, and for this they may well repose. They were the guardians of Scottish freedom, and they stood to their post. Where danger was, they were foremost. By their sermons, their conduct, both public and private, and by the proceedings of their assemblies, they stirred up the minds of men, woke them from their lethargy, formed them to habits of discussion, and excited that inquisitive and democratic spirit which is the only effectual guarantee the people can ever possess against the tyranny of those who are set over them. This was the work of the Scottish clergy, and all hail to them that did it."

This great quality, it may be admitted, the Church in Scotland has honorably preserved. It has identified itself with

Scotland Saw His Glory

the people in a way and to an extent which has not been exceeded, if indeed equalled, by any other Protestant church.

The remaining characteristic of the movement, as it affects Scotland, is the value it attached to education. For this, Scotland is indebted to Knox, and nothing could be more enlightened or liberal than the scheme drawn out by him. In the Book of Discipline, it is laid down that "no father, of what state or condition, ever he be, may use his children at his own fantasy, especially in their youth, but all must be compelled to bring up their children in learning and virtue, so that they may live their lives in profit of the Church and Commonwealth. In remote parts, the minister, or reader, is to take care that the children learn their rudiments and are instructed in the catechism. In towns, a schoolmaster, able to teach grammar and the Latin tongue, is to be attached to every church; every large town is to have a college (a secondary school) where the arts, at least logic, rhetoric, and the tongues, may be taught by approved masters, for whom honest stipends must be appointed. All education is to lead up to and be a preparation for the university. There, after a liberal training in the arts, tongues, and philosophy, each student must study the subjects in which he intends chiefly to travail for the profit of the Commonwealth."

This zeal for education the Scottish Church has honorably maintained. It insists upon a prolonged training of its own ministers, both in the arts and theology, who thus, even in the remotest parts, represent the value of education and see to its efficiency. It is mainly owing to this fact that the village schools have reached so high a standard and that for centuries the best education has been placed at the door of the humblest lad. The effect of this upon the national life has been incalculable. It has fitted the poorest for the highest walks in life. It has turned out a type of character at once strong and self-reliant. It

John Knox and the Reformation

has changed Scotland from a nation of outlaws to a nation that stands in the vanguard of progress. Whatever other countries lost through the Reformation, it will be admitted by the most candid of observers that Scotland lost least and that the middle of the sixteenth century saw the outburst of a new spiritual and national life and the founding of a church in keeping with the genius and character of the people. In Scotland, perhaps, more than in any other country, the spiritual movement of the sixteenth century reaped its finest and most lasting fruits.

Of the character of the great leader of the reform movement in Scotland, various estimates have been formed according to the bias of the persons forming them.

First, it is averred that John Knox was no saint. Certainly if he is to be judged by the medieval type of saints this would be instantly acknowledged. If saintliness of character belongs exclusively to the contemplative life and if to attain to it the individual must hide himself in cloistered retreats, must deny himself the duties of life, and leave it to others to fight its conflicts, then John Knox is the last man for whom a claim to saintliness could be sustained. But if the religious life is not incompatible with the mingling in life's affairs, with a passionate attachment to one side in a great conflict, with the disposition to strike hard blows in defense of what is known to be true, and with the willingness to suffer death itself rather than desist, then there is still hope for John Knox to be considered not only a deeply religious man, but to be recognized as a worthy leader in a great spiritual movement.

His chief offense in the eyes of those who judge him harshly is his intolerance. Most regard intolerance as a peculiarly unattractive trait in character. In one historic person only has perfect love of good and perfect hatred of evil been combined with perfect charity. Christ was able to say in the hour of conflict, when passions ran high and hearts were estranged, "He

Scotland Saw His Glory

that is not against us is on our part."[2] But this is a reach of lofty and noble tolerance of which the world possesses but one example and one alone. Certainly not even his most fervent admirer could deny that Knox was the most uncompromising of opponents and that his zeal often carried him far beyond the realm of what was true and just in conduct. Intolerance which springs from a narrow mind and a cold heart, and the deeds that are born of it, are without justice and mercy.

There is another intolerance, however, which has its source in a genuine hatred of evil, with a passionate desire to see it overthrown and the good established. It is with this latter form of intolerance that Knox must be charged. It is possible, however, to say something in his defense. There are times when to be tolerant is to commit the unpardonable sin; when men, if they have anything of God in them, must be intolerant; when the evils around them become such a menace that men lose their sense of proportion in their passionate desire to end them. No doubt, in the strife which follows, much suffers which in itself is good. In the heat of the conflict, those incensed by the battle do not pause to make fine distinctions or delicately distinguish the varying character of their foes. All who are not on their side they regard as against them. Doubtless, also, this very intolerance of evil can be carried too far and even strike against that which is not evil. This may be the inevitable mistake made by those who are passionately in earnest, but it does not condemn this form of intolerance as evil in itself. In itself it is a mark of heroism. It is the divine spirit in a man roused to heroic action. The work which Knox did would never have been done at all had it not been that in his inmost heart, burning at white heat, there was the intolerance of the intolera-

---

[2] Mark 9:40.

John Knox and the Reformation

ble. "It seems to me hard measure," says Carlyle, "that this Scottish man, now after three hundred years, should have to plead like a culprit before the world, intrinsically for having been, in such a way as it was then possible to be, the bravest of all Scotsmen! Had he been a poor half and half, he could have crouched into the corner like so many others. Scotland would have not been delivered, and Knox would have been without blame. He is the one Scotsman to whom, of all others, his country and the world owe a debt. He has to plead that Scotland would forgive him for having been worth to it any million unblamable Scotsmen that need no forgiveness! He bared his breast to the battle, had to row in galleys, wander forlorn in exile, in clouds and storms, was censured, shot at through the windows, and had a right sore fighting life. If this world were his place of recompense, then he made but a bad venture of it. But we have gotten above all those details of his battle, and living now in clearness on the fruits of his victory, we, for our own sake, ought to look through the rumors and controversies enveloping the man, into the man himself."

When we look into the man himself, we see a nature of the most noble sincerity. No one has ever doubted this or could ever doubt it. Right or wrong, Knox believed in the cause he advocated, believed in it in that way in which men willingly suffer death itself rather than relinquish the struggle. Nothing is nobler than this. When a man suffers as Knox did, when he lays his life open to daily peril, seeking for no earthly reward but the victory of the cause which to him is the cause of God, he may make a thousand mistakes, but his name will deserve to be enshrined on the pages of history, and there will be granted to him that noble immortality which attends only the great and the good.

To many, the greatness of Knox is dimmed because of his interference in political strife. The political propagandist, it is

Scotland Saw His Glory

asserted, took the place of the religious Reformer. A just recognition of the conditions then existing, however, will reveal the fact that the two were so inextricably mixed that it was impossible to be the one without the other. Not that it is meant that he was always wise, that often he would not have been better to have left public affairs alone when he rushed into them. Knox was not a perfect being. If, to be a religious Reformer, it is necessary never to make a mistake, though daily plunged in the most exciting events, then Knox comes ridiculously far short. He was not always wise; he made mistakes and was intolerant and relentless often when he might wisely have given way. But if a man is to be tried, not by the standard of perfection, but by the honesty of his intentions and the unselfishness of his aims, then Knox's mistakes will swiftly be forgotten, while his services to his country and to truth are remembered. He had no mind to meddle with politics, no further than it had religion mixed with it. What he demanded from the state was this—"the liberty of our conscience, to serve our Lord God as we shall answer to Him." In his austere figure, his flashing eyes, his stern denunciations, and his solemn threats and warnings, he resembles, as Carlyle says, "more than any of the moderns, an old Hebrew prophet. The same inflexibility, intolerance, rigid narrow-looking adherence to God's truth, stern rebuke in the name of God to all who forsake truth, an old Hebrew prophet in the guise of an Edinburgh minister of the sixteenth century. We are to take him for that, and not require him to be other."

Knox was too much a Scotsman to easily lay open his inmost heart or readily to betray the secrets of the soul, and indeed, this spiritual reticence is a marked characteristic of the movement as it is the marked characteristic of the Scottish people. To know Knox, it is necessary not only to sit in old St. Giles and hear the thunder of his voice, or watch him in

John Knox and the Reformation

council, keen, unflinching, conscious of power, and not without a secret enjoyment of it. But we have to follow him to his home, see him throw off the cares of state, and become the loving husband, the gentle father, or the kind friend. Much more have we to enter into his closet when the door is shut and when, in the silence, he opens his heart to God. Then the real nature of the man is disclosed, as for hours together he wrestles in prayer, agonizing for his country, for Christ's cause, for the maintenance of purity in the Church. There he is no longer the stern, uncompromising Calvinist, but the child, sobbing and pleading for forgiveness, acknowledging his deep unworthiness, his abject dependence upon God for daily help and guidance. Then the tears trickle down his furrowed cheeks as the melted snows of spring trickle down the wrinkled face of the mountain, leaving behind a shining pathway which seems tremulous with pity and love. It is such moments, when the soul is laid bare before God, when the white rays are thrown into the hidden depths and its inmost secrets are disclosed, that the nature of man can be truly discerned. Knox before his fellows was intolerant, unbending, austere, often even coarse. But before God, he was a broken-hearted penitent, seeking through tears and bitter self-reproaches the way to His Father's house, yet knowing full well that there was a place prepared for him, where upon entering, he would find rest. "Hast thou hope?" they asked him as he lay dying. He was too weak to answer, but lifting up his hand, he pointed upward, and in this hope he died, as by the strength of it he had lived.

The service which John Knox rendered to his country in a time of revolution and danger would be difficult to overstate. At a time when all the powerful were grasping for still more power, his voice was raised for righteousness, and that voice nothing on earth could silence. Of the part he had played, he is himself nobly conscious. "What I have been to my country,

Scotland Saw His Glory

although this ungrateful age will not know, yet the ages to come will be compelled to bear witness to the truth."

An interesting description of Knox as he appeared to a young student is given in the diary of James Melville, and refers to the year before Knox's death, when, for personal safety, he had to take refuge in St. Andrews. "Of all the benefits I had that year, was the coming of that most notable prophet and apostle of our nation, Mr. John Knox, to St. Andrews. . . . Mr. Knox would sometimes come in and repose himself in our college yard, and call us scholars unto him, and bless us, and exhort us to know God and His work in our country, and stand by the good cause, to use our time well, and learn the good instructions, and follow the good example of our masters. He was very weak. I saw him every day of his doctrine go hulie and fear, with a furring of matriks about his neck, a staff in the one hand, and good godly Richard Ballantyne, his servant, holding up the other oxter, from the Abbey to the Parish Church, and by the said Richard and another servant lifted up to the pulpit, where he behoved to lean at his first entry, but with his sermon, he was so active and vigorous that he was like to ding that pulpit in blads and fly out of it."

Perhaps the noblest testimony to his work and worth was given by one well able to estimate both. Standing in the churchyard of St. Giles beside his grave, in the presence of an enormous concourse of people who had followed the body to its last resting place, the Earl of Moray, then Regent of Scotland, offered this testimony:

"Here lyeth a man who in his life never feared the face of man, who hath been often threatened with dagge and dagger, but yet hath ended his days in peace and honour."

Chapter 2

Sixteenth Century Men of Revival

When the darkness of Popery first began to be dispersed by the rays of truth which feebly penetrated it, Scotland, like other European countries, received occasional gleams of the true light. These beams irradiated a scanty portion of the land but were generally smothered in the fires of persecution. Early in the fifteenth century, some of the opinions propagated by Wickliff were carried to Scotland. The Church was sufficiently ripe for reformation to at least feel the burden of its ceremonies and to be sensible of its corruptions, so that any man who lifted his voice against them quickly obtained willing followers.

In 1422, James Risby was put to death for denying that the Church of Rome was head of all other churches, that the bishop of that See (meaning the Pope) had pre-eminence over bishops in other countries, and that the clergy and monks ought to possess temporal power. He adopted these sentiments from Wickliff, and for his propagation of them, he forfeited his life. We do not know whether there was converting power with his preaching or the nature of the effect produced among his followers, but his execution seems to have been among the first of a series of scenes of tyranny and bloodshed arising from Papal animosity against the Truth. His fate is mentioned in the Records of the city of Glasgow.

Patrick Hamilton

The most affecting case of all the early martyrs of the Reformation was that of Patrick Hamilton, a man held in admiration and reverence by many on account of his learning, integrity, and singleness of purpose in propagating the truth that

Scotland Saw His Glory

he had been taught. His heart could not find satisfaction in the German Universities where the society of Luther and Melancthon and the guardianship of Lambert might have attracted him to pass his days, "but the zeal of God's glory did so eat him up, that he could not rest till he returned into his own country where the bright beams of the true light which, by God's grace, were planted in his heart, began most abundantly to break forth, both in public and in secret."[1] His influence was too powerful and too hateful to such men as Beaton, Archbishop of St Andrews, to be left long without a check. As he was allied to the highest rank in the kingdom, and as his holy life had filled many with reverent admiration, it required the stratagem of procuring the absence of the King and exciting the nobles into a ferment before the Archbishop dared to perpetrate his dark purpose. In 1527, this triumph of the enemy of all truth was accomplished, and the faithful, the noble, the valiant Patrick Hamilton expired at the stake because he denied the use of pilgrimages, prayers to the saints and for the dead, purgatory, etc. He died testifying that "though this death is bitter to the flesh, and fearful before men, yet it is the entrance into eternal life, which none shall possess who deny Jesus Christ before this wicked generation." He obtained the crown of martyrdom at the early age of twenty-four.

The desire of this holy man's heart was fulfilled as much by his death as it could possibly have been by his life. The "wolves who had devoured the prey" found themselves in a worse case than before, for men in all parts of the kingdom began to enquire why this flower of the land had been put to a violent death—and upon hearing the articles of faith for which he suffered, many began to question the truth and authority of

---

[1] John Gillies' *Historical Collections Relating to Remarkable Periods of the Success of the Gospel.*

Sixteenth Century Revivals

that which they had formerly implicitly believed. Presently not only novices but the subprior even in the popish seat of St. Andrews, black friars and grey, began to "smell somewhat of the verity, and espy out the vanity of the received superstitions." By this means the persecutors had even more vile work on hand, new consultations were taken, and more were sentenced to burn at the stake, for men began to speak freely. "A merry gentleman, named John Lindsay . . . familiar to James Beaton, standing by when consultation was had, said, 'My Lord, if ye burn any more, except ye follow my counsel, ye will utterly destroy yourselves; if ye will burn them, let them be burnt in hollow cellars, for the smoke of Mr. Patrick Hamilton hath infected as many as it blew upon.'"[2]

In 1543, sixteen years after the death of Hamilton, a time when many others had shown that they valued the truth as it is in Jesus more than life, an act of Parliament was obtained, which rendered it lawful for every man to use the benefit of the Scriptures in the translation which they then possessed; and "thereby did the knowledge of God wondrously increase, and God gave his Holy Spirit to simple men in great abundance."

George Wishart

Another individual upon whose faithful and undaunted labors the head of the church commanded a blessing is George Wishart. After learning the Truth at Cambridge, he began his ministrations in Ross-shire and afterwards served the populous town of Dundee. He was listened to with great admiration and the Word was proclaimed with power to many souls until Cardinal David Beaton, nephew of James and affected by an equally persecuting spirit, incited a leading man in the place to prohibit his troubling that town any more by his preaching.

---

[2] Knox's *History of the Reformation,* Vol. 1.

Scotland Saw His Glory

Wishart then went to the West and made offers of God's word to willing hearers until the Cardinal induced the Bishop of Glasgow (Dunbar) to pursue him to Ayr, with the intention of silencing him. The Earl of Glencairn and other gentlemen, hearing of the design of the Bishop, also came to Ayr and when the Reformer was excluded from the pulpit, which was taken possession of by the Prelate, he bravely went to the market-cross where he preached such a sermon that his very enemies were confounded.[3]

For some time after this, Wishart preached in various places in the West and on one occasion, finding the church of Mauchline shut against him, he prevented those of his friends who would have forced an entrance saying, "Jesus Christ is as mighty in the fields as in the church, and Himself often preached in the desert, at the seaside, and other places. It is the word of peace God sends by me, the blood of none shall be shed this day for the preaching of it." He then took his station on an earthen fence where he continued preaching to the people above three hours. God wrought so wonderfully by that sermon that one of the wickedest men in the country, the Laird of Sheld, was converted by it. It is reported that his eyes ran down with such abundance of tears, that all men wondered at him.

Presently, tidings reached Wishart that the plague had broken out in Dundee, and in spite of the importunities of friends, this servant of God went there saying, "They are now in trouble, and need comfort; perhaps the hand of God will make them now to magnify and reverence the Word of God,

---

[3]Knox's specimen of the Bishop's sermon is curious—"They say we should preich. Quhy not? Better lait thryve, nor nevir thryve. Had us still for your bischope, and we sall provyde better the nixt tyme." That which was delivered at the market-cross must have formed a striking and salutary contrast to the babblings of the poor dignitary.

Sixteenth Century Revivals

which before they lightly esteemed." He chose his preaching station at the East gate, having the whole within and the sick without. His text was, "He sent his word and healed them" (Psalm 107:20), "by which sermon he so raised up the hearts of those who heard him, that they regarded not death, but judged them more happy who should then depart, rather than such as should remain behind." He visited without reserve all those who lay in extremity and so influenced the healthy to distribute to the afflicted that he was enabled to provide for all their wants. In the very midst of these exertions, which could not have been ventured upon except by one strong in the faith, the miserable Cardinal stirred up a wicked man, one of his minions in the priesthood, to assassinate Wishart. He waited to waylay him as he descended from church after the people had departed, but his victim, being warned by the agitation of his manner and spying the hilt of the dagger, went calmly up and seized it. The caitiff fell on his knees to implore forgiveness, but news of this reaching the dispersing multitude, they burst in at the gate and would have torn him in pieces, but the man of God took the trembling villain in his arms, saying, "Whosoever hurts him shall hurt me; for he hath done me no hurt, but much good, in teaching me more heedfulness for the time to come." Thus he saved the vile priest's life. After this Wishart continued preaching in various places and everywhere the people flocked to hear him.

In 1546, the Cardinal had Wishart brought before him to give an account of his heretical and seditious doctrines. Following the example of his blessed Master, he hid not his face from shame and spitting, being exposed to the most abusive words and spiteful conduct that human animosity could suggest. A priest named Lauder was set up as his accuser. He read a scroll of accusations and curses so bitter that the poor, ignorant auditors looked to see the earth open and swallow up

Scotland Saw His Glory

Mr. Wishart. He concluded his imprecations by spitting in the face of the faithful martyr saying, "What answerest thou, thou runnagate, traitor, thief?" Wishart fell on his knees, made his prayer to God, then calmly said "Many and horrible sayings unto me a Christian man, many words abominable to hear have ye spoken this day, which not only to teach, but even to think, I ever thought a great abomination. . . ." He then gave an account of his doctrine, answering every article as far as they would give him leave to speak. But his enemies, disregarding the reason, sobriety, and godliness of his answers, condemned him to be burnt to death. After receiving this sentence he again fell on his knees and prayed audibly: "O immortal God, how long wilt thou suffer the ungodly to exercise their fury upon Thy servants, which do further Thy Word in this world; whereas they on the contrary seek to destroy the Truth, whereby Thou hast revealed Thyself to the world. O Lord, we know certainly that Thy true servants must suffer for Thy name's sake persecutions, afflictions, and troubles; yet we desire that Thou wouldst preserve and defend Thy church, which Thou hast chosen before the foundation of the world, and give Thy people grace to hear Thy Word, and to be Thy true servants in this present life. . . ." His power over the people was too well known and had become too formidable to the bishops for them to suffer him to be heard pleading his cause either with man or God. Therefore the crowd was driven out and he hurried to the castle to be kept until the executioners should have prepared their torments. Wishart requested in this interval to see the subprior who had been employed to preach before his public accusation. After some conference with him, the man was melted to tears and went to the Cardinal, not to plead for Wishart's life for that was beyond hope, but to make known his innocence to all men.

The captain of the castle came to offer him some food.

Sixteenth Century Revivals

Having accepted the offer, he used this occasion to discourse with him and some friends about the Lord's last supper and His sufferings and death for us. He exhorted them to love one another, laying aside all rancor and malice as becomes the members of Jesus Christ who continually intercedes for us to His Father. After this he blessed the bread and wine which had been prepared for the meal and distributed them in the name of the Lord, desiring them to remember that Christ died for them and to feed on Him spiritually.

His companions at this solemn hour must have been those who had received his doctrines. For those who had been accustomed to worship a wafer which was supposedly turned into the real body of Christ by an unbelieving priest, it must have seemed strange and wonderful to return to the simple ordinance of remembrance as it was instituted by the Lord Himself, especially under the circumstance of Wishart, like Christ, about to be offered up for the Truth. After giving thanks and praying for them, he retired to his chamber to wait the executioners.

His prayers and exhortations during the period approaching his death are full of love, forgiveness, and zeal. He earnestly exhorted those brethren and sisters whom he had often taught to persevere in their study of the Word of God and not be driven away by the terror of his sufferings, "for had he taught men's doctrines, he should have had greater thanks from men," but for the Word of God's sake he now suffered, not sorrowfully, but with a glad heart. He called them to observe that he would not change countenance for he did not fear those who could kill the body and after that had no more that they could do. His prayers for his accusers and murderers and his tranquil joy to the last had an affect like that of the first martyr Stephen. The bystanders and all who heard of it were filled with admiration and wonder. Like the death of Patrick Hamilton, his death aroused more persons from a state of carelessness and awakened more distrust in the church which murdered him than all his public ministrations, numerous, faithful, and efficacious as they had been. It was but two years after his return from Cambridge, fraught with divine zeal, that he was summoned by means of martyrdom to appear before his Lord in Heaven.

William Cooper

In pursuing the work of the Spirit it is notable that we are not called upon to follow it from district to district or from church to church, but rather from one faithful preacher to another. God is true to His purpose of propagating saving truth by the exertions of His servants. The next man upon whose labors the blessing of God seemed prominent is William Cooper. He lived less than half a century after Wishart. Scotland had, in 1560, held its first General Assembly. Somewhere between 1580 and 1590, the Assembly appointed Mr. Cooper to the charge of the parish of Bothkenner, in Stirlingshire. When he came there, he "found the desolation [of the parish] so great that except the walls [of the church], which were ruinous also, neither doore nor window nor pulpit nor any part of a roofe was there at all: yet it pleased God to give such a blessing to the ministry of His Word that [within six months] the hearts [of the people] thereby were stirred up cheerfully to build the Lord's house." During seven or eight years of very successful ministry in that place God begin to acquaint him with His terrors and with inward temptations so that his life was almost wasted with heaviness; yet thereby he learned to know more and more of Christ Jesus.

In 1595 he moved to the Town of Perth in the north of Scotland where for nineteen years he was a comfort to the best sort and a wound to the worst. It appears that a revival began around the year 1600. He held public meetings on Wednesday, Friday, and Saturday evenings. Concerning these gatherings he

Sixteenth Century Revivals

wrote, "It would have done a Christian's heart good to see those joyful assemblies, to have heard the zealous cryings to God among that people, with sighings, and tears, and melting hearts, and mourning eyes." Speaking of himself he says, "My witness is in Heaven, that the love of Jesus and His people made continual preaching my pleasure, and I had no such joy as in doing His work." All the time that this lively ministry was going on, the Lord still exercised Him with inward temptations and great variety of spiritual combats, the end of which, through divine mercy, was joy unspeakable, as he himself testifies: "Yea, once in the greatest extremity of horror and anguish of spirit, when I had utterly given over and looked for nothing but confusion, suddenly there did shine in the very twinkling of an eye, the bright and lightsome countenance of God, proclaiming peace, and confirming it with invincible reasons. O what a change was there in a moment! The silly soul that was even now at the brink of the pit, looking for nothing but to be swallowed up, was instantly raised up to heaven, to have fellowship with God in Christ Jesus; and from this day forward, my soul was never troubled with such extremity of terrors. This confirmation was given to me on a Saturday morning; there found I the power of religion, the certainty of the Word; there was I touched with such a lively sense of the divinity and power of the Godhead, in mercy reconciled with man, and with me in Christ, as I trust my soul shall never forget; glory, glory, glory be to the joyful deliverer of my soul out of all adversities for ever."

In the midst of his inward wrestlings Mr. Cooper was not without his combats with wicked men, but all outward trial seemed small to him after his inward experience. He never had a controversy with any man but for his sins, and the Lord assisting him, "the power of the word did so hammer down their pride," that they were all of them brought to acknowledge

Scotland Saw His Glory

their evil ways. "It was no marvel," says the quaint historian, "to see Satan stir up his wicked instruments to molest him, for he professed himself a disquieter of him and his kingdom." Mr. Cooper ceased from his labors in 1619.[4]

John Welsh

John Welsh, son of a gentleman in Nithsdale, was the cause of much affliction to his parents in boyhood. Those fine mental energies, which when sanctified by the Holy Spirit made him a man eminent for faithfulness in the church, in unsanctified days led him to various and strange excesses. The spirit of adventure was so strong in him that for a short time he actually joined the thieves who dwelt in the Debatable Ground on the English Borders. Fortunately his father received him again after much entreaty by a female friend who acted as mediator. When he determined to go to college, he promised his father that if he should break off again he would be content to have his father disown him for ever. He soon became a student of great promise and selected the ministry as the profession of his choice. His first charge was at Selkirk. Although it was for a brief time, his ministry in that place was not without fruit, albeit "he was attended by the prophet's shadow, the hatred of the wicked." A boy in the house where he boarded was so affected by his holy conduct that until old age he never forgot the impression. It was Mr. Welsh's custom, on going to bed, to lay a plaid above his bed clothes so that when he arose during the night for prayer he could cover himself with it. He used to wonder audibly how a Christian could lie in bed all night and not rise to pray. From the beginning of his ministry until his death, he reckoned the day ill spent if he had not prayed for

---

[4]Clark's *Lives*.

Sixteenth Century Revivals

seven or eight hours. For a short time he was in charge of the parish of Kirkcudbright but was transferred to Ayr in 1590, where he continued until banished.

The generation that had profited under the preaching of Wishart had passed away. Tragically, as might be expected in such a period of false doctrine, their faith had expired with them. Consequently, Welsh found the hatred of godliness so great that no one would let him a house. He was thankful for a time to find shelter under the roof of Mr. John Stewart, a merchant who was sometime provost of that borough, a man still had in remembrance as an eminent Christian, who was a great comfort and assistant to his young minister. At the time he began his work there, Ayr was the seat of faction and of bloody feuds so that no one could walk the streets in safety. Mr. Welsh, like Bernard Gilpin on the Borders, was often obliged to rush between parties of fighting men in the midst of bloodshed, his head shielded by a helmet but with no weapon except the message of peace. He adopted this singular practice which was doubtless recommended by the custom and spirit of the times, and its success prevents us from stigmatizing it as whimsical. After having, by his personal interference, terminated a skirmish and done what he could to pacify the angry passions of the combatants, he was accustomed to have a table placed in the street and, beginning with prayer, he prevailed on the parties to eat and drink together. The whole was concluded by the singing of a Psalm. After the rude people had begun to hearken to his doctrine and observe his heavenly example, he obtained such influence over them as to become their counsellor and pattern in all things so that this town of blows and animosities was presently converted into a scene of peace. We cannot pass this unusual employment of a minister of the gospel without observing the deep ways of Providence which can turn even the experience obtained by transgression to the glory of

Scotland Saw His Glory

God. How little did the youth think, when in rebellion against his father and in love with adventure, that in uniting himself with marauders on the Border, he was there at a school of training in undaunted coolness in the midst of battles, so that he might overcome the violent and shed abroad, in the name of the Prince of Peace, the spirit of peace.

Welsh was most diligent in labors, never preaching less than once every day. Having a strong constitution, he was enabled to devote all the hours he required to prayer and study without diminishing his time for exertion among his people. "But if his diligence was great," says his biographer, "so it is doubted whether his sowing in painfulness, or his harvest in success, was greatest; for if either his spiritual experience in seeking the Lord, or his fruitfulness in converting souls be considered, they will be found unparalleled in Scotland—and many years after Mr. Welsh's death, Mr. David Dickson, at that time a flourishing minister at Irvine, was frequently heard to say, when people talked to him of the success of his ministry, 'the gleaning grapes in Ayr, in Mr. Welsh's time, were far above the vintage of Irvine in his own.'

"Mr. Welsh's preaching was spiritual and searching, his utterance tender and moving. He did not much insist upon scholastic purposes and made no show of his learning. One of his hearers, who was afterwards minister at Muirkirk, said that a man could hardly hear him without weeping, his mode of address was so affecting. Sometimes before he went to preach, he would send for one or two of his elders and tell them he feared to go to the pulpit because he found himself so deserted. He would desire them to pray, and then would venture to the pulpit. These painful exercises, which were so calculated to empty him of self, were ordinarily followed with unusual assistance. He would retire to the church of Ayr, which was at some distance from the town, and not find it an irksome

Sixteenth Century Revivals

solitude to pass the whole night there in prayer. His choice of this place does not seem to have arisen from any superstition about its being a sacred edifice; but he thus obtained liberty to give full expression to his strong emotions and prayed not only in an audible but often in a loud voice.

"His wife, who was an excellent woman, a daughter of John Knox, not infrequently sought him in his midnight watchings, and has found him lying on the ground, weeping and wrestling with the Lord. On one of these occasions, when his wife found him overcharged with grief, he told her he had that to press him which she had not,—the souls of three thousand to answer for, while he knew not how it was with many of them. And at another time when she found him alone, his spirit almost overwhelmed with anguish and grief, upon her serious enquiry he said that the times that were to come on Scotland were heavy and sad, though she might not see them, and that for the contempt of the gospel."[5]

"On a certain night, being under an extraordinary pressure of spirit to pour forth his heart to God, he left his wife in bed, and going out to a garden spent most of the night in that exercise. His wife becoming at last uneasy, went to seek for him, but missing him in his ordinary place, entered other gardens by such passages as she knew; at last she heard a voice and drawing near to it could hear him speak a few words with great force and fervency accompanied with audible expressions of inward anguish, which were these, 'O God, wilt thou not give me Scotland? O God, wilt thou not give me Scotland?' She being afraid to interrupt him went back and heard not the close. At length he came home, and having returned to bed, his wife began to reprove his unmercifulness to his own body, and then enquired what it was that he prayed for, telling him that

---

[5]Fleming's *Fulfilling of the Scripture*, Vol. 1, p.364.

she had overheard him. He replied she had better have been in bed, but since she heard, he would tell her that he had endured a great fight for Scotland this night and hardly could he get a remnant reserved, 'yet,' said he, 'He will be gracious.'

"Another night he arose, but went not out of doors, but in a chamber travailed and groaned so, that his wife several times called him to bed. He, however, waited his time, and when he came she began a modest expostulation with him for tarrying. 'Hold thy peace,' said he, 'it will be well with us, but I shall never preach another preaching in Ayr.' He fell asleep, and before he awakened the messenger was come who carried him prisoner to the Castle of Edinburgh."[6]

These examples of Mr. Welsh's earnest importunity in prayer show us what must have been his influence in his day. He wrestled like Jacob of old and had power with God and prevailed. His discernment and sagacity in studying the dealings of God and the ways of men retrospectively gave him skill to perceive the probable turn that future events would take. This was so to such a degree that his calculations were almost regarded as predictions. The solemnity of his mind produced by the emergency in his country along with his deep communion with the God from whom he looked for help, cast a mysterious grandeur around his person which conferred on him an influence far above the measure of Christians in general. In these less exciting times, there are those who impute to John Welsh "monkish austerities" as if a man could not arise in the night to pray unless at the summons of a midnight vesper bell and for the purpose of repeating a certain portion of his rosary. If we consider his early history, we shall find that he was no monk either in his own person and practice or in the training of his pious father. His own spiritual condition and the state of his

---

[6]Ibid. Vol. 1, p.381.

Sixteenth Century Revivals

church are not without precedent in Scripture, for Judah exhibits the same experience: "With my soul have I desired Thee in the night; yea, with my spirit within me will I seek Thee early; for when Thy judgments are in the earth, the inhabitants of the world will learn righteousness."[7] It was a time of judgment and sore trial for the Church of Scotland. Her faithful pastors were spared to their flocks only by sufferance. They were in hourly danger of arrest, imprisonment, and banishment. Instead of speaking of "enthusiasm and fanaticism," let us rather consider that if Welsh were beside himself it was in zeal for God, and if he were sober or dejected, it was in the service of his people and of his country. Rather than speaking ill of him we ought to give thanks that he was one of the few righteous men for whose sakes, and in answer to whose intercessions, the Church of Scotland has been preserved.

Mr. Welsh and Mr. Forbes, another great witness for the truth in those days of trial, were sentenced to die at the assize at Linlithgow in 1606. While under that sentence, Mr. Welsh wrote in an exalted strain of joy to his friends the Melvilles, then in London: "Dear Brethren, we dare say by experience, and God is witness we lie not, that unspeakable is the joy that is in a free and full testimony of Christ's royal authority; unspeakable is the joy of suffering for His kingdom. We had never such joy and peace in preaching it, as we have found in suffering for it. We spoke before in knowledge, we now speak by experience, that the kingdom of God consists in peace and joy. . . . Our joy has greatly abounded since the last day (the day of their sentence of death) so that we cannot enough wonder at the riches of His free grace, that should have vouchsafed such a gift unto us, to suffer for His kingdom, in which there is joy unspeakable and glorious, and we are rather

---

[7]Isaiah 26:9.

Scotland Saw His Glory

in fear that they (the sufferings) be not continued, and so we be robbed of further consolation, than that they should increase. Surely there is great consolation in suffering for Christ; we dow[8] not express unto you the joy which our God hath caused abound in us."

His preaching in prison, both in Edinburgh and in Blackness, was not without fruit. We find his friend John Stewart following him to his place of confinement with the love that became him to such a servant of their blessed Lord.

James VI was induced to commute the sentence of death into banishment, probably because of his aversion to shed the blood of one whose reputation was so high and whose labors were held in such reverence by the church. Welsh was allowed to journey to France where he quickly learned to preach in the French language and was honored to bear witness to the truth before the King and his Court and to win a rich harvest of souls.

After some time he was allowed to return to England where he languished in London until he died. The King was often entreated to allow his return to Scotland because of his health. This boon was never granted. He was afflicted with languor and great weakness in his knees, apparently caused by his continual kneeling at prayer; though he was able to walk, he was wholly insensible in them, and the flesh became hard and horny. King James was often importuned to allow Welsh to preach, but he always refused the request until Welsh became so weak that his friends thought it impracticable. Yet as soon as he obtained permission, "he greedily embraced this liberty, and having access to a lecturer's pulpit, he went and preached both long and fervently, which was the last performance of his life; for after he had ended his sermon he returned to his chamber, and

---

[8] Are not able to.

Sixteenth Century Revivals

within two hours, quietly and without pain, resigned his spirit into His Maker's hands, in 1622, having lived fifty-two years."

During his prolonged time of languor and feebleness, he was so filled and overcome with the sensible enjoyment of God that he was sometimes overheard in prayer saying, "Lord, hold Thy hand, it is enough. Thy servant is a clay vessel, and can hold no more."

The Josiah Welsh, who was minister of Temple Patrick in North Ireland and one of the happy society of ministers who were the instruments of the revival there in 1629, was the son of this man and the heir to his father's graces and blessings.

At this remote period we cannot obtain much information concerning the people who were called under the Revival at Ayr, although we have abundant evidence of a great change being wrought there and many characters formed to holiness. But a few anecdotes are still extant of individuals who were members of Mr. Welsh's flock that furnish a sample of what fruit that vintage produced. Hugh Kennedy, who was at the time Provost of Ayr and one of Mr. Welsh's choice friends, met a man in the town who had done a most unprovoked injury to one of his sons by throwing his sea chest into the water. The Provost said in wrath to the man, "Were it not for the awe of God, and the place that I bear, I judge that you deserve that I should tread you under my feet." About two o'clock next morning the Provost came to his friend John Stewart, desiring him to go with him, telling him that he could not eat or sleep because of the injurious boasting words he had spoken to that man. He said as he had confessed his fault to God, he must now go and confess it to the man. They went together to the house and the man, hearing who called at such an untimely hour, drew his sword in bed to defend himself from the attack of the angry Provost. To his astonishment, his expected assailant fell on his knees before him and said, "Brother, I

Scotland Saw His Glory

wronged you and the office I bear, in boasting and threatening you, and I can get no rest till you forgive me;" and he would not rise till the man solemnly forgave him. It is also related of Hugh Kennedy, that being one day engaged in prayer for many hours, he came out at last to his Christian friends who had waited long for him, his countenance beaming with unusual cheerfulness. When they enquired of him relative to his long stay, he replied, "It was no wonder, for he had that day got mercy to himself and all his;" and there was evidence that it was true, for each of his children gave "large ground" to judge that they were truly godly.

While he was dying, Mr. Ferguson, a faithful minister who stood by, said to him, "You have cause, sir, to be assured that the angels of God are now waiting at the stoups[9] of this bed, to convey your soul into Abraham's bosom." The answer was, "I am sure thereof, and if the walls of this house could speak, they could tell how many sweet days I have had in secret fellowship with God, and how familiar he hath been with my soul." Mr. Welsh wrote from France of this good man: "Happy is that city, yea, happy is that nation that hath a Hugh Kennedy in it; I have myself certainly found the answers of his prayers from the Lord in my behalf."

John Stewart, the only man who would give a lodging to Mr. Welsh on his first going to Ayr, was a fast friend of Hugh Kennedy. It is instructive to look back through centuries and study the influences of Christian friendship in knitting hearts together and causing them to walk to the house of God in company. This John Stewart, having come to the inheritance of his patrimony, was so moved with the straits that many who loved the Lord Jesus were reduced to that he deliberately resolved to distribute his substance to his distressed brethren.

---

[9]Posts.

Sixteenth Century Revivals

He therefore called as many together in Edinburgh as he had means to collect—and having spent some time in prayer, took their solemn promise not to reveal what he was about to do while he lived. He told them he knew what straits many of them were in and had brought a little money to lend to each, but that they were not to repay him until he required it of them. This deed of love was not known until his death. Some time after he had thus denuded himself, the plague broke out in Ayr, in consequence of which trade fell into decay and Mr. Stewart himself got into difficulties. The profane of the place began to upbraid him saying that religion had made him poor and his giving to others, like a fool, now made him want bread. The good man, somewhat like Joshua when he prayed, "what wilt Thou do unto Thy great name," could not bear that his profession of religion should bring the good Providence of God into disrepute even with the wicked; he therefore left the country to conceal his straits and went to Rochelle, in France. When he was there he found that the obstacles to trade had reduced the price of salt and various other articles so as to encourage him to load a ship upon credit. This he did, hastening home through England to be ready to receive his cargo. After long and anxious waiting, he was informed that the vessel had fallen into the hands of the Turks. This intelligence so overcame him, from the fear that the mouths of the wicked should be opened to reproach his profession, that for many days he kept to his chamber. At last a maid, who heard among the people that John Stewart's ship was arrived in the Roads, came running and called at the door that his ship was come. "But he being at prayer, could not be moved from his Master's company till he was satisfied, and then went forth and saw it was the truth." His deep exercise of mind was not, however, to end here, for a worthy Christian and his great intimate, John Kennedy (supposed to be the seafaring son of Hugh), had gone out in a small

Scotland Saw His Glory

boat for joy to meet the ship. A storm arose, his little boat was carried out to sea, and in the judgment of all who looked on, he was supposed to be swallowed up by the raging ocean. The storm so increased that the loss of the ship was hourly expected also. This dear and gracious man was so overpowered with grief that for three days he could see no one. At last, having gone to visit the supposed widow of his friend—while they were mutually weeping and consoling each other, John Kennedy came home, having been cast away on a distant part of the coast. The ship also came safely into port. Thus God heard their cry and delivered them out of their distresses, and here at once many mercies met. The sale of his cargo enabled him to pay all his debts and returned him twenty thousand merks besides. Thus the bread on the waters was returned after many days, and the liberal heart was made to rejoice in the kind and watchful Providence of God.

On his death-bed, John Stewart exhorted all who came to visit him to be humble. Of himself he said, "I go the way of all flesh, and it may be some of you doubt nothing of my well-being; yea, I testify, that except when I slept or was on business, I was not these ten years without thoughts of God so long as I should be in going from my own house to the Cross; and yet I doubt myself and am in great agony—yea, at the brink of despair." A day or two before he died he turned his face from the company to the wall for two hours. Then Mr. John Ferguson, a grave and godly minister of that place, came in and asked what he was doing. Hearing this question he turned himself saying, "I have been fighting and working out my salvation with fear and trembling; and now I bless God it is perfected, sealed, confirmed—and all fears are gone."[10]

---

[10]Fleming's *Fulfilling of the Scriptures*, Vol. 1, p.397.

Chapter 3

The General Assembly of 1596

Scottish Presbyterian historians are agreed about the fatefulness of the year 1596 as far as the purity and prosperity of their Church is concerned. The hopefulness that marked its opening months, as well as the prophecy of coming disaster that darkened its close, are both emphasized. Writing early in the following century, Calderwood says 1596 was "a remarkable yeere to the Kirk of Scotland, both for the beginning and for the end of it. The Kirk of Scotland was now come to her perfectioun, and the greatest puritie that she ever atteaned unto, both in doctrine and discipline, so that her beautie was admirable to foraigne kirks. The assemblies of the sancts were never so glorious, nor profitable to everie one of the true members thereof than in the beginning of this yeere." The meridian of splendor, however, was soon passed. "The end of this yeere," he continues, "beganne that dooleful decay and declynning of this Kirk which has continued to this houre, proceeding from worse to worse; so that now we see such corruptiouns as we thought not to have seen in our dayes."

James Melville, nephew of the reformer, is equally emphatic in saying the year may be marked "for a speciall periodic and fatall yeir to the Kirk of Scotland." He describes "the schaw of profit" that characterized its start, and declares "the mids of it veric comfortable," "but the end of it tragicall." He finds that even nature conspired to make the year notable, for several portentous events took place during its course.

Even apart from its politico-ecclesiastical significance, 1596 should ever be held in grateful remembrance because of the noteworthy revival that was experienced throughout the greater

Scotland Saw His Glory

part of it. As already noted, various testimonies make it unquestionable that corruptions both in manners and morals had crept in. Church and State alike were suffering from them. The Reformation, with all its enthusiasm and new life, had passed more than thirty years previously. The generation that experienced it was nearly gone. With their disappearance, the impetus the movement provided practically exhausted itself. A new energizing of religious sentiment and devotion was urgently needed. This necessity, the awakening of 1596 provided.

Doubtless the movement originated with John Davidson, Minister of Prestonpans, a man well known for his personal piety and for the prominent part he took in the public affairs of his times. In spite of an almost acrid plainness of speech, Davidson had many gifts and graces of character—learning, eloquence, courage, honesty, and fidelity. Common report credited him with unusual prophetic vision and utterance.

His own ministry at Prestonpans was used by the Holy Spirit to stimulate an awakening in the district. Soon after his settlement there, the Presbytery minutes record: "The haill gentlemen being required to reform their houses and use prayers at morn and evening, with reading of the Scriptures after dinner and supper, promised to obey; and for execution thereof every minister was ordered to visit their houses and see whether it was so or not; and for behoof of the unlearned Mr. John Davidson was ordained to pen short morning and evening prayers, with graces before and after meat, to be communicated to each minister for behoof of his flock. These forms of prayer were approved by the Presbytery and ordered to be printed."

For several years he had bemoaned the grave defections of the people from spiritual religion and had especially denounced the faithlessness of the ministry. At the Synod of Fife, in September 1593, he addressed the Court and urged that "the ordinary and lawful armour of fasting and prayer" alone could

The General Assembly of 1596

protect the land from the consequences of "the negligence and profainnesse" of its pastors, whom he characterized as "the mirriest and carelesest men in Scotland." Preaching before the Assembly of 1594, he attacked those ministers who avoided what might be considered false doctrine, "yitt the truth was so unfaithfulie delivered and so coldlie that their flockes were consumed with hunger." With his soul moved to its depths by what he knew would be the fatal issues of the prevailing corruptions, he brought the whole matter before his own Presbytery of Haddington and prevailed upon them to overture the General Assembly regarding it.

The overture they prepared was apparently principally of Davidson's composition and showed commendable restraint in many directions. While he was thought by some to be nothing but a "firebrand," the document demonstrates that he was a man of great sensitivity, earnestness, and practical wisdom. The nation was truly in great spiritual peril, but some were unwise enough to believe that its true peril lay in the physical realm, the country being in fear of a Spanish attack on its liberties. The overture recognized the necessity of making suitable provision against the outward danger but considered a few lines sufficient for that subject. It was the conviction of the Presbytery that little good could result from the use of outward means in resisting an enemy until a reformation of morals and manners in true repentance and faith had brought men into right relationship with God. Thus it gave its strength to calling the attention of the Assembly to the "grosse sinnes" that prevailed in all estates of the realm. The aristocracy, magistrates, ministers, and people stood in like condemnation. The overture urged the General Assembly to make all needed preparations for "universall repentance and earnest turning to God." The whole tone of the document shows the sincerity and the anxiety of the memorialists. They were deeply convinced of the perilous position in which the spiritual interests of the nation stood.

The General Assembly was convened in St. Giles' Cathedral, Edinburgh, on Monday, March 24, 1596. The interior of the old church had been altered greatly in appearance since the days of the papal ascendancy for the eastern extremity had been partitioned off to serve as a parish church and was variously known as the "East" or "Little" Church. The ministry of Robert Bruce conferred distinction upon it, and it was generally identified with his name, just as in later days the baser uses to which it was put caused it to be nicknamed "Haddo's Hole." It was in this section of St. Giles' that the Assembly met. No one would call it a comfortable place. Its floor was of earth, and a due regard to the health of those who worshipped in it, as well as that of the venerable fathers and brethren of the Assembly, caused the Town Council to cover its bareness with rushes. It is important to know this because it has frequently been charged that religious emotion is nothing but the product of the light and heat of the hall in which it occurs. The General Assembly of 1596 could definitely rule those factors out.

Robert Pont, Minister of St. Cuthbert's, who had frequently presided over the deliberations of the Assembly, was chosen Moderator. He was the worthy head of a worthy convocation. In the struggle for religious liberty he had borne his share. He had also shown much aptitude in the department of sacred learning. With him were men whose services on behalf of national religion and of their common Presbyterianism have made their names outstanding—Andrew Melville; James Melville; Nicol Dalgleish; Robert Bruce; David Lindsay; James Nicolson, the ex-moderator; Robert Rollock, the Principal of Edinburgh University; Patrick Simson, the Church historian; and among many others, though to be placed in a different category, Thomas Buchanan.

The General Assembly of 1596

Some difference of opinion emerged at the beginning of the Assembly as to the precise business which had brought it together. The Moderator thought that the Spanish danger should have first place in their deliberations. Although he was supported in this contention by several of his brethren, the large majority determined that its main business was the communication from the Presbytery of Haddington and the state of religion and morals to which it called attention. This was certainly to the credit of the members. The Church leaders of the time are too often spoken of as mere ecclesiastics, bent only on the triumph of their own form of church polity and little moved by the deeper matters of personal devotion to Christ. If anything was needed to dispose of that slander, the proceedings of this Assembly would furnish what was necessary.

Having thus arranged its chief business, the Assembly showed its confidence in Davidson by a unanimous request that he would "give up the particular catalogue of the cheefe offences and corruptiouns in all estats." This he produced on Wednesday. The Assembly approved the document, making only one amendment to it suggested by Andrew Melville, that "the censure answerable to the offense" should be added in each case. For this purpose, the whole was remitted to a committee consisting of nine members of the house—Nicol Dalgleish, Peter Blackburn, Walter Balcalquall, John Mackquherne, Adam Johnston, John Knox, James Law, John Johnston, and John Davidson—brethren, as James Melville describes them, "of sharpest and best insight."

It was an extraordinary paper that came under the notice of the Assembly. It spared no sin and mitigated no offence. It spoke boldly regarding king, queen, noble, judge, and peasant with equal impartiality and with like incisiveness. Its compilers have in this matter, as well as in their general policy towards their countrymen, been accused of undue censoriousness and with having much of the spirit of the Pharisee. The charge is groundless for, as is befitting to men in dead earnest, the document dealt mainly with the order to which they themselves belonged. The space devoted to the offenses of the ministry alone is much larger than that given to the rest of the realm. There is no reason to believe that the long array of sins and shortcomings is set down with any exaggeration whatsoever. Men whose consciences are aflame with the sense of convicted sin are not as a rule careful of the terms in which they make acknowledgment of their transgressions. There is in the document a Pauline sincerity about the way in which offences are baldly named and blame for them accepted. Surely any Church about which such things can be affirmed needs humiliation and reformation.

What can be said about a ministry concerning whom an influential assembly records the following verdict?—"That such as are light and wantoun in behaviour, as in gorgeous and light apparrell, in speeche, in using light and profane companie, unlawfull gaining, as dancing, cairding, dyeing, and suche like, not beseeming the gravitie of a pastor, be sharpelie and gravelie reproved by the presbytrie, according to the degree thereof: and continuing therein after due admonitioun, that he be deprived as slanderous to the gospell. That ministers being found swearers or banners, profainers of the Sabboth, drunkards, fighters, guiltie of all these, or anie of them, to be deposed simpliciter: and siclyke, leers, detractors, flatterers, breakers of promises, brawlers and quarrellers, after admonitioun continuing therein, incurre the same punishment." To such a black catalogue, other faults like trading for "filthie gain," keeping of public inns, and exacting excessive usury were added. Not only were positive transgressions named, but the Assembly approved of a list of sins of omission to be dealt with. They deplored the case of those ministers "as sall be found not given to their

The General Assembly of 1596

booke and studie of Scriptures, not carefull to have bookes, not givin to sanctification and prayer, that studie not to be powerfull and spirituall, not applying the doctrine to his corruptiouns, which is the pastorall gift, obscure and too scholastick before the people, cold and wanting zeale, negligent in visiting the sicke, cairing for the poore, or indiscreit in choosing parts of the Word not meetest for the flocke, flatterers, and dissembling as publict sinnes, and speciallie of great personages in their congregatiouns, for flatterie of for feare." The picture is an altogether sordid one. No wonder souls like John Davidson were moved to wrath and sorrow.

This terrible indictment came before the Assembly again on Friday the 26th. What could the brethren do before what they universally acknowledged was unanswerable? True to scriptural tradition, they determined "that there should be a humiliation among the ministrie before their departure." But who should lead the Assembly in this great act of confession? The names of the best men among them were presented one after the other —saintly Robert Bruce, learned Robert Rollock, statesmanlike Andrew Melville, Patrick Simson, James Nicolson, and John Davidson. By a vote, Principal Rollock was set apart for the high office, but he absolutely refused the duty. The Assembly then fell back on Davidson and would take no denial from him. He urged that the act, being fixed for Tuesday of the following week, would allow him no time for adequate preparation, as he had "to ryde home to his congregatioun to teache" on the intervening Sabbath. But the Assembly judged that the man who best knew the sins would best help them to make due confession to God concerning them. They insisted on his undertaking the duty, passing the following ordinance:

"Concerning the defectiouns in the ministrie, the same being at length read out, reasoned and considered, the brethrein concluded the same, agreing therewith. And in respect that, by

Scotland Saw His Glory

God's grace, they intend reformatioun, and to see the kirk and ministrie purged, to the effect the work may have the better successe, they think it necessar that this Assemblie be humbled for wanting suche care as became, in suche points as are sett doun, and some zealous and godlie brother in doctrine and lay them out for their better humiliatioun; and that they make solemne promise before the Majestie of God, and make new covenant with Him, for a more carefull and reverent discharge of their ministrie. To the which effect was chosin Mr. Johne Davidsone, and Tuisday nixt, at nyne houres in the morning, appointed in the New Kirk for that effect, whereunto none is to resort but the ministrie. The forme to be advised the morne in privie conference."[1]

Tuesday morning came in due course. On the preceding Saturday, the form of procedure had been agreed upon in private conference, and the Assembly knew what was expected of it. The meeting began at nine o'clock and lasted for more than four hours. Great care was taken to exclude all who had no right of entrance, only one of the two doors leading into the Little Kirk being opened. Consequently, "few were present except the ministrie, the whole amounting to foure hundredth persons, all ministers or choice professors." We can easily imagine the solemnity that pervaded the company. They had met to acknowledge before the high God, not only personal transgressions, but the sins of their order.

John Davidson proved an expert in deepening the sense of defection and shortcoming. After prayer, he read the thirteenth and thirty-fourth chapters of Ezekiel, passages that must have struck to the quick, for they dealt with lying prophets and shepherds that feed themselves and not the flock. We have only the baldest outline of the discourse that followed, but there can

---

[1] Calderwood, Vol. 5, p.401.

The General Assembly of 1596

be no doubt as to the way in which the leader pressed the likeness home. "He was verie moving in applicatioun to the present tymes," says the historian, "so that within an houre after they entered the Kirk, they looked with another countenance than that wherewith they entered." The preacher was quick to note the pulse of his audience and, ending his discourse, exhorted the brethren to silent meditation and confession. Old St. Giles' saw a strange sight during the next quarter of an hour. Emotion overcame the men: "There were suche sighes and sobbs, with shedding of teares among the most part of all estats that were present, everie one provoking another by their example, and the teacher himself by his example, that the Kirk resounded, so that the place might worthilie have beene called Bochim; for the like of that day was never seene in Scotland since the Reformation, as everie man confessed. There have been manie dayes of humiliatioun for present or immanent dangers, but the like for sinne and defectioun was there never seen."[2] Scotland had been afraid of having her bearded men weep, but surely these were gracious tears that boded well for the religion of the land.[3]

After prayer, Davidson again addressed the penitent Assembly—this time from Luke twelve, the parable of the faithful and wise steward. His words were delivered "with rare assistance of God's Spirit." If the former discourse had been for the breaking down, this was for building up. His broken-hearted

---

[2] Calderwood, Vol. 5, p.407.

[3] Mr. Andrew Lang finds occasion for sneering at the events of the day: "These impressive scenes," he says, "displayed the sincere belief of the Assembly that they represented the people of Israel. Scotland was their promised land, to extirpate Amalekites was their bounded duty. . . . *(History of Scotland,* Vol. 2, p.406.)

audience was wonderfully comforted. When they were about to disperse in great cheer, Davidson called upon them "to hold up their hands to testify their entering in a new league with God." Every hand but one was joyfully held up to take the covenant. It must have been a moving scene—a whole church through its representative ministry and eldership reconsecrating itself to God. The jarring note in the day's harmony came from Thomas Buchanan, nephew of the historian. He was either "not moved" or "despised that exercise."[4] In later days, he turned aside from the stricter defence of his party, and chroniclers saw in that defection and in his subsequent tragic death, the fruit of his scorn of the doings of this memorable Assembly.

Considerable misunderstanding has arisen concerning the nature of the covenant made. Church historians like M'Crie the younger, and recent writers like Dr. King Hewison, Hill Burton, and Andrew Lang, refer to it in ambiguous terms and have described the transaction as if it were a renewal of the National Covenant of 1580 or of that part of it known as the "King's Confession," The "Second Confession of Faith," or the "Negative Confession." This is entirely mistaken. We do not have the exact terms of the covenant—if indeed it was reduced to writing or even to words—but there is no room for doubt as to its nature and intent. The Assembly had its political outlook and its national duties to perform, but on that morning of March 30th, 1596, the members were examining their own and their neighbors personal transgressions and backslidings rather than attempting to discuss matters of national and international

---

[4]This was quite in accord with Buchanan's known opinions. At the Synod of Fife, held on Sept. 25th, 1593, when Davidson had impassionately indicted "the coldness and negligence of the ministrie," Buchanan had been unsympathetic. Davidson's "feare," he said, "was no sound argument in suche maters." Calderwood, p.261.

The General Assembly of 1596

importance. Spottiswood makes the distinction quite clear. "This is the covenant that by some is so often objected and said to be violated by those that gave obedience to the canons of the Church, albeit in it there is not a word or syllable that sounds either to confirming of the Church government then in use or to the rejecting of that which since has been established. . . . By this covenant all did bind themselves to abide by the possession of the truth and to walk according to the same, as God should enable them. But for the rules of policy or ceremonies serving to good order or decency, let inspection be taken of the Register which is extant, and it shall plainly appear that at the time there was not so much as any mention thereof made." The Assembly's own description of the act is that the members "entered into a new covenant with God, protesting to walke more warilie in their ways and more diligentlie in their charges." James Melville who was present and took the covenant is equally clear: it was "a entring of new againe in covenant with their God in Jesus Christ, the grait Pastor of the saulles and Mediator of the Covenant. . . ." Row merely says that the Assembly "renewed a covenant with God and ingaged themselves for tyme to come." Calderwood, more shortly still, calls it "a new league with God." Such a bond required no words, simultaneously spoken or otherwise; it need not have been more than the vow of the heart spoken in the ear of God.

After such a wonderful experience, it was natural that the Assembly should wish that any impulse and desire for a renewed and consecrated life which they had felt should be shared by their brethren. At the afternoon session they enjoyed "the brethren of the synodall assemblies to make the like solemne humiliatioun and protestatioun as was observed by the Generall, at their nixt conveening; and so manie as be not at their synod to doe it at their presbytereis."[5] As it turned out, the exercise was not confined to presbyteries, but widened out beyond ministers to their congregations.

Unfortunately, it is impossible to know the exact extent to which the Assembly's injunction was obeyed. Many helpful records disappeared and others remain inaccessible, but enough evidence exists to show that the movement was widespread. Dr. M'Crie enthusiastically says that the "ordinance was obeyed with an alacrity and ardor which spread from synod to synod, from presbytery to presbytery, and from parish to parish: the inhabitants of one city saying to another, 'Come and let us join ourselves to the Lord in a perpetual covenant that shall not be forgotten, until all Scotland, like Judah of old, rejoiced at the oath.'"[6] Synods, presbyteries, and congregations participated, although Scot declares that the injunction "was not universally put into execution."[7] The Records of the Presbytery of Stirling, for example, detail the steps taken against Lady Livingston who was justly suspected of favoring the Papacy. Part of the charge brought against her on July 28, 1596, was that by riding to Edinburgh, she "prophanit ye last Sabboth quhair on the holie communion was ministrat and the new covenant maid in all the kirks within thir bounds." James Melville was forced to lament, "I dar nocht bot mark it, howbeit against my will, that the Ministers of Edinburche and Kirk thairof neglected and omitted this actioun of the Covenant, with the effect of a feirfull desolatioun, if we dar judge!"[8]

It was customary to join the dispensation of the Sacrament with the taking of the covenant. Thus at Anstruther the minutes

---

[5]Calderwood, Vol. 5, p.408.
[6]*The Story of the Scottish Church,* p.37.
[7]Scott, *Apologetical Narration,* p.66.
[8]Melville's *Diary,* p.368.

The General Assembly of 1596

of the Kirk session read: "We thought meet to enter in tryell of ourselfes for the better preparation to the Covenant and Lorde's Supper." James Melville mourns that "the Ministers of Edinburche and Kirk thairof" omitted the sacred office and, in the omission, finds the cause of the "feirful desolatioun" that in a few months fell upon them. The blame of their neglect, however, could not be laid at the door of the Presbytery, for they had solemnly enjoined its observance—"It is concluditt, according to the act of Generall Assemblie, a covenant salbe renewitt in all the bounds of this Presbitrie and that upon the vii. of October next."

It is to James Melville, however, that we owe a detailed account of how the covenant may have been taken in the subordinate courts of the Church. He was connected with the Synod of Fife and the Presbytery of St. Andrews, and he enters fully into the steps these bodies, as well as his own congregation at Kilrenny, took to carry out the recommendations of the Assembly. The Synod of Fife acted on lines that followed closely the procedure of the General Assembly. It met in Dunfermline in May 1596 with James Melville as moderator, a man who was in thorough sympathy with the movement and who, as chairman, proved as suitable in the office as John Davidson had been in the higher court. Under his guidance, the Synod set about the work in a methodical and earnest manner. Adequate preparation for the members taking the covenant in a right state of mind was made. Wednesday, May 12, was set apart for a preliminary service to be conducted by David Ferguson of Dunfermline, one of the original veterans of the Reformation and the oldest minister in the Church. The principal meeting was appointed for the following day.

The brethren came to the chief gathering fasting, but they were rewarded for their "preceise abstinence." At four in the afternoon, as the diarist quaintly records, they dispersed "als

Scotland Saw His Glory

full of spirituall joy in the saull as emptie of corporall fuid." The proceedings were commenced by David Black who preached a copious, powerful, percing, and pertinent" discourse. Then entering on the main business of the day, Melville took as his subject the covenant made by Israel at the instigation of Joshua. The effect of his words was just as appropriate to the occasion. "The Lord," he says, "steirit upe sic a motioun of hart, that all were forcit to fall down before the Lord, with sobbes and teares in aboundance, everie man mightelie commovit with the affectionnes of thair conscience in the presence of thair God, in private meditatioun, rypping out thair wayes, confessing and acknawlaging thair unworthines and craving earnestlie grace for ammendiment, and that for a lang space." Melville continued his exhortations, and then the covenant was suitably entered into—"Be lifting upe of the hand, everie an testified befor God, and mutualie an to the uther, the sinceare and earnest purpose of the hart to studie till amend and serve God better in tyme to come, bathe in their privat persones and in the office of that grait Ministerie of God's honour, and salvatioun of the peiple concredit to thame."[9]

After suitable addresses by John Davidson and Patrick Simson, who were present by order of the Assembly, and by David Ferguson, David Black, and Andrew Melville, all outstanding members of the Court, the Synod broke up with an "ernest prayer powred out be the Moderator for getting of grace to remember, practise and pey the vows thair maid, and after hartlie thankgiffing for that memorable benefit of God."

During the third week of July, the Presbytery of St. Andrews, under Melville's direction, obeyed the injunction of the Supreme Court. The same solemn scenes were enacted.

---

[9] Melville's *Diary*, p.355,356.

The General Assembly of 1596

Gentlemen, burgesses, barons, and ministers took the covenant, each testifying to a "trew conversioun and change of mynd."

The procedure adopted by congregations was necessarily somewhat different. For example, in Kilrenny, the month of August was devoted to teaching the people. The nature of the covenant was carefully explained and shown to carry with it all that was subsequently summed up in the phrase, *the federal relationship of God and the believer.* To be outside the covenant meant that "maist miserable esteat of nature, without God, without Chryst, a chylde of wrathe, alian from the comounweill of his peiple, under the slaverie of the devill and sinne, and, finallie a faggot of hellesfyre." To be within the band was to be acknowledged as the servant and child of God. Whether by raising of hand, partaking of the Supper, or any other outward means, the Covenant was renewed in those days.

Thus a gracious wave of returning to God swept over the land. We do not learn much of the personal effects the movement had—the time being yet far distant when formal records were made of methods, incidents, and results, but who can doubt that sincere facing of these matters by the community would permanently affect it for good? Nobody was left outside the scope of this beneficent opportunity. Many ministers had at least four occasions in which they could renew their covenant with God; all of them had three. No class was left out, and the common people had the privilege brought to their very doors.

Note again the words of Calderwood with which this chapter began: 1596 was "a remarkable yeere to the Kirk of Scotland, both for the beginning and for the end of it. The Kirk of Scotland was now come to her perfectioun, and the greatest puritie that she ever atteaned unto, both in doctrine and discipline, so that her beautie was admirable to foraigne kirks. The assemblies of the sancts were never so glorious, nor profitable to everie one of the true members thereof than in the beginning of this yeere." But things changed: "The end of this yeere beganne that dooleful decay and declynning of this Kirk which has continued to this houre, proceeding from worse to worse; so that now we see such corruptiouns as we thought not to have seen in our dayes."[10] Thus this widespread revival came at a most opportune time for Scotland. Many regarded it as God's own preparation for the sore trials which were soon to fall upon His faithful Church. Clearly it braced ministers and people alike for the disappointments they had so soon and unexpectedly to face.

The benefits of the Revival of 1596 were not limited to Scotland. As is true of every great work of the Spirit of God, the remembrance of God's mighty acts by future generations is both inspiring and instructive. Clearly, Jonathan Edwards was thus affected when in writing of New England revivals of the eighteenth century he refers to the General Assembly of 1596, showing that violent emotion resulting in "great outcries" is not an uncommon accompaniment of religious conviction: "Particularly I think fit here to insert a testimony of my honoured father, of what he remembers formerly to have heard. 'I well remember that one, Mr. Alexander Allan, a Scots gentleman of good credit that dwelt formerly in this town, showed me a letter that came from Scotland, that gave an account of a sermon preached in the city of Edinburgh, in the time of the sitting of the General Assembly of divines in that kingdom, that so affected the people that there was a great and loud cry made throughout the Assembly.'"

Surely the people of God are never in greater danger than when forgetting His gracious deeds and glorious works done in former generations.

---

[10]Vol. 5, p.387.

Chapter 4

Stewarton, 1625[1]

Notable as Stewarton is in the annals of revival, it has little or nothing otherwise to commend it. The parish in all probability took its name from the village that nestles near its center. It lies in the upper half of the basin of the Annick, a stream which rises in the low hills separating the shires of Renfrew and Ayr and loses itself in the Water of Irvine, a short distance above the town of that name. Today,[2] the long grey village numbers close to 5,000 inhabitants. In the days of the revival, it was little more than a cluster of houses that surrounded the parish church. For many years, its sturdy townsmen were chiefly weavers and bonnet makers with a reputation for the excellence of their workmanship. Their industry fell on evil days, but at the time of the revival, it was as flourishing as its opportunities allowed. It is recorded that in 1630 the bonnet makers of Stewarton formed "a small but powerful combination, supporting their own immediate interests with the utmost pertinacity and with a cordial contempt for the welfare of others that is amusing, just from its simplicity and want of reflection."

After passing the village, the Annick, or the Stewarton Water as it is usually called, winds through the valley for eight miles to Irvine. For most of this distance, it forms the boundary line between the parishes of Dreghorn and Irvine which, with

---

[1]This is the usual year assigned to the beginning of the movement. Stevenson (*History of Church and State in Scotland,* p.120), however, points out that both Wodrow and Crawford, the Church historian, give 1630. There seems to be no valid reason for departing from the traditional date.

[2]1918.

Scotland Saw His Glory

Stewarton, may be said to comprise the whole valley. As becomes a pastoral region, the population is scattered and of no great number. When the fires of the revival crept up both sides of the Annick, the inhabitants were fewer still. The district, however, had as an advantage the fact that it lay on one of the main highways from the west country. It was, in consequence, a center from which religious impressions spread easily.

The minister of Stewarton in 1625 was William Castlelaw. Unfortunately, we know very little about him, although what we do know shows he was a man of considerable parts as well as of endearing disposition. He was minister of the Kirk of Stewarton as early as December 21, 1616. By the time of the revival, he was well acquainted with the spiritual needs of his people and had the interests both of religion and of learning thoroughly at heart. In 1632 he gave 20 pounds—a large sum in those days—toward building the library of Glasgow University. At his death in July 1642, his own books were valued at 80 pounds. Although he acknowledged the pretensions of the prelacy by exercising his office under the bishops, he was nevertheless a man of evangelical piety and zeal.

An anecdote regarding Castlelaw lets in much light on his character. Robert Blair, a regent in Glasgow University and afterwards well known as a preacher, tells how in 1623 he had become suspected by the authorities and was in great anxiety about the proceedings to be taken against him. He had often preached in the Stewarton pulpit and was well acquainted with its pastor. One evening, in the midst of his perplexity, Castlelaw dropped in on him in his house in Glasgow. He stayed the night, and next morning the brethren started together for Dumbarton. Looking back on that journey years afterwards, Blair recalled with delight the companionship he enjoyed by the way. "That day," he exclaims, "I was so sweetly comforted that for the most part of the way (it being ten miles) we did cheerfully sing Psalms." More than a dozen years afterwards, Castlelaw's Presbytery was much exercised over the order commanding the use of Laud's *Service Book.* They determined, after much perturbation and hesitation, to "supplicat in the name of us all for a suspension" of the edict. Castlelaw was chosen to lay the petition before the Privy Council. So successful were his representations that, yielding to his and other pressure, the Council modified their order and declared that "the ministers were alone to buy the Books for their own information, but not for any present use in their parishes." From all this, it appears that Castlelaw was a man well fitted to direct the revival when it broke out among his people.

Fleming says that the revival appeared in Stewarton parish first, and "after through much of that country, particularly at Irvine." If this is so, it explains why the whole movement is named the "Stewarton Revival." But facts seem against Fleming. The course of the revival is usually described as being from Irvine up to the banks of the Annick. Stewarton parish may have benefited most, and its minister may have had the sore experience of having sowed and of seeing another reap, but the center of interest lay for the most part in Irvine. The name most intimately connected with the revival is that of David Dickson, whose memory is still fragrant in the west, even after a lapse of nearly three centuries. Mr. Dickson had been formerly Professor of Moral Philosophy in the University of Glasgow, but on receiving a call from the town of Irvine to be their minister, he resigned his chair in the college and was ordained to the pastoral office. By 1625 he had succeeded in obtaining an extraordinary hold on the affections of the entire neighborhood. The year of his settlement, 1618, was also that of the passing of the *Five Articles of Perth,* which Dickson at once found it to be his duty to denounce. In due course, he was summoned before the Court of High Commission. The scenes that took place in his parish on the Sabbath before he left showed, in no equivocal fashion, the love his parishioners had for him. "During the whole time of sermon," says Calderwood, "there was weeping and lamentations: scarce one within the doors could hold up his head. That whole day the women were going up and down the kirk-yaird and under stairs grieving as if their husbands had been newly buried." The same grief broke out anew next morning when "Mr. David" was leaping upon his horse "to proceed to Edinburgh."

On January 9, 1622, Dickson was sentenced to banishment to the parish of Turiff, in the north of Scotland. His statement at the time clearly reflected his conviction, "The will of the Lord be done; though ye cast me off, the Lord will take me up. Send me whither you will, I hope my Master will go with me; and as He has been with me heretofore, He will be with me still, as being His own weak servant." The Master whom he so dearly loved and so faithfully served, having much people in Irvine and its vicinity who were to be to Him for a name and a praise, did not permit His servant to remain long in banishment. Having the hearts of all men in His hand, turning them whithersoever He wills, He stirred up the Earl of Eglintoun, the magistrates, and others of the town of Irvine, to petition for his release from the sentence of banishment. Through the overruling providence of God, their request was granted, and in July 1623, he was allowed to return to his work.

Dickson came back with a new enthusiasm for his ministry. He had found both Turiff's climate and religion cold. "He was afterwards wont to observe that the devils in the north were much worse than the devils in the west, for studying one day would have served him at Irvine, but it required two days of study for preaching at Turiff." The revival broke out in 1625. The movement has been represented in some quarters as "a mere popular commotion against the purposes of Charles I and

Stewarton, 1625

the Court who were attempting to impose Episcopacy on an unwilling people." It is quite possible that the plans and methods of the government forced a deeper examination of the essentials of the faith and drove men into closer touch with Christ. It is certain that the persecution which Dickson endured made him a more eager preacher, and his parishioners a people more willing to receive his message. Dickson's sermons had hooks in them. The English merchant who heard Robert Blair and Samuel Rutherford and was captivated by their styles, also heard Dickson. He described the preacher as a "well-favored old man with a long beard," adding, "that man showed me all my heart." As an author, he has his own place even today, and his career as professor, both before and after his Irvine pastorate, proves his scholarship;[3] but his best "books," he said, were the lives of his people. He believed in what is called "Scriptural preaching" and founded his short discourse on texts of reasonable length. He considered simplicity and directness essential. The results achieved show that he was not mistaken in his methods. Gifted with great preaching ability and with an unusually attractive personality, it is not astonishing that he drew crowds to hear him, especially at communion seasons when "all the most eminent and serious Christians from all corners" of the land came to Irvine. What took place some years later in the neighboring parish of Fenwick, under the spell of William Guthrie's piety and eloquence, happened also at Irvine. Many came and settled permanently in the town so that, as Wodrow quaintly puts it, "they might be under the drop of his ministry."

---

[3] Nothing is more conspicuous in the story of these early revivals than the weight of the men who led them, alike in preaching ability, scholarship, and personal impressiveness of character.

Scotland Saw His Glory

After some months of such preaching, the work of grace began. Conversions became frequent and continuous. Fleming's testimony is most explicit: "It can be said (which divers ministers and Christians yet alive can witness) that, for a considerable time, few Sabbaths did pass without some evidently converted, and some convincing proofs of the power of God accompanying His Word." So eager were the people to hear the way of salvation that they were not content with the ordinary ministrations of the sanctuary. They pressed for private dealing by the preacher, and the manse became thronged with men and women anxious about their spiritual condition. "Upon the Sabbath evenings," says Wodrow in the passage cited above, "many persons, under soul distress, used to resort to his house after sermon, when usually he spent an hour or two in answering their cases, and directing and comforting those who were cast down, in all which he had an extraordinary talent; indeed, he had the tongue of the learned, and knew how to speak a word in season to the weary soul. In a large hall he had in his house at Irvine, there would have been, as I am informed by old Christians, several scores of serious Christians waiting for him when he came from the church."

Encouraged by this demonstration of the work of the Spirit, Dickson started services on Mondays. It was the day of the weekly market, and the town was usually crowded with visitors from the surrounding districts. We are told that the hour of meeting was judiciously arranged so that it would not interfere with the proper business of the market-place. Full advantage was taken of the privilege, and the church became even more crowded than it was on the Sabbath. Irvine was a goodly distance from Stewarton, but the people of that parish attended eagerly and regularly. Robert Blair, who knew the facts firsthand says: "As many of them as were able to travel went to the Monday market at Irvine with some little commodities

Stewarton, 1625

such as they had; but their chief intention was to hear the lecture that ended before the market began, and by their example, many of that parish (their minister encouraging them to it) and out of other parishes went thither, whereby the power of religion was spread over that part of the country."

It is probable that when the "wark" assumed these proportions, help was given from the outside. The task was one of some delicacy, but fortunately those who took part in it were men whose judgement and experience could be trusted. We know how two of those who came to assist regarded what they saw. Blair tells how Robert Boyd, of Trochrigg, Principal of the College of Glasgow, a man "of . . . austere-like carriage but of a most tender heart . . . came from his house in Carrick to meet with" the converts, and "having conferred with them, both men and women, blessed God for the grace of God in them." Blair himself confesses his indebtedness to these simple peasants who had come under the power of God. "I had much conference with them and profited more by them than I think they did by me." "I bless God," he adds, "that ever I was acquainted with that people. . . . I was helped thereby to relieve, according to my power, them that were in need, and to sympathize tenderly with such as I knew to be tempted and lying under heavy pressures of conscience, whereby I still learned more of the wicked wiles of Satan and of the blessed ways of God."

At least two gracious ladies gave welcome assistance. Both belonged to the landed gentry of the neighborhood. The first was Lady Robertland, by which name is evidently meant Margaret Fleming, wife of David Cunningham of Robertland,[4]

---

[4] It was a custom of courtesy at the time to give territorial titles to the ladies of proprietors, even though they had no such right at law. The final vestige of this practice was removed at the beginning of the nineteenth century.

an estate which lay in close proximity to the village of Stewarton. Gathering up the impressions of this lady after nearly a century, Wodrow names her "an extraordinary Christian." Blair, who occasionally resided at the mansion-house when he visited Stewarton, speaks of her as "that famous saint," and John Livingstone who knew her well, describes her as a "Christian deeply exercised in her mind." She was a women of many trials, but also a woman of many privileges in her sorrows. "She did often get very signal outgates from her troubles," we are told.

Lady Robertland did all she could for those who had been convinced by the Spirit. She acted as hostess for the ministers and moved among the poorer classes with words of encouragement and advice. Livingstone especially records that "she was a great help to the poor people of Stewarton when they were awakened." Her gift was "a strange way of continuing a spiritual discourse under similitude of worldly things," which probably means that she made large use of parable and illustration in her talks with the people. How great a help these private conversations and personal interviews were it is not difficult to understand. That she had her own times of spiritual depression would make her all the wiser a counsellor—"many battles brought many victories" to herself.

The second lady was Anna, Countess of Eglintoun. She was the daughter of the first Earl of Linlithgow and had been a maid of honor to the queen of James VI. Her reputation for piety was very great. She took a deep interest in those who came under the influence of the revival and "did much countenance them." Her husband, who afterwards was among the very first to affix his signature to the National Covenant of 1638, shared in her interest. Blair has a strange way of describing the part the Earl played, saying the Countess succeeded in persuading him to "forego his hunting and hawking" that he might have

Stewarton, 1625

conversation with the converts. Hopefully, the Earl's absorption in the sport was not so great as to need much pressure. At any rate, his verdict was favorable to what he saw and heard. He "protested that he never spoke with the like of them: he wondered at the wisdom they manifested in their speech."

In spite, however, of these expressions of praise, Stewarton was not exempt from the dangers to which all revivals are exposed. The intense movements of the soul are ever prone to play upon the nervous system and produce effects which show themselves in physical prostrations and in various forms of excitement. These excesses and extravagances made due appearance in Stewarton. "Many," says Fleming, "were so choked and taken by the heart through terror, the Spirit in such measure convincing them of sin in hearing of the Word, that they have been made to fall over and thus carried out of the church." Blair speaks of "great terrors and deep exercise of conscience," and Wodrow of "excesses both in time of sermon and in families." As was natural, these phenomena, as well as the whole course of the movement, gave scoffers their opportunity and the awakening was nicknamed the "Stewarton sickness," and those that were affected the "daft folk of Stewarton."

The work, however, was under the guidance of men who were strong in intellect and in caution, and the worst effects were warded off. Dickson, Boyd, and Blair did their best to discourage undue excitement. When Blair and Livingston were called upon to cope with similar circumstances a year or two later in Ireland, they took strong measures, and a conference which they called together agreed that the unwelcome manifestations were the work of the devil. The Scottish brethren had no difficulty in coming to a similar conclusion, and so successful were they in putting down unseemly disturbances, that Wodrow testifies "they were enabled to act so prudent a part as Satan's design was much disappointed."

Scotland Saw His Glory

For at least five years the general attention to religion continued in the valley and its neighborhood. Marked changes took place in character and conduct. Mockers of religion and many who had led dissolute lives became sober, respectable, and God-fearing. Stewarton and Irvine were made centers of pilgrimages for many over the whole country. The result was that "solid, serious religion flourished mightily in the West of Scotland." Fleming beautifully compares the work to the effects "of a spreading moorburn",[5] which "put a lustre on these parts of the country." Dickson bore himself through it all with the modesty that became a true servant of Christ. He was under no delusion as to the cause of the success that had attended his ministry. Castlelaw could stand aside and see another preferred, and Dickson looked with joy at the wonderful influence exerted earlier by John Welch of Ayr. More than once he is reported to have observed that "the vintage of Irvine was not equal to the gleanings, and not once to be compared to the harvest at Ayr in Mr. John Welch's time, when indeed the gospel had wonderful success in conviction, conversion, and confirmation."

"This great spring time of the gospel," says Fleming, did not last for a short time merely, but continued many years . . . and like a spreading stream, increasing as it flows, and fertilizing all within its reach, so did the power of godliness advance from one place to another, increasing in its progress, and throwing a marvelous lustre over those parts of the country." The fame of this revival brought many from distant parts of the country who, when they came and witnessed the gladdening sight of so many turned from darkness to light and walking in the fear of the Lord and comfort of the Holy Ghost, thanked God, took courage, and became more earnest in prayer than ever for the descent of the Spirit on other parts of the Church. The remem-

---

[5]The burning of heather.

Stewarton, 1625

brance of the gracious promise, that "for all these things I will be inquired of by the House of Israel to do it for them," would quicken their importunities at the throne of grace—that God for Christ's sake would come and visit that vine which His own right hand had planted and make it fruitful and fill the whole land.

How long the effects of the revival remained in the community is unknown. By the time of Patrick Warner, who was settled over the parish in 1688, they had entirely disappeared. Indeed, the heart of that good man was almost broken by the godlessness that was rampant around him. In sending out an edition of his predecessor Alexander Nisbet's book on *Ecclesiastes,* he reviews the many religious privileges the parish had had. He speaks of the learned and devoted ministers set over it, saying, "By all which it appears that the people of this place have had a long and clear day of the gospel among them." Then, making his earnest appeal to the reader, he continues, "If, therefore, thou be one that livest near God, I beg prayer on their behalf, least, if otherwise, because of their barrenness, the Kingdom of God should be taken from them." So intolerable did Warner find the situation that he retired. Reid, the minister of the neighboring parish of Stevenston, preached the church vacant in February 1763, and among other biting things said, "Oh, but the people of Irvine must be sadly degenerated! Would your forefathers have treated an honest minister of the gospel at such a rate?" But, thank God, the tide did turn again. William McKnight, minister at Irvine, took part in the Revival at Cambuslang in 1742, and before long Irvine itself shared in the blessing.

Chapter 5

The Kirk of Shotts, 1630

That there was some connection between the Stewarton Revival and the remarkable movement that took place at the Kirk of Shotts on Monday, June 21, 1630, is more than probable. Some echo of what had taken place at Irvine must have reached the upland parish, for it lay on the high road of communication between the capital and the west country, and travellers to and fro could hardly miss dropping some intelligence regarding it. A direct line of connection between the two movements can be found in the person of John Livingston whose sermon was the chief agency in the awakening at Shotts. He was a friend of the ministers at both places. He had preached more than once at Shotts before 1630 and had himself come under the influence of the Revival at Stewarton. In the course of his autobiography, he tells how he could not give any date for his conversion but adds: "I do remember one night in the Dean of Kilmarnock, having been most of the day before in company with some of the people of Stewarton, who were under rare and sad exercises of mind, I lay down in some heaviness that I had never had experience of such thing. That night, in the midst of my sleep, there came upon me such a terror of the wrath of God that, if it had increased a small degree higher or continued a minute longer, I had been in as dreadful a condition as ever living man was in; but it instantly removed, and I thought it was said to me within my heart, 'See what a fool thou art to desire the thing thou couldst not endure.'" It may not, therefore, be unduly pressing probabilities to conclude that the true origin of the work of grace at Shotts

Scotland Saw His Glory

is to be found in David Dickson's labors among the people of Stewarton and Irvine.

The Kirk of Shotts—which must be distinguished from the village built at the railway station of Shotts some miles distant—is a moorland village on the bare watershed which divides the valley of the Clyde from the Lothians. The present church stands out conspicuously and can be seen for miles around, as no doubt its predecessors did on the same site. During the closing years of the sixteenth century, the parish had been somewhat unhappy in its ministers. An ordained preacher was not settled over it until thirty years after the Reformation, and even then the difficulties of the parishioners did not end, for four successive ministries lasted only two years each. At length, in 1599, John Home was ordained to the charge, and his term of office was destined to last his lifetime—he died in 1640. In 1630, accordingly, Home was a man well advanced in years. Robert Blair and John Livingston went to assist him at a sacrament in 1632. He was then described as "an aged and infirm man." What personal part he took in the revival is unknown. Wodrow speaks of him as "a man of easy temper," and it is probable that, like William Castlelaw of Stewarton, he had the grace given him to stand aside when the critical time came.

The steps which led up to the revival are, according to a uniform tradition, well defined and display quite markedly from what small beginnings such movements may arise. The manse stood on the highway which led through the parish. As there was no house of entertainment for a considerable distance along the road on either side of Shotts, the minister seems to have been in the habit of aiding travellers in their need. Several ladies of rank were specially indebted to his friendly offices, notably on one occasion when they had to remain overnight at the manse owing to the breakdown of their carriage. They were

Kirk of Shoots, 1630

struck with the inconvenience and dilapidation of the minister's house and determined to procure better accommodation for him. They succeeded so well that a new manse was erected. On its completion, Home waited on the ladies to express his gratitude and to ascertain if there was any way of showing his sense of the obligation under which he lay. All the ladies asked was that certain well-known preachers, whom they named, should be invited to assist at the approaching sacrament. To this Home readily agreed.

The chief of these "honorable women" was the widowed Marchioness of Hamilton, a lady of outstanding character, with a strong attachment to the Covenanting cause. Another was Lady Culross, whose name occurs in the subsequent story. She was a daughter of Sir James Melville of Hallhill, the well-known diplomat of the reign of Queen Mary, and had married John Colville, heir to the barony of Colville of Culross. Livingston, who was her close friend, has given her a niche among his *Memorable Characteristics,* and testifies to her piety. "Of all that ever I saw, she was the most unwearied in religious exercises, and the more she attained to access to God, she hungered the more." She was well known to her contemporaries as the author of *Ane Godlie Dreame,* of which several editions had appeared before 1630.

The names of just two ministers invited to the communion are known to us. David Dickson came with all the work at Irvine behind him. The other was the veteran Robert Bruce, then over 70 years of age and widely recognized as a statesman and winner of souls. It was said of him by his own generation that no man had more demonstration of the Spirit accompanying his preaching, and that none had more seals to his ministry. Calderwood speaks of "the many thousands" he won for Christ —most notable among whom perhaps was the famous Alexander Henderson.

Scotland Saw His Glory

Though not an ordained minister, John Livingston was also invited to be present. He was only twenty-seven years of age but already had a great reputation as a preacher. For communions he was much in request, and it was not the fault of the people if he were not already settled over a congregation. Several calls had been addressed to him, but "all were obstructed by those in power," for Livingston had not commended himself to the bishops. So inveterate was their hostility to him that in 1627 he had been ordered to "desist preaching" altogether. The command, however, had not closed his mouth, and he had conducted services all over the Lowlands. At that time of the revival, he was acting as chaplain to the Countess of Wigton at her mansion house at Cumbernauld.

The report of the exceptional character of the gathering spread far and wide, and numbers of all ranks flocked to Shotts. Unfortunately, no record of the meetings that took place prior to the Sabbath or of those of the Sabbath itself remains. The only note that indicates the nature and effect of the exercises is that there was much prayer. Livingston himself reports that he was "in company with some Christians who spent the night in prayer and conference" on the Sabbath evening. This gathering probably refers to the one he himself describes in his "Memorable Characteristics" in his reference to Lady Culross. "At the communion in the Shotts in June 1630," he says, "when the night after the Sabbath was spent in prayer by a great many Christians, in a large room where her bed was, and in the morning all going apart for their private devotion, she went into the bed, and drew the curtains, that she might set herself to prayer. William Ridge of Adderny coming into the room, and hearing her have great motion on her, although she spake not out, he desired her to speak out, saying that there was none in the room but him and her woman, as at the time there was no other. She did soe, and the door being opened, the room filled

Kirk of Shoots, 1630

full. She continued in prayer, with wonderful assistance, for large three hours' time."

So evident was the interest created at the various services and conferences that a desire took hold of the people to give special expression to their thanksgiving. Communion seasons had up to that time usually ended with the Sabbath day, but the ministers readily agreed to the wish of the congregation and one of their number was selected to preach that Monday.[1]

When Monday morning came, the preacher appointed was unable, through illness, to undertake the duty assigned to him, and at the suggestion of Lady Culross, John Livingston was asked to take his place. Livingston was startled at the thought of speaking before so many veterans in the art. He had modelled his preaching upon that of Robert Bruce, amongst others, and he did not care to appear before his teacher. It was only with difficulty that he consented. He then withdrew for meditation. "When I was alone in the fields about eight or nine o'clock," he tells us, "there came such a misgiving spirit upon me, considering my unworthiness and weakness, and the multitude and expectation of the people, that I was consulting with myself to have stolen away somewhere and declined that day's preaching." In his flight, he had actually passed some

---

[1] It is usually said that this service was the origin of the Monday thanksgiving service after communion. It may have settled a growing practice, but it is probable that the service existed before. Fleming's phrase is that the sermon on Monday was then "not usually practiced" (*Fulfillment of Scripture*, Vol. 2, p.96). An article in the *Reformed Presbyterian Magazine*, 1866, p 103 (probably by the late Rev. J. H. Thomson, author of the *Martyr Graves of Scotland*), entitled *Origin of the Communion Services,* says: "It is generally said to have been first introduced by Livingston at the Kirk of Shotts, June 21, 1630; but from his autobiography as well as from that of Robert Blair it seems to have been common both in Scotland and among the Presbyterians in Ireland."

craigs, which tradition still points out, and was just losing sight of the church when the thought occurred to his mind that he was "distrusting God." At the same time, the words seemed to be spoken in his ear, "Was I ever a barren wilderness or a land of darkness?" and he stopped and turned back.

The service was held in the open-air at the west end of the churchyard. The grassy turf which sloped somewhat quickly away on all sides accommodated the worshippers and provided a natural amphitheater for them. The sermon Livingston preached has become one of Scotland's historic discourses. So great a mark did it make that its preacher has been spoken of as "single sermon Livingston." He chose as his text Ezekiel 36:25,26—"Then will I sprinkle clean water upon you, and ye shall be clean: from all your filthiness, and from all your idols, will I cleanse you. A new heart also will I give you, and a new spirit will I put within you: and I will take away the stony heart out of your flesh, and I will give you an heart of flesh." The discourse lasted for an hour and a half at least. "In the end," he says, "offering to close with some works of exhortation, I was led on about ane hour's time in ane strain of exhortation and warning with such liberty and melting of heart as I never had the like in publick all my life." The crisis of the discourse was produced by an incident that took place during its delivery. Some rain commenced to fall, and the congregation, beginning "to stickle a little," drew their cloaks more securely round them. Like a true preacher, Livingston saw his opportunity. "What a mercy it is," he cried, "that the Lord sifts that rain throu these heavens on us, and does not rain down fire and brimstone as He did on Sodom and Gomorrah." Speaking of the matter long afterwards, when he was an exile in Holland, Livingston ascribed the great results of the sermon to this passing incident. He acknowledged that he never spent much time in the preparation of his discourses. He believed more in "getting his

Kirk of Shoots, 1630

heart brought into the right disposition," adding that he thought the "hunger of the hearers helped him more than his own preparation." It may be a dangerous doctrine for most ministers, but its wisdom was proved on this occasion. The passing reference was so unmistakably used that Livingston was afterwards constrained to advise that "when you are strongly pressed to say anything you have not premeditated, do not offer to stop it. You know not what God has to do with it."

Fleming describes what took place as "a strange unusual motion of the hearers," which is his way of saying that considerable manifestation of feeling took place in the congregation. Livingston uses the same word. Speaking of the taking of the National Covenant at Lanark in 1638, he says: "Except one day at the Kirk of Shotts, I never saw such motions from the Spirit of God." The phrase may not include those physical perturbations which appeared at Stewarton, although James Robe has this sentence: "An aged man told me last summer [1742] that an old man who had lived about the Shotts, whom he served in his younger years, told him that several upon that remarkable Monday after sermon lay so long as if they had been dead, that their friends and others scarce thought they would recover." Whatever may have been the nature of the commotion, Livingston must have been reminded of his own experience at his first communion when "there come such a trembling upon me that all my body shook." Five hundred is usually given as the number of those who that day experienced a saving change.

Few details have come down regarding individual cases. The records of those that have may be transcribed in full. Writing under date May 1711, Wodrow has the following— "Mr. John Paisley tells me he had it from the person himself, frequently, John Johnstoun ane eminent Christian in Paisley. He was very young and apprenticed to a merchant in Glasgow, who was very much sett for the Bishops and had been educated

Scotland Saw His Glory

this way himself. He was sent in by his master to Edinburgh about some business and behoved to walk in on foot. He came from Glasgow, the Communion Monday after the Shotts Communion. and when he saw the meeting afarr off, hearing of it that it was a Puritan meeting, he says his heart rose against them in spite and malice. When he came nearer he cursed them in his heart, and when he came within hearing of the voice he cursed them in words: and yet (just like the Apostle Paul being full of rage and spite) soe free is the grace of God, he found ane inclination to goe near and hear what was said: and he was not a quarter of one hour there till the Lord touched his heart by the Word: and, said he, 'I gote that which I never cast again!' There he was converted and all this country know what ane eminent and usefull Christian he was."

Dr. Gillies gives two examples. One relates to "a poor man, a horse-hirer in Glasgow, whom a gentlewoman had employed to carry her to Shotts. In time of sermon he had taken out his horse to feed at a distance from the tent; when the power of God was so much felt in the latter part of the sermon, he apprehended that there was a more than ordinary concern among the people; something he felt strike him in such a way as he could not account for; he hastily rose up and ran into the congregation, where he was made sharer of what God was distributing among them that day."

The other is a moving story indeed. "On that remarkable Monday, three gay young gentlemen of Glasgow were travelling to Edinburgh, for the purpose of enjoying the public diversions there. They stopped to breakfast at Shotts. One of them proposed to his associates to stay and hear the young man who was to preach while their horses rested. And that they might not lose time, they agreed to quit the worship at the end of the sermon and not wait for the concluding devotional exercises. But the power of God so arrested them, that they

Kirk of Shoots, 1630

could not quit the spot till all was over. When they returned to the public house to take their horses, they called for some refreshment; but when it was placed on the table, they all looked to each other, no one durst touch it till a blessing was asked, and as it was not their manner formerly to be careful about such things, one of them at last proposed—'I think we should ask a blessing to our drink.' The others readily agreed, and put it upon one of the company to do it, which he at once agreed to. When they had done they could not rise until another should return thanks. They went on their way more sober and sedate than usual, but none of them mentioned their inward concern to another, only now and then they remarked, 'Was it now a great sermon we heard?' or, 'I never heard the like of it.' They went to Edinburgh, but instead of plunging into light amusements, as they had designed, they kept their rooms the great part of two days while they remained; and then, being quite weary of Edinburgh, they returned home. They still did not open their minds to each other on their way, and when they reached home they kept their apartments, and came little abroad. At last one of them visited another, and discovered to him what God had done for him at Shotts. The other frankly owned the concern he was brought under at the same time. Both of them went to the third, whom they found in the same case, and they three agreed directly to begin a fellowship meeting. They continued to have a practice suitable to their profession as long as they lived, and some of them lived to an advanced age, and were eminent and useful in Glasgow."

Livingston never ceased to be thankful for that day at Shotts. In his later years he said he never wished to see in writing any of the discourses he had preached except two. Both of them were delivered at Monday thanksgiving services after communion. One was this Shotts discourse and the other was preached at Holywood in Ireland, which resulted in the conversion of well-nigh one thousand persons. It is urgent to note that, on both of these occasions, Livingston spent the whole night before in conference and prayer with other Christians and had no opportunity for any more than ordinary preparation. The immediate effect on himself, however, was painful. He seems to have become stunned and frightened at the extraordinary results. In a day or two he, characteristically started to see his friend, David Dickson, at Irvine. On the Thursday he preached at Kilmarnock, where "some little stamp" of the inspiration he had been under remained. On the following Monday at Irvine, however, he was so "deserted" that he determined to give up preaching for a time. Searching for a reason for this strange experience, he concluded that it was the chastisement of the Lord for his pride of heart. But Dickson was wiser and insisted on his friend continuing his work "to get amends of the devil." Livingston was persuaded and succeeded in preaching next Sabbath with "some tolerable freedom."

The work of grace did not end with the departure of Livingston. There is abundant evidence that it spread over the whole countryside. Fleming's words are most poignant: "I must . . . mention that solemn communion at the Kirk of Shotts, at which time there was so convincing an appearance of God, and downpouring of the Spirit . . . which did follow the ordinances, especially on Monday, 21st of June, when there was a strange unusual motion of the hearers, who in a great multitude were there convened of divers ranks. It was known, as I can speak on sure ground, that near five hundred had at that time as discernable change wrought on them, of whom most proved lively Christians afterwards. It was the sowing of a seed through Clydesdale, so that many of the most eminent Christians of that country could date either their conversion or some remarkable confirmation in their case from that day. It was the more remarkable that one, after much reluctance, by a special and

Kirk of Shoots, 1630

unexpected Providence, was called to preach that sermon on the Monday, which was not then usually practiced; and that the night before, by most of the Christians there, was spent in prayer; so that the work of that Monday might be discerned as a convincing return to prayer."[2] The work had results in the mansion houses of the nobility as well as in the cottage of the peasant. "While these Christians were upon the stage," says Walker in his Preface to *Peden's Life,* "they would have little time when they met, but they would have had some notes of that sermon."

Eight years later, when the covenant was being signed over Scotland, one of the strongholds of the movement lay in the immediate neighborhood, and a banner inscribed "For the Parish of Shotts" flew at Bothwell Bridge.

Andrew Gray of Chrystoun wrote of the period: "Two springs of the revival of religion in this corner were the famous sermon at the Kirk of Shotts, and the labours of Mr. Robert Bruce. As at the sermon at Shotts, a good number of people were by grace made acquainted with the life and power of religion, so several of them were eminently good men, and remarkable not only for a pious, inoffensive behaviour, but also for their abounding in all good fruits which pure and undefiled religion enables its sincere followers to produce. This made them not only esteemed and revered by many of their neighbours, but also produced some respect for religion itself, from which they procured many advantages, its followers being readier to do them in all kind of good offices than other people. Among other good fruits, you cannot doubt a strong inclination to promote the spiritual good of others was a principal one. As the labourers were then few in this part of God's vineyard. He seemed to have inspired these private Christians with an

---

[2]Fleming's *Fulfillment of the Scriptures.*

uncommon degree of love to the souls of men, inciting them to labour by all proper methods, to bring others acquainted with that grace which had produced such blessed effects on themselves; and their labours were not without considerable effect. They were called the Puritans of the Muir of Bothwell, perhaps by way of reproach, by those who were ill affected towards them."

Messrs. Bennet, Ramsay, and Carstairs were contemporaries of Bruce and Livingston but continued ministry sometime after their passing. They were mutually helpful in promoting a lively work of grace in the west. It is said of the ministry of Mr. Thomas Melvin of Calder that in a few years the worship of God was so generally set up in families in his parish that it was counted a scandal to such as neglected it. It is also reported that the number of praying societies rose from one to eight or ten under his pastoral leadership.

These men were blessed in extending the knowledge of the gospel by the more ordinary means; but as our focus is on singular effusions of divine grace, we need to note what happened on a Monday after the celebration of the Lord's Supper at Kirkintilloch: "The people being detained in church by a sudden fall of rain, Mr. Carstairs (not their own minister, but the minister of Cathcart) stept into the pulpit, and in an extemporaneous discourse, wherein he described the nature of faith, and cautioned them against mistakes about it, especially against depending on a sort of faith that they had all their days, and knew not how they came by, declaring faith to be a work of the Spirit of God with power—there arose a mighty commotion in the congregation; many were brought into a deep concern about their soul's condition, the good fruit of which appeared in their after life and conversation.

"A similiar instance is remembered at Calder, where the same Mr. Carstairs officiated for Mr. Melvin, who had been

Kirk of Shoots, 1630

taken with a fit of sickness during the sacramental solemnities. While they were singing part of the 24th Psalm, 'Ye gates lift up your heads,' &c., before the blessing of the elements, there was a mighty melting of heart seized the congregation, and the Spirit of God, like a mighty wind, burst open the everlasting doors, and took possession of the hearts of sinners, several people from that day dating their first soul-concern and conversion. Mr. Carstairs used to say, he had three days of heaven upon earth, and one of them was at Calder. The exemplary life and conversation of the clergymen we have mentioned, as well as their labours and zeal for winning souls to Christ, raised the credit of their ministry high among good people. They loved them as their own souls, attended the ordinances with earnestness and joy, and considered the want of them as the greatest loss they could possibly sustain. This appeared when, after their ministers were turned out at the Restoration, multitudes attended their preaching in the fields at the hazard of their lives."[3]

In regard to this wide and continued influence, George Barclay, one of the covenanting preachers, is most explicit. He is reported by Walker as saying that "above all places in Scotland, he found the greatest gale upon his spirit upon the water Clyde, which he attributed much to the plentiful, successful prayers of some of the old Christians and their offspring, who got a merciful cast of free grace, when casts were a dealing at the Kirk of Shotts, the 20th of June 1630, which perfumed and gave a scent to the overward of Clydesdale above all other places, but alas! is now much gone!"

The fame of the time became not only a cause of thanksgiving but also the hope of less spiritual days. In 1736 the newly constituted Associate Presbytery looked back with longing eyes

---

[3]Gillies's *Historical Collections*, Vol. 1, p.314.

Scotland Saw His Glory

on the period as a time when the gospel had more than ordinary power and success. And Patrick Walker, speaking for himself and fretting under the lukewarmness of religion at the beginning of the same century, was persuaded that "if ever the Lord pity this weather-beaten Sardis, Laodicean Church and send forth a thaw wind and spring tide day of the gospel to thaw the frozen face of affairs, as was at Stewarton, and spread through the West of Scotland, as muirburn a hundred years since, and at the Kirk of Shotts five years thereafter," it would result "that these and many other things that now are wersh and unsavoury will come in request again."

Chapter 6

Cambuslang, 1742

Perhaps no century has been more harshly spoken of than the eighteenth. Carlyle, in his vehement language, described it as the age "of lying, of sham, the fraudulent bankrupt century, the reign of Beelzebub, the peculiar era of cant." One of its most distinguished sons, the great Bishop Butler, especially deplored its spiritual poverty. "It is come," he said, "I know not how, to be taken for granted by many persons that Christianity is not so much a subject for enquiry, but that it is now at length discovered to be fictitious. And accordingly they treat it as if, in the present age, this were an agreed point among all people of discernment, and nothing remained but to set it up as a principal subject of mirth and ridicule, as it were, by way of reprisals for having so long interrupted the pleasures of the world." This is a verdict with which Principal Cairns, who made the century a special study, generally agrees when he says: "What the first centuries are in the history of Christianity, the eighteenth is in the history of unbelief." Its morals were little better than its religion. "The historian of moral and religious progress," says Mark Pattison, "is under the necessity of depicting the period as one of decay in religion, licentiousness of morals, public corruption, profaneness of language—a day of 'rebuke and blasphemy.' It was an age destitute of depth or earnestness; an age whose poetry was without romance, whose philosophy was without insight, and whose public men were without character; an age of 'light without love,' whose 'very merits were of the earth, earthy.'"

Scotland, on the whole, shared in the prevailing conditions. Ebenezer Erskine may have been somewhat biased, but his description of his native land was—"generally lifeless, lukewarm, and upsitten." He was probably right, for it was the day of the Moderate—the man who had no profound belief in anything, and whose life corresponded faithfully to his negative religion.

And yet this maligned century was not altogether fruitless in what makes for the success of the Kingdom of God. In England, it witnessed the rise and amazing progress of Methodism which rescued evangelical religion from threatened destruction. Scotland, in like manner, saw the origin of both branches of the Secession Church and the spiritual impulse which their creation afforded. Notable revivals of religion were visited upon the people throughout the whole country and were as wells of water in a dry and parched land.

The first motions of revival appeared in America. As early as 1730, a revival had occurred at Freehold, New Jersey. It was followed in 1734 by the better-known work under Jonathan Edwards in New England. These awakenings were the heralds of a religious movement that was to spread over all England and Wales. From about 1730 onwards, the Principality heard the gospel from a succession of men like Griffith Jones, Daniel Rowland, Howell Harris, and Howell Davies. George Whitefield was converted about seven weeks after Easter, 1735, and John Wesley on May 24, 1738. Both itinerated after their conversions, preaching everywhere throughout the land. On the invitation of the Seceders, Whitefield visited Scotland in the autumn of 1741 and, in both the east and the west, had remarkable success.

It would be hard to tell what connection existed between these movements and the awakening in Cambuslang in 1742. For want of a better word, it may be said that revivals are infectious, and accounts of the success of the gospel in America and England may have made similar events possible for the

Cambuslang, 1742

Lanarkshire village. Quickening was in the air, and direct contact may not therefore have been required. Whitefield did indeed work both in England and at Cambuslang, but the Cambuslang "Wark" began four months after he had brought his first Scottish visit to a close and had been running its course for nearly five months before he returned for his second campaign.

The parish had a notable connection with evangelical religion having been the scene of the ministry of Robert Fleming, the author of *The Fulfilling of Scripture,* a work from which quotations have already been made. For several years before the revival, societies for prayer had existed in the district, but it was on the whole in a pitiful state when the Rev. William M'Culloch was settled over it in 1731. For the preceding eight years a contest had been carried on between the Duke of Hamilton, who held the patronage of the parish, and the people regarding the succession to the charge. It was only when the nominee of the patron accepted presentation to the parish of West Linton that he gave way, and M'Culloch, "whom the people were for," was admitted. The former incumbent had been unfit for ministerial service for some time before his death in 1723, and for nearly sixteen years, the parish had been without real supervision. Wodrow gives as evidence of the condition of neglect which prevailed that he had been told "there was not one under sixteen years of age who ever had been catechized"—a process that at one time held a distinct place in the religious education of young and old alike.

The opening years of the ministry thus begun gave little promise that special blessing would come to the neighborhood through it. Unfortunately, the wrangling that had preceded the settlement did not end with M'Culloch's ordination. Certain of the parishioners continued their opposition to him, and for ten years, friction existed in a more or less acute state. The sacrament was not dispensed for the first three years of M'Culloch's ministry. When the Presbytery made enquiry into the matter, he defended his action on the ground that he had insufficient elders to begin with and that, during the second year, he thought it needful to instruct the people and get better acquainted with them before administering the rite. Matters reached a crisis in 1739 when an open rupture took place in the session. It is impossible now to discover what was the subject of dispute or to follow the proceedings taken. About 1745, when a better day had dawned, the session considered that it would not "answer any valuable purpose of edification to transmit to posterity the remembrance of that unhappy breach" and destroyed all the papers connected with the matter, especially in that "all parties . . . signified their desire that it might be buried in oblivion."

M'Culloch's personal qualifications for his office were not such as to mark him out as a probable leader in a great revival movement. He seems to have been possessed of more than average scholarship, but for the pulpit he had virtually no gifts. His voice was thin and weak and his utterance slow. His son, Dr. Robert M'Culloch of Dairsie, published a selection of his father's sermons in 1793. In the sketch prefixed to this volume, he acknowledged that his father was "not a very ready speaker; though eminent for learning and piety, he was not eloquent. Thoughtful and studious, he delivered the truths of God faithfully: but his manner was slow and cautious, very different from that of popular orators."

It was the jesting manner of the time to nickname an unpopular preacher a "yill minister," because "his rising to speak during field preachings at communions was taken by many as the signal to seek refreshment." This uncomplimentary nickname attached itself to M'Culloch. The published sermons bear out this general verdict. They are in no way distinguished for eloquence or profundity of thought. Two of them are

Cambuslang, 1742

marked as having been delivered at Cambuslang in the year of the revival, but unfortunately they are no guides to the actual words then spoken. The son says his father "in some cases considerably altered the first copy," and he especially mentions that one of the two had undergone much change. When M'Culloch died in 1771, however, his people did not remember his slow and halting speech. The only eulogy they carved upon his tombstone, as it stands today in Cambuslang Churchyard, reads—"He was eminently successful in preaching the gospel."

M'Culloch's own spiritual condition was not satisfactory when he began his ministry. Wodrow tells a strange story of a distressing interview he had with him less than four months after his ordination. It would appear that the burden of his parish had already begun to lie heavily upon M'Culloch. He had conscientiously tried to do his duty, but he had felt himself unfitted for the responsibility, and he came to the older man for advice and help. "Since his ordination he had been preaching on conversion and the nature of it, which, he tells me, he had not thoroughly considered and gone to the bottom of before, and now he thinks he is perfectly a stranger to this great work." So deep had been his misgivings about entering on the ministry at all that he had almost fled the country before his ordination. The active discharge of his duties had only increased this sense of unworthiness, for "he is also much damped in conversation with his people and their telling him experiences which he has been a stranger to, amidst all he wants not like seals to his ministry." Wodrow came to the conclusion that his confidant's case presented "a mixture of bodily and very heavy spiritual distress" and gave him suitable advice. "I presumed to say he had more of a call to the ministry than severall had atteaned to, and I took him to be of a thinking, melancholy disposition, and ready to dip too farr into things. I asked him if he could deny but that the glory of Christ and the good of souls wer not in his eye on entring the ministry. He could not deny it." In ending his story, Wodrow concludes that M'Culloch's "life has been all along grave, serious, and contemplative. We who are ministers have much need of such an instance to quicken and awaken us."

No further glimpse is available of M'Culloch's spiritual history until ten years later, when we see him in the full assurance of faith in the midst of the revival movement.

M'Culloch began sowing the seed of the revival as early as the autumn of 1740. He had followed with great eagerness the course of the religious awakenings in England and America under Whitefield and Jonathan Edwards and had been in correspondence with both of these leaders. What he learned, he generally communicated to his congregation on Sabbath evening after the sermon. He took an active share in that part of Whitefield's first Scottish campaign (September 1741) which related to Glasgow and afterwards wrote the evangelist that "fifty persons had been converted by his ten sermons in Glasgow and that many others had been convinced of sin and were seeking salvation." Among these converts were some of his own parishioners.

In addition to all this, M'Culloch set himself deliberately to educate his people on the vital matters of the faith. "The minister in his ordinary course of sermon for nearly a twelve-month before the work began," says the first attested record of the movement "had been preaching on those subjects which tend most directly to explain the nature, and prove the necessity, of regeneration according to the different lights in which that important matter is represented in Holy Scripture." So diligent was M'Culloch in work of this kind that, in December 1741, he started the publication of a little journal named the *Weekly History* and circulated it far and wide at the price of one halfpenny—probably the first religious periodical to appear in Scotland.

Cambuslang, 1742

Many in the parish seconded the efforts of their minister in the way best open to them—they met frequently for prayer. "A Gentleman in the Gorbals of Glasgow" who had firsthand knowledge of the condition of expectancy that existed wrote, "The people there have been wonderfully given to private, secret, and social prayer and religious conferences, assembling themselves as the manner of some is, and considering one another to provoke to love and good works. . . . There has been unusual wrestling and pouring forth of their hearts in prayer."

As a result of all these efforts, a more than ordinary interest was observed during 1741 in the services M'Culloch conducted. The congregations increased in size. The church was small and in bad repair, and when the weather permitted, the congregation adjourned to the high banks of the burn which flowed past the churchyard. Railway lines and modern buildings have now changed the area, but then the place was "peculiarly well adapted for the purpose. It is a green brae on the east side of a deep ravine near the church, scooped out by nature in the form of an amphitheater." Here, for some months, M'Culloch spoke to large gatherings, and the spot acquired the name of the "preaching" or "conversion braes."

As 1741 closed and 1742 opened, M'Culloch discovered that the fallow ground was being broken up and that the people were becoming ever more accessible to gospel influences. At the end of January, a petition, chiefly under the direction of Robert Bowman, a weaver, and Ingram More, a shoemaker who had been one of Whitefield's converts at Glasgow during the preceding summer, was sent through the parish for signatures. It was signed by ninety heads of families out of a total of about eight hundred persons, and M'Culloch gladly consented to its request.

A beginning was made on the first Thursday of February. Two meetings passed, and a few, in anxiety about their religious condition, sought interviews with the minister each evening. It was on Thursday, the 18th, however, that unmistakable evidence was first given of a work of grace begun. The sermon, which was on the text, "And this is His name whereby He shall be called, the Lord our Righteousness" (Jeremiah 23:6), passed without anything unusual occurring, although it appears to have made a great impression. The preacher came to his last public prayer. Apparently he was oppressed with the failure of all his planning and praying, for he cried—"Who hath believed our report, or to whom is the arm of the Lord revealed? Where is the fruit of my labour among this people?" It was the spark that was needed. Immediately the church was filled with the sound of weeping. That night the manse was crowded with about fifty "wounded" souls, as the spiritually afflicted came to be called. So manifestly was this eighteenth day of February 1742 the beginning of great things for the parish that, until M'Culloch died, the nearest Sabbath to the date was held by the congregation as its anniversary. On these memorial days, M'Culloch used to read from the pulpit a paper in which he said the day "was observed partly as a day of thanksgiving for the remarkable season of grace to many in the British Colonies, and particularly in this small corner in the years 1741 and 1742."

A report of these proceedings spread widely, and the interest aroused drew numbers to Cambuslang. Many came long distances. To meet the evident needs of the situation, M'Culloch was compelled to institute daily services which continued practically without interruption for the next six or seven months.[1] The church, we are told, was seldom empty, and

---

[1] Unfortunately the Session records for the period of the revival are missing. Some information regarding the number of the services can, however, be gleaned from the treasurer's statement of the church-door

Cambuslang, 1742

the manse continued to be crowded. An unfriendly critic of the movement, who was an eye-witness, says that after each service, M'Culloch went to the manse "where he takes down in writ the names of the new ones, their designation, place of abode, time, and manner of their being seized, and continues most part of the night teaching and exhorting them."[2] All this, of necessity, involved a tremendous strain upon the resources of one man. Happily, M'Culloch was not allowed to face the labor alone. He had the help of two probationers, James Young and Alexander Duncan, and of several ministers from the neighborhood. As the meetings went on, however, it was noted that M'Culloch seemed "to renew his strength, and notwithstanding of extraordinary fatigue and toil, he seems to be more than ordinarily lively, prompt, and extemporary in all the parts of his ministerial work." By the beginning of May, the number of the awakened was over three hundred.

We have several glimpses into the meetings that were held in the church and on the braes during this time. No effort appears to have been made to maintain silence on the part of the congregation. Some clapped their hands and broke into cries as they were touched by what they heard. M'Culloch was accused of having done nothing to restrain the outbursts, but rather of doing his best to increase them. He is reported to have said that the congregation should not "stifle or smother their convictions but encourage them." More sustained interruptions

---

collections. From this it appears that a daily service was maintained without interruption from February 26 to March 18; in April on all but ten days, in May on all but eight, and in June on all but eleven. From Thursday, February 4, to August 29 services were conducted altogether on 120 days.

[2]Two beautifully written manuscript volumes of "cases" prepared by M'Culloch are preserved in the New College Library, Edinburgh. Dr. Duncan Macfarlan printed long excerpts in his *Revivals of the Eighteenth Century*.

were common, and members of the congregation seem to have both exhorted and prayed. The hostile critic before mentioned gives this example: "I was present at one of their meetings when a weaver, leaning over the same tent where the minister was preaching, conversed with some people at a distance so as to be heard of the whole congregation, and when one who stood at a great distance from the tent said that he wished these people (meaning the people under convictions and those who were speaking to them) would compose themselves so as they and others might hear the sermon, the clergyman who was preaching answered, 'If ever ye had known what it was to have an awakened conscience, ye would have known that to be impossible,'"

Boys are said to have prayed in public. One elder from a neighboring parish was summarily stopped in the midst of his petitions because, by using the phrase, "If it be a work of God," he appeared to cast doubt on the divine origin of the movement. The meetings sometimes lasted until six o'clock in the morning. Dr. Meek, M'Culloch's successor in the pastorate, and a man who had no evangelical sympathies, laid stress upon this sentence from the critic's statement: "All the 'wounded souls' (as they are commonly designed) are regularly brought out when sermon begins, guarded by Ingram More and Robert Bowman (most part of them having their heads tied about with napkins), and all placed together on forms before the tent, near which stand several dishes full of water for the use of those that faint. There they continue crying all the time of sermon, psalms, and prayers."

Meantime, the report of the work had spread to various parts of Scotland, and ministers from Dundee, Edinburgh, Glasgow, Irvine, and elsewhere came to see it with their own eyes. Mindful of future generations as well as of hostile criticism at the time, M'Culloch, at the beginning of April,

Cambuslang, 1742

asked for letters of attestation from some of those who thus had personal experience of the movement. Robe printed nine of these attestations. They are all avowedly from men who were in complete sympathy with both methods and results. All lay stress upon the deep sense of sin shown by the penitents and ascribe to this cause the bodily distress into which so many fell.

The well-known John Willison of Dundee, in a lengthy report said, "Seeing some are desirous to know my thoughts of the work at Cambuslang, I am willing to own that I have travelled a good way to inquire and get satisfaction about it. And having resided several days in Mr. McCulloch's house, I had occasion to converse with many who had been awakened and under conviction there; I found several in darkness and great distress about their soul's condition, and with many tears bewailing their sins and original corruption, and especially the sin of unbelief, and slighting of precious Christ. Others I found in a most desirable frame, overcome with a sense of the wonderful love and loveliness of Jesus Christ, even sick of love, and inviting all about them to help them to praise Him. I spoke also with many who had got relief from their soul trouble, and in whom the gracious work of the Spirit of God appeared in the fruits and effects of it, according to my apprehension; such as their ingenuous confessing of their former evil ways, and professing a hatred to sin; very low and abasing thoughts of themselves; renouncing the vanities of the world, and all their own doings and righteousness, and relying wholly upon Christ for righteousness and strength; and expressing great love to Christ, to the Bible, to secret prayer, to the people of God, and to His image, in whomsoever it was, without respect of persons or parties; and also love to their enemies. I conversed with some who had been very wicked and scandalous, but now wonderfully changed; though some were rude and boisterous before, they now had the meekness and mildness of the Lamb about them, and though I conversed with a great number, both men and women, old and young, I could observe nothing visionary or enthusiastic about them for their discourses were solid, and experiences Scriptural; I had heard much of this surprising work by letters, and by eye-witnesses, before I came, but all that made slight impressions on me when compared with what I was eye and ear-witness to myself. Upon the whole, I look upon the work at Cambuslang, to be a most singular and marvelous outpouring of the Holy Spirit, which Christ has promised; and I pray it may be a happy forerunner of a general reviving of the work of God in this poor decayed Church, and a blessed means of union among all the lovers of our dear Jesus."

Hamilton of Glasgow "could never observe the least disorder in their judgments." M'Knight of Irvine declared "the surprising work . . . is of God." MacLaurin of Glasgow noted that the movement was already bearing fruit in better conduct and that the awakened were having "a strict regard to the precepts of both tables of the Divine Law: herein exercising themselves to have 'consciences void of offence toward God and toward men.'"

And so the work went on during the spring and early summer. The crowds that flocked to Cambuslang were extraordinary. Writing on April 28, M'Culloch reports to Whitefield that "some have computed the number present during the last two Lord's Days as nine or ten thousand."

It was customary at the time to observe the Sacrament of the Lord's Supper only once a year, and it was determined that the annual communion should be held on July 11. Whitefield had by that date accomplished six weeks of his second visit to Scotland, and even greater results than on the preceding year had attended his ministry. M'Culloch, who had been in correspondence with him during the winter, invited the evange-

Cambuslang, 1742

list to assist him. Whitefield readily consented. He arrived at Cambuslang at midday on the Tuesday before the day appointed for the Sacrament and preached three times ere the night closed. The effect was extraordinary. He had been accustomed to outbursts of fervor in America where he had spent the preceding winter. The way in which the Cambuslang crowds were swayed outdid his American experiences. "For about an hour and half," he said, "there was such weeping, so many falling into deep distress and manifesting it in various ways, that description is impossible. The people seemed to be smitten by scores. They were carried off and brought into the house like wounded soldiers taken from the field of battle. Their agonies and cries were deeply affecting." Preaching was continued far into the night and "throughout the whole of the night might the voice of prayer and praise be still heard in the fields."

Whitefield was absent on Wednesday and Thursday but returned on Friday evening. Next day, he preached to an enormous gathering which he calculated numbered 20,000. So great a number assembled on the Sabbath that the use of the Church was impossible, and the sacrament was dispensed on the "braes." Two tents were set up, and throughout that long summer day, preaching and serving the tables was continued. Help was given by local ministers as well as by Dr. Alexander Webster of Edinburgh. Altogether, seventeen tables were served, the number of communicants being about 1,700.

Monday, however, was the great day. Like the Monday at Shotts, it was prepared for by much prayer, and the sound of worshipping companies could be heard all through the preceding night. In the morning Whitefield preached. The experience of that day beggared all he had seen before. "The motion," he said, "passed swift as lightening from one end of the audience to the other. You might have seen thousands bathed in tears, some wringing their hands, some almost swooning, and others crying out and mourning over a pierced Saviour." "Our glorious Immanuel," wrote M'Culloch, adopting one of Whitefield's phrases, "is still going on to make numerous conquest in this place. It is not quite five months since the work began and during that time I have reason to believe that upwards of five hundred souls have been awakened, brought under deep conviction of sin and a feeling sense of their lost condition."

The general effect of this July communion was so good that both Whitefield and Webster urged on M'Culloch the desirability of repeating the celebration at an early date. To do so would run counter to established custom, and M'Culloch did not come to a decision all at once. The new life, however, had run in channels that were unusual in several ways, and it did not require much pressure on M'Culloch to create a precedent in this direction also. On Sabbath, July 18, the session met and fixed August 15 for a second observance of the Lord's Supper.

Great preparations were made that the celebration should be carried out worthily. When the day came, expectations were amply fulfilled. On Sabbath, the crowds were enormous. The number stated to be present varies. M'Culloch himself says, "Some have called it fifty thousand, some forty, and the lowest estimate I hear of, with which Mr. Whitefield agrees, who has been used to great multitudes and accustomed to form a judgement of their number, makes them to have been upward of thirty thousand."[3] Communicants came from all quarters.

---

[3] The presence of crowds is reflected in the collections taken. The offering on an ordinary Sabbath varied between three to twelve pounds, Scots. On the first Communion Sabbath it stood at 117 lbs. 12 shillings and on the second at 194 lbs. 2 shillings. The legal allowance for communion elements was 33 lbs. 3s; for those two communions 103 lbs. 13s 4d required to be expended. The total collections for February - December 1741 amounted to 146 lbs. 13s 9d: for the same period in 1742 the sum raised was 1445 lbs. 17s 9d—all which figures are in Scots money. (Session

Cambuslang, 1742

Multitudes flocked in from the surrounding districts. Two hundred journeyed from Edinburgh; Kilmarnock, Irvine, and Stewarton each sent one hundred. Among the crowds were strangers from England and Ireland. The number who sat at the tables was about three thousand.[4] So impressive were the scenes witnessed that [Dr.] John Erskine of Edinburgh did not hesitate to take the events of this communion for *The Visible Signs of*

Records.)

[4] A curious sidelight is thrown upon the numbers present at these communions by an action at the instance of Hamilton of Westburn (the same name appears as opposing the settlement of M'Culloch in 1731 - Wodrow's *Analecta,* Vol. 4, p.189) against the minister and Kirk-Session of Cambuslang, which came before the Court of Session on November 22, 1752. The pursuer objected to certain payments made by the defendants in 1742, and desired the Court to reduce them on the ground that the poor of the parish had suffered by the expenditure. The payments included "two guineas for the use of a field to preach in, the congregation being so numerous that the church-yard could not contain them," a fee to a constable for keeping the peace, and a sum of seventeen shillings for repairing a park dyke broken down by the crowd, as well as an extra expenditure for communion elements. Although it was stated that the poor's fund had been helped by changing its stock of 500 lbs. to 5000 lbs. through the contributions of the congregations that then assembled, the Court nevertheless sustained Hamilton's plea as to the first three items but repelled his objection to the last. It does seem to have been a somewhat mean action and did not have the sympathy of one of the judges, Lord Elchies. Lord Elchies, in his comments on the case, reports a discussion of his colleagues which takes the reader back to the days of Charles II. "Some of the Lords," he says, "highly condemned the practice of preaching in the fields, and proposed that we should put a mark of our disapprobation on it, but I thought that we had no power to approve or disapprove of his preaching in the fields, that was the province only of his superiors in church (and most of the Court agreed with me)." Elchies' *Decisions of Court of Session,* I.s.v. *Kirk Session;* Vol. 2, p.238.

Scotland Saw His Glory

the Lord's Return to Scotland, as he entitles his anonymous pamphlet.

"The ministers who assisted at this solemnity were Mr. Whitefield, Mr. Webster from Edinburgh, Mr. MacLaurin and Mr. Gillies from Glasgow, Mr. Robe from Kilsyth, Mr. Currie from Kinglassie, Mr. M'Knight from Irvine, Mr. Bonner from Torphichen, Mr. Hamilton from Douglas, Mr. Henderson from Blantyre, Mr. Maxwell from Rutherglen, and Mr. Adam from Cathcart,"—all evangelical ministers. "All of them appeared to be very much assisted in their work. Four of them preached on the fast day; four on the Saturday; on Sabbath, I cannot tell how many; and five on Monday; on which last day it was computed that above twenty-four ministers and preachers were present."

Also of interest are the names of some of the elders who helped their brethren of Cambuslang. As early as March ninth, it was noted that those awakened had "consisted most of illiterate folk or of those formerly of no very great note for Christian knowledge, profession, or practice of religion." This communion gives the other side, for some of these assisting elders were "persons of rank and distinction." They included the Hon. Charles Erskine, Bruce of Kennet, Gillon of Wallhouse, and Warner of Ardeer.

"Old Mr. Bonner, though so frail that he took three days to ride eighteen miles from Torphichen to Cambuslang, was so set upon coming here, that he could by no means stay away; and when he was helped up to the tent, preached three times with great life; and returned with much satisfaction and joy."

Worship was conducted at three centers. "One tent was placed at the lower extremity of the amphitheater, and near the joining of the two rivulets, and here the sacrament was administered; a second tent was erected in the churchyard; and a third in a green field to the west of the first tent." The impression

Cambuslang, 1742

conveyed to the minds of the chief agents seems to indicate that the whole proceedings were more ordinary and much quieter than at the first communion. M'Culloch says, "There was a great deal of outward decency and regularity observable at the tables. . . . The thing most remarkable was the spiritual glory of this solemnity—I mean the gracious and sensible presence of God. Not a few were awakened to a sense of sin and of their lost and perishing condition without a Saviour. Others had their bands loosed, and were brought into the marvelous liberty of the sons of God." And Whitefield, writing to a correspondent a fortnight later, declared, "Such a passover has not been heard of. . . . On Monday, at seven in the morning, the Rev. Mr. Webster preached, and there was a great commotion, and also in the third sermon which I preached. A very great and serious concern was visible throughout the whole assembly."

Compared with what both had written on the former occasion, this was restrained language. Had the movement begun to show signs of falling off? Dr. James Meek says conclusively that it ended with this second communion. "The Cambuslang work continued for six months, that is, from 18th February till the second communion. Few or none were convicted or converted after this last period. The daily preachings and exhortations, except the weekly lecture, ceased. Public worship, however, was kept in the open fields till the month of November, when the inclemency of the weather rendered it necessary to repair to the Kirk." The strange absence of accounts of further events, either from M'Culloch or Robe, seems to imply that this statement is on the whole correct, and that before 1742 had ended, religious concerns had resumed their ordinary course in the parish. For a time, the numbers attending the annual communions continued large, but they also fell off as the years passed. In 1743 the attendance was 2,000; in 1744 about 1,500; in 1745 about 1,300; in 1746 about 1,200, the disturbed state of the country having little effect on the size of the congregations. In 1751 the number of communicants still exceeded that before 1742.

But though the revival had thus exhausted itself, its results did not disappear with it. Particular stress is laid by those who were favorable to the work on the reformation of manners which it brought about, and several testimonies could easily be advanced to that effect. There is abundance of evidence also that the change wrought in many lives was permanent and that the good effects of the movement could be traced until near the close of the century.

Thus, under the date, Cambuslang, October 9, 1748, Whitefield writes: "At present I am in the place where the great awakening was about six years ago. The fruits of it yet remain."

In about 1750, the land of Holland was visited with a revival which encountered much opposition. One of the arguments used against it was the necessarily ephemeral nature of all impressions created under such condition. To meet the objection, Robe of Kilsyth was asked to provide evidence of the permanent character of the work at Cambuslang. That and other motives induced him to collect testimonies in 1751. Nine years had elapsed, and the interval was considered long enough to furnish reliable information. While the results were not all that might be hoped for, there being a number who appeared to have fallen away, a sufficient number had remained faithful to their profession to place the value of the work beyond dispute. M'Culloch wrote: "I do not talk of them at random, nor speak of their number in a loose, general, and confused way; but have now before me, at the writing of this, April 27, 1751, a list of about 400 persons awakened here at Cambuslang in 1742 who from that time to the time of their death, or to this, that is for these nine years past, have been enabled to behave in a good measure as becometh the gospel." Meetings for prayer increased

Cambuslang, 1742

in 1742 from three to more than a dozen, and in the year M'Culloch reported, there still remained six of these. The session cordially endorsed their minister's statement and sent it forth with their attestation, explaining at the same time that the fall in the number of prayer meetings was due largely to the varying changes in the life of the parish.

If additional testimony is needed, it may be found in the words of M'Culloch son, the minister of Dairsie, and in what Dr. Robertson, one of M'Culloch's successors in the parish, found when he entered on the work in 1795. In the dedication of the volume of his father's sermons, which the former published in 1793, he writes: "Though I cannot possibly have the least recollection of anything that occurred at that period [1742], yet having spent about twenty years of my life in that parish, I have had the best opportunity of strictly inquiring into facts and of impartially examining the evidences of their truth and reality." He cordially adopts the result to which Dr. Webster arrived in his booklet, *Divine Influence the True Spring of the Extraordinary Work at Cambuslang,* namely, that many had been radically and permanently changed in character and life. The author of the *New Statistical Account* records the experience of the then minister of Cambuslang: "When Dr. Robertson entered on the charge of the parish, a number of the converts of 1742 still lived and gave evidence of the piety and consistency of their conduct and the reality of the saving change wrought on their hearts."

As shall be shown in another chapter, a storm of controversy arose over the happenings at Cambuslang. These events need not be defended in every particular, but of this there is surely certainty—the movement was a work of God for many sinful men and women. It is reported that the aged Rev. John Bonner, minister of Torphichen, while standing on the stairhead of the manse before he left Cambuslang after the second communion,

Scotland Saw His Glory

explained, "Now lettest thou thy servant depart in peace, for mine eyes have seen thy salvation." That is perhaps the best available commentary on whole transaction.

Chapter 7

Kilsyth, 1742

The Revival at Kilsyth may be regarded as part of the religious awakening that originated, so far as Scotland was concerned, at Cambuslang. It had, however, a prior history and distinctive features that give it the right of being considered a separate movement. In any case, its story stands by itself and can be told with only the slightest reference to what took place at Cambuslang. If it is compared with the Lanarksire Revival, it may suffer somewhat in the matter of numbers as well as in the attention given to its progress by the wider public of Scotland, but it is in no wise behind in the quality of the results achieved.

The parish had this notable connection with the past revival history of Scotland: it was the birthplace of John Livingston, of Shotts fame. Its hills, too, had witnessed Montrose inflict one of the bloodiest defeats sustained by the Covenanters. Hill Burton says it was the cavalier boast that not an unmounted enemy escaped during the pitiless pursuit. The local historian is therefore justified in pointing out that "the parish of Kilsyth being of all the parishes in Scotland the most heavily drenched in covenanting blood, there is a certain spiritual propriety that it should also have been the scene of the richest outpouring of the heavenly grace."

The name that stands out in solitary prominence in connection with the revival is that of James Robe, minister of the parish. His father was Michael Robe, who for over twelve years was one of his predecessors in the same office, removing in 1690 to the adjacent parish of Cumbernauld. The son was licensed by the Presbytery of Linlithgow towards the end of

Scotland Saw His Glory

1709 and was ordained to Kilsyth on April 24, 1713. He died on May 26, 1753 at the age of sixty-five and was consequently a man of advanced years and experience when the revival broke out in his congregation in 1742.

Fortunately for us and those that follow, Robe was a scholarly man, methodical in his habits, and with farseeing views of his duty as a witness of the religious events that were taking place in his own parish and elsewhere. It is due almost entirely to his care and devotion that the comparatively full accounts we have are available. His *Narrative* may not be arranged in a manner that can satisfy a story told in chronological sequence, but it is, nevertheless, a perfect quarry of facts and impressions regarding the work done at this time all over the land.[1] No small part of its interest lies in the picture which Robe unconsciously draws of himself. We see him resourceful and laborious. Not only had he to toil daily among the anxious and prepare suitable addresses for his people, but his pen was never allowed to be idle. He had to answer attacks and take a chief part in the controversy the revivals aroused, as well as to support the almost intolerable burden of recording the individual cases that came under his notice. Yet he never seemed to weary and never lost the freshness of joy which months of awakening almost daily brought to him. "Though I was wearied when I went to bed," he gratefully wrote, "yet, like the labouring man, my rest was sweet to me. The Lord gave me the sleep of His beloved, and I was fresh by the morning."

---

[1] The *Narrative* was in the end a growth or compilation, and this may explain its form. It included pamphlets published at the time as well as extracts from contributions to the *Glasgow Weekly History* and to Robe's own journal, the *Christian Monthly History*. It has appeared in several editions. Glasgow, 1789-90 and 1840, the latter being edited by Dr. Buchanan.

Kilsyth, 1742

As an introduction to his story, Robe sketches the religious history of his parish previous to the revival. On the whole it is a melancholy recital. For a time after his settlement, the people, he says, "appeared to profit under gospel ordinances by the blessing of the Lord upon them." To provide all suitable encouragement, the Session set up several meetings for prayer. Under the date of December 3, 1721, their minutes runs: "In order to the bearing down of sin and renewing the power of godliness, it is enacted by the Session that societies for prayer and conference be set up in the congregation, and that they form themselves with a particular eye to the reformation of the manners of the congregation and to the provoking others to love and good works, and that this work may be managed for the glory of God in attaining these ends." Robe himself does not seem to have had a share in conducting the meetings, although he drew up rules for their guidance.

The promise that lay in these things, however, came to nothing, and the people drifted into indifference. Calamities that were fitted to startle them into wakefulness fell upon them, but they passed apparently unnoticed. The minister anxiously saw that each visitation left the community further removed from religious interests. At the end of 1732, a malignant fever carried off large numbers of the inhabitants, sixty being buried within the space of three weeks. "What made this dispensation more threatening was that the most religious and judicious Christians in the congregation were removed from us thereby." Robe lived in hope that his parishioners would have spiritual wit enough to profit by the discipline that this and other disasters provided, but the years passed and instead of growing better, he found to his alarm that the morals of his people were gradually becoming worse. "Theft and other immoralities broke forth and increased to a terrible height. The return of plenty had no better influence upon us: we were going on frowardly in the way of our own hearts." The societies for prayer had long since ceased to exist.

Robe traces the preparations made for the revival back to a series of discourses on regeneration which, like his friend M'Culloch of Cambuslang, he preached to his people. "It is probable that both ministers were influenced by Doddridge's *Letters on Regeneration*, which were at that time in the enjoyment of a considerable popularity." Robe began his sermons in 1740, and as the method he employed cannot fail to be of interest, his description of them is quoted in full. "The method I followed by the divine direction, was, first, to press the importance and necessity of [regeneration], which I did from John iii. 3. Next, I shewed the mysteriousness of the way and manner of the Holy Spirit in effecting it, from John iii. 8. I proceeded, thirdly, to explain and apply the various Scripture views and expressions of it: as first, being born again, from the forequoted John iii. 8; secondly, a resurrection, from Rev. xx. 6; thirdly, a new creation, from Eph. ii. 10; fourthly, Christ's conquest of the sinner to Himself, from Psalm cx. 3; fifthly, the circumcision of the heart, from Ezek. xliv. 9. This was also intended to show the necessity of regeneration in order to the receiving of the Lord's Supper worthily, to be dispensed in the congregation about that time. Here this subject was interrupted until the end of the last year [1741], when I, resuming it, preached regeneration as it is, sixthly, the taking away the stony heart and the giving the heart of flesh, from Ezek. xi. 19; seventhly, the putting of God's law in the mind and writing it in the heart, from Heb. viii. 10." Probably a single sermon did not suffice for each of these topics. The time had not yet passed when several services were devoted to the exposition and illustration of one text, and Robe would follow that custom.

The disappointed minister could see no direct results from these discourses. The people listened, approved the doctrine,

Kilsyth, 1742

and went on placidly in the old way. Then came the spring of 1742 and the news of what had been going forward at Cambuslang. Robe did his best to interest his congregation in the work, but for a time he spoke to deaf ears—"Few of the people under my charge," he says, "went to Cambuslang, notwithstanding of what they heard me say of it." This was all the more grievous to the minister, because the parishes round his own could count cases of conversion brought about by visits to that favored spot.

During the month of April, indications were not wanting that a change in the spiritual life of the community was imminent. Robe noticed a greater eagerness among his hearers, and proposals were made for the resuscitation of the long-dead prayer societies. More particularly, the well-known John Willison was laid hold of on his way home to Dundee from Cambuslang, where he had spent several days, and made to preach on the morning of Friday, April 15. The notice calling the meeting was very short, but a "great multitude," nevertheless, convened. "He preached a distinct, plain, and moving sermon from Psalm xl. 2,3," says Robe. "Several of those now awakened date their first serious concern about their souls from their hearing this sermon and the blessing of the Lord upon it." During the next three weeks, some decided cases of anxiety showed themselves.

For part of the week preceding Sabbath, May 16, Robe was at Cambuslang and on the way home was providentially directed to a house where much spiritual distress existed among the servants. He dealt as best he could with them, and no doubt that experience as well as what he had seen at Cambuslang, had its influence upon him when next he stood in his own pulpit. In the forenoon, his text was Galatians 4:19, and the sermon was a continuation of a series on the same passage. In the afternoon he preached from John 5:40: "Ye will not come unto me that ye might have life." It was the breaking up of the ice of long years. "An extraordinary power of the Spirit from on high accompanied the Word preached," says Robe. "There was a great mourning in the congregation as for an only son. Many cried out, and these were not only women, but some strong and stout-hearted young men and some betwixt forty and fifty." A contemporary pamphlet says that "above twenty-seven were under visible concern for their salvation" and adds this interesting note: "some of which number were of the minister's own family."

Robe had long before prepared himself for an emergency like this, and he accordingly had those who were in distress brought into his barn. The anxious, however, proved too numerous for him to deal with unaided, and he had again to adjourn to the church while he sent for his neighbor, the Rev. John Oughterson of Cumbernauld. For a time Robe prayed with the distressed and made them sing Psalms, but when he tried to address them, the noise of weeping completely drowned his voice. He, therefore, determined to deal with them one by one "in his closet." The others, he left in the church under the supervision of his elders who had instructions to sing and pray with them but on no account to address them. By all these arrangements, Robe hoped to "cut off occasion of calumny and objection from them who seemed to desire it."

This was the beginning of a great work at Kilsyth. Almost from the first visible movement among the people, its magnitude placed it beyond the strength of one man. Robe accordingly sought the help of neighboring ministers, and they gladly came to his assistance. So great was the need of the people that he had also to institute week-day services which for a time were restricted to Wednesdays. To the first, held on May 19, he summoned the venerable John M'Laurin, minister of Ramshorn, Glasgow, and this was for M'Laurin the beginning of a close

Kilsyth, 1742

association with the work. Robe, however, soon discovered that his people's appetite was not being satisfied by the extra services of one week-day and that they were seeking elsewhere what they could not obtain at home. "I therefore embraced," he says, "every opportunity of strangers coming to the place to give sermon to the people." Careful lest fault should be found with this arrangement on the score of interference with the necessary secular employment of the district, Robe held these additional services in the evening. When harvest operations began, he was particularly concerned lest they should cause hindrance to the labors of the field. "I made enquiry," he says, "at some husbandmen, living in different parts of the parish, if now, when harvest was begun, they observed any part of the work and labour of the parish undone, or further behind, through the frequent attendance upon public ordinances, or by the means of the many awakened and spiritually distressed in the congregation. They replied that there was no such thing to be seen; as also, that they had heard the poorest say that their work went better on than ordinary, and that they found not any lack. They believed also that their hay harvest, which is a considerable labour in this parish, was got a third part of time sooner over than ordinary, and noticed the singular goodness of God therein."

The work at Kilsyth beginning three months after that of Cambuslang, Robe was well acquainted with all the objections which events at the latter place had raised. He had given considerable thought to the whole matter and had determined on his own course of action should his own congregation be favored with a like revival. He could discover no theoretical reason for denouncing bodily seizures and accordingly made special arrangements to deal with them if they occurred. The afflicted were to be removed from the congregation as speedily as possible and conveyed to some place where each case could receive adequate attention. In this way, he thought he would minimize the scandal such irregularities had caused and at the same time preserve order among the worshippers. But when the movement actually came, circumstances proved too strong for him. He confesses that when swoonings and other phenomena presented themselves, "it proved at first very uneasy to me; it appeared unpleasant, yea even shocking." He still found no reason for condemning them absolutely, although he discovered that removing the distressed caused even more disturbance than leaving them alone, for it gave opportunity for unseemly curiosity and "the people's attention was much lessened in hearing the Word." Robe had forthwith to abandon his plans.

The work of awakening having begun, it went on rapidly. Many came from long distances. Converts are named who had journeyed form Kirkintilloch, Denny, Larbert, Stirling, Fifeshire, and even distant Muthill. On May twenty-eighth, Robe reported that his list of awakened persons amounted to seventy-six, forty-eight of whom belonged to his own parish. On June eighth, the latter had risen to sixty. Results did not depend on any special preacher or even on the mood in which he preached. Under the date of June ninth, Robe says: "I find when I am weakest and have least expectation from my sermon, the Lord sheweth Himself most. I preached from John xvi. 11. I was far from being pleased with the composure," and yet he adds, "we have had a glorious day this day." On Tuesday, June 15, Whitefield preached at Kilsyth, and his note to his friend John Cennick reads: "On Tuesday, twice at Kilsyth to 10,000 but such a commotion, I believe, you never saw. O what agonies and cries were there!" In fact, so manifest were the results that Wednesday June 30, was held as a special day of

Kilsyth, 1742

thanksgiving.[2] "I looked upon it," says Robe, "as a token for good that we had a great congregation, seeing it was set apart for solemn thanksgiving to God. I am persuaded that it was the best observed day of thanksgiving, in every shape, ever was in Kilsyth, yet vastly short of what should have been rendered according to the benefit."

At the beginning of July, arrangements were made for the celebration of the Sacrament. The Sabbath on the fourth was set apart as a special day of preparation. The impression made on the congregation by the services was very great. "Yesterday," wrote Robe, "was a Bochim in the congregation for unworthy communicating." We have no special account of the Sacrament itself, but we are assured that the work of awakening continued.

Robe attended the memorable second communion at Cambuslang on August fifteenth. While there, he was strongly advised by M'Culloch to have a second communion at Kilsyth also. But Robe had his objections. He had "a rooted aversion," he said, "to anything that looked like affecting popularity," and it was only when one of his own Session approached him that he brought the matter before that body. "After this the Session met again and again to pray and deliberate about it. I was informed that it was the earnest desire of the generality of the parish to have it. They urged that the Lord had wrought great and extraordinary things in the congregation this summer in a work of conviction and conversion; and they thought that the most solemn and extraordinary thanksgiving was due to Him

---

[2]The Kirk-Session minutes make little or no mention of the revival. One of the few entries, however, refers to this appointment: "The Session agree that Wednesday, the 30th of June, be set apart for solemn public thanksgiving in this congregation for the extraordinary outpouring of the Spirit of God upon this and other congregations in the neighborhood and the success of the gospel here." *Kirk-Session Records,* June 27, 1742.

Scotland Saw His Glory

from them, and which they could not offer to Him in a more solemn manner than in this ordinance of thanksgiving. They declared also that they were willing to bear a considerable part of the charges and offered to bear the whole, if it had been accepted." Under this pressure Robe consented. The Session appointed October third for the ordinance. The minute runs: "The Session having met according to appointment, after John Lapsly, John Grindlay, and Alexander Patrick prayed, they, at the general desire of the parish, unanimously agreed that the Sacrament of the Lord's Supper be given a second time in this place, the first Sabbath of October, and for several weighty reasons, particularly the extraordinary outpouring of the Holy Spirit upon numbers here, and further agree that the expense of the elements be taken off the collection."

Though the Sacrament was held somewhat late in the season, the weather seems to have been propitious, for most of the services took place in the open air. The account of that interesting solemnity given by Mr. Robe is truly heart stirring: "I was assisted on the occasion by the Rev. Mr. MacLaurin of Glasgow, Mr. James Warden of Calder, Mr. John Warden of Campsie, Mr. James Burnside of Kirkintilloch, Mr. James Mackie of St. Ninians, Mr. John Smith of Larbert, Mr. Spiers of Linlithgow, Mr. Thomas Gillespie of Carnock,[3] Mr. Hunter of Saline, Mr. M'Culloch of Cambuslang, and Mr. Porteous of Monivaird. Upon the fast-day, sermon was in the fields to a very numerous and attentive audience, by three ministers, without any intermission because of the shortness of the day.

---

[3] In later years, Gillespie was the founder of the Relief Church. His attitude is in striking contrast to that of those who formed the other branch of the Seccession. "Mr. Robe mentions that of all who visited him and lent him assistance, Mr. Gillespie was the one who most signally appeared as the instrument of God."

Kilsyth, 1742

Upon the Friday evening, there was a sermon in the kirk, and there was a good deal of concern among the people. Upon Saturday there was sermon both in the kirk and in the fields.

"Upon the Lord's day the public service began about half-past eight in the morning, and continued without intermission till half-past eight in the evening. I preached the action sermon by the divine direction and assistance, from Eph. ii. 7, 'That in the ages to come He might show the exceeding riches of His grace, in His kindness towards us, through Christ Jesus.' There were about twenty-two services, each consisting of about seventy persons.[4] The evening sermon began immediately after the last table-service. And although I desired that the congregation in the fields should be dismissed after the last service, yet they chose rather to continue together till all was over. During all the services there was the most desirable frame and observable concern among the people that had ever been anywhere seen. It began to be considerable when Mr. Warden of Campsie preached, and it continued and greatly increased while Mr. Spiers preached, who concluded the public work of the day in the fields.

"On Monday there were sermons both in the kirk and in the fields. There was a good deal of observable concern; and several were brought under spiritual distress in the fields. In the evening, two ministers preached to the numerous distressed convened in the kirk. On Tuesday morning there was a sermon preached and a discourse by another minister, containing suitable instructions and directions both to the awakened and to those who had never attained to any sight or sense of their sin and danger.

"The spiritual fruits of this solemn and extraordinary dispensation of Word and Sacrament were truly animating.

---

[4] By this reckoning, some 1,540 persons actually received the elements.

Scotland Saw His Glory

Many secure sinners were awakened. Zion's mighty King brought the wheel of the law over them and sent them home with broken and contrite hearts. Some who came hither in a state of spiritual distress and law-work, felt such a time of the Mediator's power as enabled them to embrace Jesus Christ with such distinctness as to know that they had done it. Many had the love of Christ so shed abroad in their hearts by the Holy Ghost that they could not contain, but were constrained to break forth in floods of tears in the most significant expressions of their own vileness and unworthiness and of the deep sense they had of the exceeding riches of God's grace in His kindness towards them by Christ Jesus."

"There were many strangers from a great distance," says Robe, "who came hither to keep this feast to the Lord; several of them of note and distinction in the world, of great penetration and judgment, and long experience in the Christian life, who declared themselves well satisfied with what they had heard, seen, and felt by the Lord's mercy in this place." Whitefield received news of it and wrote: "Glory be to His great name! We have seen much of His power in Scotland. The work in the west goes on and increases. Last Sabbath and Monday things greater than ever were seen at Kilsyth."

Few particulars are available regarding the progress of the work during the winter of 1742, but it proceeded steadily. Robe wrote on the 18th of April 1743 that "public and discernible awakenings continue in this congregation, reaching even some of the elder sort, particularly yesterday when there appeared a general concern upon the congregation." In November of the same year, Robe started the publication of a monthly magazine giving revival news both at home and abroad. In the first number, there appears a resume of progress during the preceding six months. The author has to confess to a considerable falling off in interest. "There was a great difference," he writes,

Kilsyth, 1742

"between this and the former summer as to the numbers of the awakened in this and the neighboring congregations. During that season the number of the awakened was like the cutting down and reaping in the harvests; it was in handfuls. But now it was only like the gleaning grapes when the vintage is done, and as the shaking of on olive tree, two or three being in the top of the uppermost bough, four or five in the utmost fruitful branches thereof." He says also that although outcries continued, no case of "convulsive motions or hystericisms" had occurred since the preceding February. At the Sacrament in July, several were converted, and when that ordinance was repeated in August, there was a rekindling of the old flame.[5] "During all the days about that solemn time, there was a discernible serious concern amongst the people. Not a few were awakened, and some of them from parishes at a considerable distance. Upon the Lord's day, there was a most considerable concern and unusual motion amongst the people that hath been ever seen in the remembrance of man." The numbers attending must have been very great, for the communicants were over 1,600. The figures certainly say much regarding the vitality of the movement, for this number exceeded that of the corresponding celebration of the preceding year. The Sacrament dispensed at Cambuslang on the first anniversary of the great August communion of 1742 showed a very considerable reduction in numbers.

---

[5] The Kirk Session minute in reference to this second celebration for 1743 runs, ". . .It being represented by several members of the Session that it is the universal desire and inclination of the congregation that it [the Lord's Supper] should be given again, and that from the consideration of the extraordinary satisfaction that the Lord's people have had here, both last time and formerly, and other considerations, the Session unanimously agreed that it be given a second time upon the third Sabbath of August next."

Scotland Saw His Glory

In December 1743, Robe could report that "the Lord is yet remarkably amongst us," but the succeeding year showed no signs of special grace. The church building was in a state of decay, and the people were obliged for the most part to worship in the fields. The winter of 1744 proved exceptionally severe, yet the congregations continued "numerous and attentive," notwithstanding the trying circumstances in which they had oftentimes to meet. A terrible catastrophe seemed imminent on the last Sabbath of December. "By a dreadful blast of wind, we were threatened with an immediate fall of the roof of the kirk, and there was a great outcry of the people for fear of their lives." Fortunately the congregation left the building without hurt, but unfortunately the experience did not have the spiritual results which Robe evidently expected. The people gathered in the open air, and he preached a sermon appropriate to the occasion, but "there was no person awakened or any impression made upon the spirits of any unconverted sinners." Robe's inference is that this was "certain evidence that no fears of immediate death, no fright about the temporal life, will awaken sinners or give them uneasy convictions of their sin and misery without the Spirit of the Lord." It also seems to show that the impetus of the revival had exhausted itself, although cases of conversion took place throughout 1745.

The evidence is strong that this revival was of a very solid nature. It was far removed from enthusiastic fanaticism, on the one hand, and presumptuous Antinomianism, on the other. The experience of many made it unequivocally manifest that "the Lord Himself had given the Word." Deep humility, hatred of all sin, love of holiness, aspirations after conformity to the image of God, fervent prayers, and endeavors that others might be brought to the same views and the same enjoyments characterized the greater number of the individuals with whom Robe was called to converse. Indeed, the views of sin and of the way of

Kilsyth, 1742

salvation entertained by the individuals brought under the power of this blessed work of the Spirit were, generally speaking, of the most Scriptural and enlightened description.

One man, being asked "what he took closing with Christ to be," made this most intelligent reply: "I take closing with Christ to be a receiving of Him as a Prophet, to teach me the way of salvation; as a Priest, to atone for me, and to be my righteousness in the sight of God; and as a King to rule over me and to subdue sin and corruption in me; and that without Christ's righteousness imputed, I can never be accepted in the sight of God."

A woman who was brought distinctly to receive and rest alone upon Christ for salvation expressed herself by saying, "Worldly thoughts are away from me now, and oh that they would never return again! Ten thousand worlds could not give me the love and joy with which Christ now fills me." When asked some questions by Mr. Robe, she said, "Sir, though you put questions to me, as was done to Peter, Christ, who knows my heart, knows that I do love Him, and I am resolved, in the strength of imparted promised grace, to show my love to Him by keeping His commandments." She sometimes gave utterance to such words as, "He is my sure portion, whom I have chosen forever. Oh, what hath He done for me! I desire to have all the world brought to Him, that they too may partake of His rich and sovereign grace."

Although the greater number, like the awakened at the day of Pentecost or like the convicted jailer at Philippi, were made to cry out under a sense of sin and apprehension of coming wrath and could not conceal their distress, yet many more were brought to Jesus in a more gentle and silent manner, whose cases were not made known to Mr. Robe until after they had obtained peace in believing. To illustrate, a woman who was brought to concern on May sixteenth waited upon Mr. Robe the following week, manifesting great anxiety for the salvation of her soul. "I was," says he, "much pleased with the character of her convictions, with her knowledge, and the longing desires she expressed after Jesus Christ. I said to her, 'Essay to accept of Christ, bestir yourself, rise up at His call and invite Him to enter into your heart, into your soul.' Although I did not intend or mean this, she arose with great composure, stood and prayed in a most scriptural style. She acknowledged sin, original and actual, her utter want of righteousness, the wonderfulness of God's patience to her. She prayed for mercy to be drawn to Jesus Christ, and that she might be clothed with His white raiment. Sometimes in her address, she would say—'Sweet Jesus;' 'He is precious;' 'He is altogether lovely.' She first came to sensible relief from a sermon I preached on John xvi. 10, 'Of righteousness, because I go to My Father, and ye see Me no more.' In her return home that day, these words were strongly impressed on her mind—'My heart is fixed, O God, my heart is fixed; I will sing and give praise.' She fell down upon her knees; her heart being filled with joy in the Lord, and her mouth with His praise."

Mr. Robe describes the case of a man who "came first under conviction by hearing the doctrine of regeneration stated, as it is in the writing of God's law upon the sinner's heart, from Heb. viii. 10. He was made distinctly to see that it was not as yet written upon his heart, and that if he would be happy hereafter, it was indispensably necessary that it should be so. Upon the evening of the day when he received his first impressions, he conversed with a friend concerning the resurrection, the general judgment, and the sad state in which impenitent sinners must be throughout eternity. By such converse his impressions were deepened. Every sermon and every awakening experienced by his neighbours was blessed for the same end. He told me that he could apply to himself the

Kilsyth, 1742

greater part of a sermon he heard from me concerning the Spirit's convincing the world of sin: such as, that He usually begins with one sin, and after that proceeds to convince of particular sins. He was convinced of the sins of his heart, and of the evil nature of sin. He was not so much distressed about sin, as exposing himself to hell, but he felt particularly grieved as it was an insult offered to a holy God. He got such a sight of the filthiness of sin, as to loathe himself on account of it. He was also convinced of the great sin of unbelief, of the sinfulness of the least thought of iniquity, though not consented thereto; of the evil of self-conceit, a sense of the sinfulness of which stuck as long with him, as he termed it, as anything else. He was also sensible of his inability to help himself, of his own want of righteousness, and that he could not work out a righteousness for himself. He was brought to see the sufficiency of Christ's righteousness, and that He, to use his own words, was always ready, if we would but trust in Him. Seeing that he had not informed any one of his spiritual distress till he got relief by believing in Christ, I asked what it was that kept up his spirit under fear and trouble of mind, continuing so long. He told me that when his heart was like to burst in prayer, that word came constantly in his mind and encouraged him to wait for the Lord with patience and hope: 'I waited patiently for the Lord, and He inclined unto me, and heard my cry.' His first relief came in this manner. In the Society for Prayer of which he had become a member, he inquired, 'What was the most proper exercise for a person under convictions?' to which it was replied by a very judicious Christian, 'That it was to behold the Lamb of God,' which he essayed to do. When I gave, in a public discourse, the marks of those who had Christ formed in them, he said that by the help of the Spirit he could apply them all to himself, and that during prayer and after sermon, he was in a frame surprising to himself; that his whole heart and affections went out in closing with Jesus Christ, and that he was filled with rejoicing and wonder at His love."

Knowing how the spiritual results of such a movement would be watched and criticized, Robe was careful all along to place them beyond dispute so far as that was possible. Four months after the beginning of the revival, he provided himself with an attestation drawn up by the heritors and the Session of the parish. They witnessed to a remarkable change in the conduct of the villagers. Crime had largely ceased, private jealousies and feuds had been composed; secret and public prayer was common, and young and old alike had been moved to better living. The magistrate of Kilsyth certified "that so much of the spirit of mildness and friendship prevails amongst the people in this place that there hath been no pleas before our court for these several months past, whereas formerly a great many were brought before me every week."

When more time had elapsed and a better opportunity was accordingly afforded for judging of the probable permanency of the work, Robe's verdict is very satisfactory. He tells how he maintained communication with the various praying societies throughout the parish, receiving monthly reports from each. "At this present time, the eighth of December [1743], I can testify and declare that of the many I conceived good hopes of, from what I knew of them myself and heard of them from others, there is not one—blessed be the Lord, Who keeps the people from falling, for it—against whom I can conclude total apostasy or want of grace from anything that hath befallen them. They are within half-a-dozen whom I have had to rebuke."

In 1751 Robe and his Session again made enquiry into the steadfastness of the converts. The longer interval better enabled the chaff to be sifted from the wheat, and a mixed story required to be told. On the one hand, the general community had again fallen into ways of dissipation and irreligion to such

Kilsyth, 1742

an extent that certain sins abounded "more than ever I knew in this place, unless it was at the time of my first coming to it." Some of those who had apparently come under conviction had become backsliders, and others had been seized with spiritual deadness. Several of the praying societies had been given up. The reason for this last was not altogether unsatisfactory, although "in some instances persons have forsaken these meetings, and particular meetings have ceased without being able to assign any satisfactory reason for it." Much of this state of affairs was no doubt due to the reaction which usually follows a season of high privilege, but it was not all discouraging. At a meeting of Session held on March 19, 1751, Robe submitted a list of more than a hundred persons "who were the most of them brought under notorious spiritual concern in the years 1741 and 1743." After examining the names, the Session testified that they still "had their conversation as becometh the gospel: as also that four or five of the said list who were removed by death behaved until their said removal as became good Christians." Surely the result was notable after the testing of eight years, and Robe had reason to be satisfied.

It was, in fact, impossible that such a general turning to God could fail to produce results that stretched far down the years. As late as 1793, the parish minister of the day declared he was happy to have it in his power to say that "there are persons yet alive who have proved by the uniform tenor of their lives" that they had been true to the profession they made half a century before. The influence of Kilsyth, too, was felt in many parts of Scotland, and when again the town was visited with spiritual blessing in 1839 no small part of that effect was due to what had happened a century before.

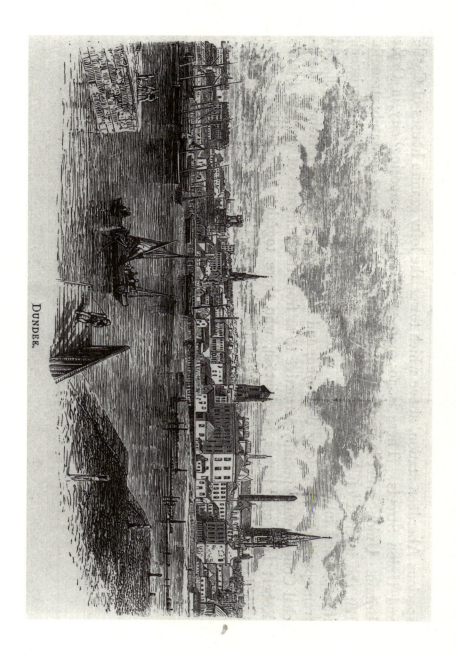

Chapter 8

Beyond Cambuslang and Kilsyth, 1742

In dealing with the spread of the Revival of 1742 throughout Scotland, it is necessary to remember that there was more than one place from which spiritual impulses might be propagated. Whitefield had itinerated through the central districts in the summer and autumn of 1741. His preaching had everywhere been accompanied with remarkable power. Before he was able to return in June 1742, the work of awakening had begun both at Cambuslang and Kilsyth and had already spread to their immediate neighborhoods. Whitefield took up his labors again at Edinburgh, and the immense crowds that waited on his ministry soon numbered many converts among them. In a short time, he was able to take part in the work going on in the west. His advent there may be looked upon as joining into one the various movements that were proceeding in the south country.

It is impossible to discover what exact share Edinburgh and the east took in the extension of the revival to other parts of Scotland. Willison of Dundee testified that considerable interest in spiritual things was shown throughout the region around the capital even before Whitefield's first visit. He reports: "In the year 1740 and afterwards, promising tokens began to appear of a revival of Christianity, for in Edinburgh and elsewhere some new praying societies were set up, and sundry students did associate with them." But the part Edinburgh played in sending the gospel beyond its borders seems to have been comparatively small. It is true that Robe, the chief historian of the whole movement, resided in the west and would naturally give prominence to what came under his notice. But even this will not account for the almost uniform silence concerning the part

Scotland Saw His Glory

Edinburgh played. The capital, in fact, did little else than accept the good brought to its doors. It was mostly from Cambuslang and Kilsyth that the impulse spread over Scotland.

The gales of the Spirit blow how and where they will. Thus It may be useless to attempt discovering how the divine influence was conveyed from one district to another. But this may be said with certainty, the news of the awakenings at Cambuslang and Kilsyth spread rapidly over the country and attracted many to these places who wanted to see for themselves what was happening. Some of these visitors underwent a saving change and could not be silent on their experiences when they returned home. In many cases ministers carried the news to their parishes. One example, showing how the revival reached the far north in this way, may suffice. Mr. John Sutherland, minister at Golspie, had wrought long among his people without apparent results. "On receiving the intelligence of the revival elsewhere," he says, "I read to my people concerning the American revivals, and those at Cambuslang and Kilsyth, and told them what I had myself witnessed at the two last places, and at Muthill, when I was on my way to the Assembly." At first, no results were apparent, but meetings for prayer were begun. "When our hopes had well-nigh failed us, a merciful God breathed on the dry bones." M'Culloch's little journal containing Robe's accounts of particular cases of anxiety and conversion also found its way to remote places and did much to stir up a spirit of expectancy. Busy as Robe himself was, he nevertheless found time to write many personal letters, and in several cases these had interesting results. On June 14, 1742, Willison of Dundee wrote to inform him that neighboring ministers were "proposing to keep parochial thanksgiving days for the good news you and others are sending us," adding that he was scheduled to be present at such a

Beyond Cambuslang and Kilsyth, 1742

service in Strathmartin on the following Wednesday. It was by such means that the revival reached various parts of Scotland.

Glasgow was in the near neighborhood of Cambuslang and came early under its influence. The city had the good fortune to possess several ministers of outstanding evangelical sympathies. The venerable Dr. John Maclaurin had long been settled over Ramshorn Parish, while his son-in-law, Dr. John Gillies, the compiler of the well-known *Historical Collections* regarding revivals, was minister of the College Parish, and Dr. John Hamilton of the Barony. All these welcomed the revival and did their best to extend its operations throughout the town. Communication between Maclaurin and Jonathan Edwards and other like-minded Americans was frequent and intimate. Gillies informs us that when Maclaurin "received their accounts he spread them among his acquaintances," and that he "met once a week with some Christian friends to receive and communicate religious intelligence, and to converse on religious subjects, which he did with inimitable spirit and cheerfulness." Societies for prayer were also greatly encouraged. In spite, however, of all this desire and preparation, there is no evidence that the city was greatly stirred when the revival broke out in its neighborhood. Nine years afterwards, Gillies issued a small periodical for the benefit of his parishioners, and in one of the numbers, he somewhat sorrowfully reminded his people that in 1742 "there was but little revival here, comparatively speaking, when the Lord was watering His vineyard round about us."

It is probable that the number joining the Church or sitting at the Lord's table at any special time is not the safest guide in estimating the value of a work of grace. Judged by this standard, however, it is plain that Glasgow did profit to some extent by the revival movement. On September 13, 1742, Dr. Hamilton wrote that his "parish has had some share in this good work. There have been above a hundred new communicants among us this summer who never did partake of the blessed sacrament before; which is five times as many as ever I admitted in any former year; most of them were awakened at Cambuslang, some of them in their own church." From an account which appeared in Robe's *Christian Monthly History*, it is evident that this accession to the membership of the Church was general over the city. The number of tables required in all the churches at the October communion of 1743 was eighteen more than usual, showing an increase of 1,200 communicants. So far as available accounts indicate, the extravagances which roused hostility at Cambuslang were wholly absent from the Glasgow congregations. The nearest approach to excitement noted is what is said to have taken place at this same October communion: "There was a more than ordinary concern to be observed upon many, both in hearing the Word and receiving the sacrament, and several are said to have felt effects of more than ordinary presence of the Lord's grace and spirit."

But if the revival was not very extensive in Glasgow, there is ample evidence that its fruits were of the most satisfactory kind in individual cases. Dr. Gillies gives his personal testimony to the perseverance of several who were converted at the time. "I am now personally acquainted with several of you," he wrote to his congregation in 1751, "who were subjects of it, and who continue, to the glory of free grace, to bring forth the fruits of a sober, righteous, and godly conversation. I know there are some melancholy instances of backsliding; our Lord had plainly taught us to expect such things. But that the revival which was at Cambuslang and other places in this country in 1742 'has come to nothing, has not been followed with any good fruit in people's lives,' you and I both know this to be otherwise." In the same year, Dr. Maclaurin supplied corroboration of the permanent value of the work done, even while

Beyond Cambuslang and Kilsyth, 1742

admitting that some had gone back on their profession. On March 26, 1751, twenty-five elders of the city forwarded to Robe a letter in which they witnessed not only to the perseverance of those who came under saving impressions in 1742, but also to the marked additions to the membership of the Church. It is evident that these good men looked back to their experiences with considerable pleasure. They especially rejoiced that "a very uncommon liberty, life, and strength was bestowed upon numbers of the ministers."

While the revival was at its height, hardly a parish in the neighborhood of Cambuslang missed participation in it. The ministers of East Kilbride, Blantyre, Bothwell, and Cathcart helped in the work directly, and many people from the other parishes visited Cambuslang. As early as May 7, 1742, William Hamilton, minister at Bothwell, reports that "there are a good number of my people who have been awakened at Cambuslang," and that as a direct consequence of the interest shown "there are some new societies for prayer and Christian conference set up in this congregation wherein several persons besides these awakened at Cambuslang have joined." Two elders belonging to Old Monkland, in the absence of a settled minister, testified "that there is a considerable number of persons belonging to this parish who have been awakened at Cambuslang to a deep concern about their salvation." And these are only samples of what was taking place over all the district. Under the date of September 13, 1742, Hamilton of the Barony wrote to Thomas Prince of Boston that he believed "in less than two months after the commencement of the work there were few parishes within twelve miles of Cambuslang but had some more or fewer awakened there to a very deep, piercing sense of sin." Including "many at a much greater distance," he thinks the number of those who had been awakened by that time amounted to over two thousand.

Scotland Saw His Glory

It is interesting to read that the Ayrshire district, which was the chief scene of the *Stewarton Sickness of 1626,* was a century later partaker in the *Cambuslang Wark* also. The country lying between Cambuslang and Irvine was only partially touched, but the revival had many fruits around Kilmarnock. Some time in the autumn of 1742, Robe writes, "In the town of Irvine, there were a few awakened first at Cambuslang; but now there are a good many awakened that never were at Cambuslang and are in very great distress and anguish of soul like those at Cambuslang and in this country [Kilsyth]. They are happy under the inspection and care of their worthy minister, the Rev. Mr. M'Kneight. In the parish of Long Dreghorn and other parishes about, there are several awakened. In the town of Kilmarnock, there are about fifty from that place awakened at Cambuslang, but there have been many more since in their own congregations." As has already been stated, it was calculated that three hundred were present at the second Cambuslang communion from Irvine, Stewarton, and Kilmarnock. Whitefield evidently was attracted by the hopeful condition which the whole district was reported to be in, for on leaving Cambuslang, he started on a preaching tour through it. Writing from Cambuslang on August 27, 1742, he says, "On Thursday, August 19th, I preached twice at Greenock; on Friday, three times at Kilbride; on Saturday, once at Kilbride and twice at Stevenston. On Sunday, August 22nd, four times at Irvine; on Monday, once at Irvine and three times at Kilmarnock; on Tuesday, once at Kilmarnock and four times at Stewarton; on Wednesday, once at Stewarton and twice at Mearns; and yesterday, twice at this place. I never preached with so much apparent success before. The work seems to spread more and more. . . . At Irvine, Kilbride, Kilmarnock, and Stewarton the concern was great; at the last three, very extraordinary."

Beyond Cambuslang and Kilsyth, 1742

The work around Irvine and Kilmarnock seems to have reached its peak in the autumn of 1742. No great advance was made between then and the autumn of 1743 if we may judge by a report printed by Robe of the communion held at that time: "The number of communicants was much the same as when it was last given, but about 200 or 300 more than in former times, which is reckoned betwixt a fourth and a fifth part increased beyond former years."

Beyond Cambuslang and Kilsyth, the fire of the revival burned brightly to the north and northeast of Glasgow. The parishes which lie in the valley through which the old Roman wall once ran were all affected, and the movement spread to the south shore of the Forth, from Stirling to Linlithgow.

The case of the parish of Baldernock deserves to be particularly noticed. Few of the people had visited those places in which the revivals took place; and although for some years there had been no regular pastor, yet about ninety individuals were brought under the quickening influence of the Spirit of Promise. Mr. Wallace, who had previously labored among them in holy things for about fifty years, had been faithful and zealous. Perhaps the many conversions that now took place might be remotely traced to his ministrations. The seed which lies long concealed may spring up in an abundant harvest.

In the absence of a regular ministry, God can accomplish His purposes of mercy with weak as well as with powerful means. He raised up and qualified Mr. James Forsyth, who occupied the humble but honorable station of parochial schoolmaster as the instrument of carrying forward, in that perish, the good work that had made such advances in the surrounding country. He was evidently a good man. He had been long distinguished for godliness. His experience of the preciousness of Christ prompted him to embrace the opportunity which his profession furnished of diffusing the knowledge of that Name and of that Salvation which he knew to be so essential to the true happiness of the people with whom he was brought in contact. He partook of the joy with which the news of God's dealings with His Church was received by such as had themselves tasted that the Lord is gracious. In the peculiar circumstances of the parish, he endeavored, by every means in his power, to infuse the same spiritual life among the people. He spoke with earnestness and power, especially to the young, about their lost condition by nature and by practice and about the love of God manifested in the gift of His Son for the salvation of sinners ready to perish. The Holy Spirit was pleased to convey these simple but impressive truths to the souls of his interested charges who, in their turn, were enabled to leave a testimony to the truth in the consciences of the adult population.

Mr. Forsyth's own account, detailed in letters to Mr. Robe, is impressive: "Since the first of February last, I endeavoured, to the utmost of my power, to instruct the children under my charge in the first principles of religion—that they were born in a state of sin and misery, and strangers to God by nature. I pressed them, with every argument I could think of, to give up their sinful ways and to flee to Jesus Christ by faith and repentance; and, by the blessing of God, my efforts were not made in vain. Glory to His holy name, that which was spoken in much weakness, was accompanied by the power of His Holy Spirit. I likewise warned them against the commission of known sin. I told them the danger of persisting contrary to the voice of conscience and the plain dictates of the Word of God; assuring them, that if they did so, their sin would one day find them out.

"These exhortations, frequently repeated, made at last some impressions on their young hearts. This was used as a means in God's hand for bringing the elder sort to a more serious

Beyond Cambuslang and Kilsyth, 1742

concern and a greater diligence in religious duties. One of the school-boys who went to Cambuslang in March was the first awakened. He, a short time thereafter, asked permission to meet with two or three of the other boys in the school-room, for the purpose of praying and singing psalms. I had great pleasure in granting this request. Very soon after, a few more of the boys manifested deep concern for their souls; and in fourteen days after the opening of this youthful prayer meeting, ten or twelve were hopefully awakened; none of them were above thirteen years of age—a few of them were so young as eight or nine. These associated together for devotional duties. Their love for these services increased; so much so, that they met sometimes three times a-day—early in the morning—at noon, during the interval of school hours—and in the evening. These soon forsook all their childish fancies and plays and were known to their school companions by their general appearance, by their walk and conversation.

"All this had a happy effect upon the other children. Many were awakened by their means. They became remarkable for tenderness of conscience. A word of terror occurring in their lessons would sometimes make them cry out and weep bitterly. Some of them could give a most intelligent account of their experience of divine truth. They were sensible of the sin of their nature, of their actual transgressions, and even of the sin of unbelief; for when I would exhort them to believe in Christ, who was both able and willing to save them to the uttermost, they would reply, in the most affecting terms, that they knew He was both able and willing, but their hearts were so hard that they could not believe aright of themselves, till God gave them the new heart—that they could do nothing for their hard hearts."

In reporting on the situation among the adults, Mr. Forsyth wrote, "Some were awakened at Cambuslang, others at Calder and Kirkintilloch, but the greater number at the private meetings for prayer held in the parish. These meetings were held twice a-week, and all were admitted who chose to attend. . . . Many who attended were blessed with the communications of divine grace, and made to experience the image and the earnest of the fellowship that is above. Two young women who had been at Cambuslang, and who brought back an evil report, saying they wondered what made the people cry out, on the 22nd of June, came to one of these meetings in Baldernock, as was supposed, with no good design. Before a quarter of an hour had elapsed, they were brought under serious conviction and continued in distress during the remaining exercises of the evening."

These details of the awakening in Baldernock furnish an impressive commentary on the words of Scripture: "Not by might, nor by power, but by My Spirit, saith the Lord" and "I will have mercy on whom I will have mercy, and I will have compassion on whom I will have compassion." They should stimulate every Christian in his own sphere to labor for Christ, trusting that the divine Spirit will come "and leave a blessing behind Him."

The movement continued all summer and seems to have been especially pleasing to Robe. He thought it ought to be noted for the instruction of the regular ministry, "seeing," he says, "that though the Lord maketh especially the preaching of the Word an effectual means of convicting and converting sinners, and of building up them that are converted, yet He also blesseth the reading of the Word, Christian communion, and religious education by parents, schoolmasters, and others for the foresaid blessed ends."

The work was notable in the parish of Calder in that it broke out unexpectedly at a meeting held on May 11, 1742, when neither people nor preacher were prepared for it. Mr.

Beyond Cambuslang and Kilsyth, 1742

Warden, the minister, was accustomed to give a weekly lecture in a small village at some distance from the church. This lecture he announced from the pulpit on the Sabbath day. He had kept his appointment week after week and found the congregation had dwindled away, so that in a state of deep discouragement on the occasion just before the revival, he added in a voice of tender pathos after his intimation, "But why should I tell you, for you will not come." In this state of feeling he went to the place, having resolved to discontinue the lecture. The people, having been touched with pity for the evident sorrow and disappointment of their minister, said to each other, "Poor body, let us go this time." He, unconscious of this purpose of theirs, went unprepared with a sermon and was much dismayed when on looking into the room he found it crowded. "Oh," cried he in the genuine simplicity of his character, "I have often been here with a sermon when there were no folks, and now when there are plenty of folks I have no sermon." He retired into the wood at a little distance, earnestly to implore divine direction and blessing. Immediately he returned to the people and preached from these words which had been suggested to his mind while in the wood: "Unto you, O men, I call; and my voice is to the sons of men."[1] From this text he opened up the fullness, the freeness, the grace of the gospel proclamation. The Holy Spirit accompanied the word spoken with power. Many were brought under His humbling influence and ultimately made to bow to the scepter of Jesus.

In Campsie there were 100 anxious souls before the end of August, some of them having been first brought under the influence of the truth at Kilsyth. The annual communion that year was notable, for the attendance was doubled. A correspondent reports that at one of the services "the Spirit of the Lord,

---

[1] Proverbs 8:4.

like a mighty, rushing wind, filled the house in such a manner that almost the whole congregation was melted into a flood of tears, accompanied with bitter outcries on the part of some newly awakened. The minister was obliged to stop; and, after a few exhortations, ended the lecture and left behind him a multitude of distressed souls, thirsting for a soul-satisfying discovery of the dear Redeemer." Throughout the following year, a few were added to the company of believers, and the minister rejoiced that "there still remains a fond desire after ordinances and a singular attention in hearing which gives room to hope that the gospel is yet doing good." In 1747 the minister was transferred to Perth and soon after wrote informing Robe that up to the time of his leaving Campsie he had known of only four who had been false to their profession.

In May, 1742, Mr. MacLaurin of Glasgow and Mr. Robe of Kilsyth preached in town of Kirkintilloch on the Fast Day previous to the dispensation of the Supper. Mr. Burnside, the minister of the parish, preached in the evening. The work of conviction that day was general and powerful. In the words of Mr. Robe, "Zion's mighty King did appear in His glory and majesty, and His arrows were sharp in the heart of His enemies." Many were awakened and brought under spiritual distress. Shortly after, one hundred and twenty are reported "under a more than ordinary concern about their salvation," including many "praying young."

At about the same time, the village and parish of Cumbernauld similarly shared in the blessing that came to Kilsyth, for there were fourteen or fifteen awakened there under the preaching of Mr. Whitefield.

In the neighborhood of Stirling, there appears to have been a wide interest in the revival, and several parishes participated in it—chiefly St. Ninians, Denny, Larbert, and Dunipace.

Beyond Cambuslang and Kilsyth, 1742

At the dispensation of the Supper in St. Ninians on the first Sabbath of August in the same year, there were several awakened by means of the sermons on the Saturday, many more on the Sabbath, and a far greater number on the Monday, which was, on the testimony of Mr. Robe, "one of the greatest days of the Mediator's power ever beheld." On Thursday immediately following, at the usual week-day lecture, a considerable number more were awakened. Mr. Mackie, the minister of the parish, was instrumental in leading many of the inquirers to "the Lamb of God, who taketh away the sin of the world." Some time after, Mr. Mackie states, "Impressions upon the people are far from wearing off. Their behaviour is such that their enemies themselves cannot find fault with it. It gives me great pleasure to hear them pray and converse. Our audience is most attentive to the preaching of the Word."

Perhaps the greatest impression was made in Gargunnock, whose minister was Mr. John Warden, a man described by Robe as having "always had a singular dexterity in instructing and dealing with the consciences of the people under his charge." In spite, however, of this fidelity and skill on the part of their minister, many of the parishioners were aroused far from Gargunnock. "There were some of them," writes Robe, "first of all awakened at Kilsyth, when the Lord's Supper was given upon the second Sabbath of July; others at Campsie, when it was given upon the last Sabbath of the said month; others at St. Ninians, when that sacrament was given upon the first Sabbath of August. Upon the Thursday thereafter there were eighteen awakened in their own congregation while the Rev. Mr. John Warden, their own aged and diligent pastor, preached to them." In a letter dated March 17th the following year, Mr. Warden wrote, "The concern in a great measure continues; fellowship meetings increase; and even the meetings for prayer among the children. The impression among the people, in general, is still apparent, by a diligent attendance upon ordinances, love to our God and Redeemer, and to all the children of our Lord's family; crying to Christ, and rejoicing in Him; and all this associated with a sober and blameless walk and conversation. A few are under spiritual concern in the parish of Kippen, and there is some stir in the parish of Monivaird."

At the western extremity of the same county, the influence of the revival was felt in the parishes of Fintry and Killearn.

The awakening in southern Perthshire seems to have been centered in Muthill, although several of the neighboring parishes shared in the movement. William Halley, the minister of Muthill, was in frequent communication with Robe, and his letters furnish an adequate account of the progress of the work in his district.

It would appear that Halley discovered revival impulses in his congregation as far back as January 1742, but it was not until the July sacrament that distinct and unmistakable evidence was forthcoming that a work of grace had begun. At the ordinance, Halley reported, "Our conquering Redeemer made some visible inroads upon the kingdom of Satan." From that time "an unusual power attended the Word preached every Sabbath day, few, if any, Sabbaths having passed but some have been awakened." Evening services were held, and these proved even more fruitful than the ordinary diets of worship. "For immediately after public worship is over, such crowds of people come to the manse as fill the house and the close before the doors, discovering a great thirst after the Word and such an unusual concern in hearing of it that their mourning cries frequently drown my voice, so that I am obliged frequently to stop till they compose themselves. . . . I am taken up in dealing with them for some hours after the meeting is dismissed." The movement was so intense and widespread in the parish that, at

Beyond Cambuslang and Kilsyth, 1742

least once, Robe ranks the work done there with that of Cambuslang and Kilsyth themselves.

The work continued over the winter and was carried for some distance into the following year. So eager were the people that even the long nights and the dark journeys across the moors could not prevent them waiting on the means of grace. Praying societies increased both in Muthill itself and in the neighboring parishes of Crieff, Monivaird, and Auchterarder. Meetings especially fitted for young people were held and met with a gratifying response. In October 1742 Halley could say that "such a praying disposition as appears amongst this people, both young and old, was never seen nor heard of before, which gives me ground to expect more of the divine influences." Nor was he disappointed. More than a year afterwards, on November 28, 1743, he had to say that "though the public awakenings are much ceased with us, which I never expected would long continue, I hope these wrought upon in this congregation are persevering and bringing forth agreeable fruits. Our praying societies are in a flourishing condition. . . . The hungry-like attention to the Word preached still continues in the congregation. The ordinances are most punctually attended, although the parish be very large and the roads bad." In the following January, the minister could still report large congregations, adding, "the like has not been seen here before." As late as February 1751, he testified to the good work done and to the perseverance of many saints. "I am fully persuaded," he says, "that the gracious fruits of that glorious work will abide with many in this congregation to eternal ages."

The revival also leapt the Grampians and found a place prepared for it in Easter Ross and its neighborhood. The whole region has long been known as one of the most religiously favored districts in the north of Scotland. It has had a succession of evangelical ministers, and the people have shown a more than ordinary appreciation of the truth they declared. "Experimental religion is there well understood," wrote Dr. Sievewright in 1822. Without doubt, part of this heartiness is due to the labor of some devoted ministers in the first half of the eighteenth century, whose work was in a measure crowned by the Revival of 1742.

John Balfour became minister of the parish of Nigg in 1729. Tradition still speaks of him as a man of eminent gifts and devoted piety. Almost from the beginning, his ministry was fruitful, but it was not until 1739 that the concern among his people was such as to attract attention. Writing in 1744, Balfour could give several interesting particulars of the progress of events. "The general meeting for prayer and spiritual conference," he said, "which some time consisted only of the members of Session and a few others, became at length so numerous that about three years ago it was necessary to divide it into two, each of which is since considerably increased. Besides these general meetings . . . there are ten societies which meet in several places of the parish every Saturday for prayer and other religious exercises. . . . Worship is kept up in all the families of the parish except three or four." Four months later he writes that "the work of awakening has proceeded upon new subjects more currently than in any former period." In January 1745 he reports "to the praise of sovereign grace that matters proceed still in my parish as formerly. New awakenings continue, and these formerly awakened persevere."

This religious interest acted so greatly upon the morality of the parish that Balfour had to tell of the absence of crime and of the diligence of the people in their secular callings. The celebration of the sacrament among them became a notable event for the whole neighborhood. An interesting story is told of one of these gatherings. "Thousands were assembled at the tent, the tables were in the open air, and Mr. Balfour presided.

Beyond Cambuslang and Kilsyth, 1742

The communion services in those days were short; but there were so many tables that, ere the last was finished, night was at hand. The instant it was served and a couple of verses sung, Mr Balfour stood up in the tent and said, 'There is no time for an address—let us pray.' And lifting up his eyes to heaven, he said, 'O Lord, we have now done what Thou hast commanded us; do Thou all that Thou hast promised, for the Lord Jesus Christ's sake, Amen.' And then, after praise, he pronounced the benediction and dismissed the immense assembly. Aged Christians were wont to say that they had never heard any prayer which so thrilled their hearts as this brief but comprehensive appeal to God." Unfortunately, this good work was largely ended on the death of Balfour in 1752 by the placing of an unsuitable successor to him in the parish.

The movement in the neighboring parish of Rosskeen showed itself abruptly in the autumn of 1742. "From the harvest of 1742 to Martinmass 1743 or thereby . . . there came a surprising revival and stir among the people; about the number of six and thirty men and women fell under a concern about their salvation during that period." The minister has left on record the texts that were "blest most for their awakening." They were Hosea 13:13, Galatians 4:19, and John 3:3— "especially the first of these subjects was the principal means of the first stir." A feature of the revival was a children's prayer meeting to which some adults were drawn.

The record of what took place in the parish of Rosemarkie is unfortunately deficient. Such had been the state of the parish that the minister was forced to say: "The least gracious revival is the more remarkable to me as I had been groaning under the burden of laboring in vain." The tide turned at the communion of July 1743. Between that date and May 1 of the following year, thirty persons had waited on the minister "under convictions and awakenings of conscience through the Word," not including several other "serious people" who had not yet sought his counsel. That greater things were still in store is apparent to the minister. "I am the more earnest in this longing expectation," he says, "when I observe the steadfast eyes, the piercing looks, the seemingly serious and greedy desires of many in the congregation at times of hearing the Word who as yet have discovered their concern of soul in no other way." Hopeful appearances were also showing themselves in several of the other parishes—Logie, Alness, Killearn, Avoch, and Kilmuir, as well as in the town of Cromarty.

North of the Dornoch Firth, Golspie and Rogart are especially mentioned as having partaken of the blessing. The work began in the former district as early as 1740. Soon afterwards, those who had been awakened formed themselves into a praying society because they themselves had "fallen under sad decays of soul" and because "others in the parish were remaining under their former stupidity." Prayer brought its reward, for in 1743-4 there was a distinct revival of religion in the parish.

We have, however, more detailed information about Golspie. It contained the seat of the Earls of Sutherland, whose family were well-known for their religious sympathies in the seventeenth century. They had given a cordial welcome to those who had to flee from the south country to avoid persecution. "These refugees might with safety have returned to their native country after the happy Revolution: yet such was their gratitude to the foresaid noble family that they chused rather to spend the remainder of their days in their respective callings under the wings that covered them in their distress. Hereby, through the blessing of God, religion flourished in the parish during the forty years' ministry of Mr. Walter Dunoon." Dunoon was succeeded by John Sutherland, whose name has already been mentioned. He was acknowledged to be a good man, but his

Beyond Cambuslang and Kilsyth, 1742

parishioners noticed that his pleading "lacked something—that it was not, after all, the voice of the Chief Shepherd." Sutherland came to the knowledge of his defect in a strange way. In the course of his visitation, he overheard a catechist and some friends praying that their minister might be given God's own Spirit. "He left the door without discovering himself, and on Monday visited the catechist and asked for an explanation. The catechist frankly told him all, and Mr. Sutherland said with beautiful simplicity, 'Will you allow me to come to your meeting and join you in that prayer?' The catechist and his friends cheerfully consented to this. Mr. Sutherland joined the meeting, and it was not long till these godly people felt that what was once lacking was now richly supplied"—perhaps the only time in the whole story of these Scottish revivals that the taught became the teacher.

As already told, Sutherland carried the news of Cambuslang, Kilsyth, and Muthill personally to his own parish. He was, in addition, much influenced by what he saw and heard of the success of the praying societies at Nigg and resolved to institute them among his people. For a time it seemed as if there was to be no result, but at last his reward came. Between November 1744 and May 1745, no fewer than seventy persons waited on the minister "under various exercises of soul" while many others did not declare themselves.

There are other places throughout Scotland named as having come under revival influences at this time, Aberdeen, Dundee, and Coldingham in Berwickshire among the rest, but particulars are wanting.

If the revival as a whole did not continue beyond 1745, it nevertheless handed on a custom which must have helped to retain some of its influences longer than would otherwise have been possible. In 1744 a Concert of Prayer was entered into by some like-minded ministers. They were drawn from both

Scotland Saw His Glory

England and Scotland and eventually included some American preachers as well. These men were moved to this course by the evident power which prayer had exercised during the revival as well as by the neglect it had suffered before the movement began. They were constrained to argue that great as was the blessing which had reached them, it might have been greater still if it had been more earnestly pleaded and prepared for. "If before the late revivals prayer for such blessings was so much neglected that in some respects it may be said, the Lord was found of people when they sought Him not and did wonderful things which we looked not for, may it not be hoped, if there be an abundant united seeking and looking for Him, a seeking His face, and that with all the heart, that we shall find? He has not commanded the house of Jacob to do this in vain, and that, as He never was, He never will be a barren wilderness nor a land of darkness to them who long for Him." The agreement runs into eight sections, but its main provision is that those adhering to it, shall for the next two years ending November 1, 1746, set apart a weekly and a quarterly portion of time for prayer for revival and quickening. It was not a new idea, for such unions binding their members to pray for some particular object had previously existed. This present Concert was found to stimulate intercession and was renewed more than once. Even the dark times that succeeded the revival did not quench the zeal of those faithful petitioners. On June 3, 1754, the Bond was again signed, this time for a further period of seven years. The answer took long in coming, for the century had to close before Scotland again experienced times of refreshing from the presence of the Lord.

Chapter 9

The Cambuslang Controversy

Even after the lapse of more than a century and a half, the work at Cambuslang has its detractors as well as its defenders. A recent magazine writer described it in unqualified terms as "an orgy of fanaticism." Hill Burton, the supposed historian, uses similar hard words. He speaks of it as "one of those strange and melancholy exhibitions called religious revivals with which, fortunately, Scotland has been but rarely, and but casually visited" and says it "exhibited the usual phenomena of such orgies—the profuse fits of weeping and trembling, the endemic epilepsies and faintings, the contortions and howls, with terrible symptoms of contrition emitted by old, obdurate sinners awakened with a sudden lighting-flash to all the horrors of their condition."[1] Such denunciations are mere echoes of the warfare that was waged while the work lasted and are hardly less bitter or less restrained than contemporary attacks.

As might have been expected, all within the parish of Cambuslang did not approve of the doings of their minister and his followers. Participants in the prayer meetings held before the second communion prayed especially for those who "unhappily opposed the work here and in other parts." Opposition was both secular and religious. Among other things, complaint was made that those engaged in the work and their converts were

---

[1] Hill Burton's grievous bias naturally led him to write in this strain, but it is inexcusable when, misunderstanding the local name for the open-air pulpit used by the preachers, he speaks of Whitefield being "in an encampment of tents on the hillside!"

guilty of "idleness and neglect of civil affairs." Webster of Edinburgh undertook to answer this charge saying any apparent neglect was merely temporary and that "even when the number of the distressed, and the circumstances of the case required more than ordinary attendance upon prayer and exhortation, this was so arranged as to occasion little or no interruption in their labor—of which their present plentiful crop is sufficient evidence." M'Culloch apparently had this accusation in mind when nine years later he described his plans. Speaking of his weekly lecture which was still going on, he says, it continued "all the year round, and even in harvest too, only altering the time of it then to the evening, to which the reapers came running from the fields, where they had been toiling all day. At other times of the year, some servants, of their own free motion and choice, are known sometimes to have stayed up all night at their master's work that they might have liberty to attend the weekly lecture next day without giving their master cause to complain."

So persistent was this misrepresentation that Dr. Robertson thought it necessary to contradict it as late as 1831. "When I came to the parish, which was in 1795 . . . I found one uniform tradition among the old people who then distinctly remembered the work, viz, that the labour of the parish was never in a more forward state than in 1742, and that the poors' roll was far from being enlarged by the events which took place in the course of that season. In admitting this, indeed, they give this explanation, that the farmer had not then such a constant succession of labor, as now, when so much green crop is sown. What the farmer would deduct from the labor of one day he would make up by the superior industry of another, and in harvest the reapers would, in the evening, have come to church with their sickles on their shoulders to hear a sermon."

However, almost from the beginning, serious objection was made on other grounds. A furious pamphlet controversy set in,

The Cambuslang Controversy

and tracts for or against came hot and fast from the press. Pulpits all over the south country rang with the clamor. Hardly a circumstance connected with the movement escaped hostile criticism and censure. Some condemned the open way in which expression was given to religious feelings: "an ostentation," it was argued, "inconsistent with the true devotion of a humble and contrite heart recommended in Scripture." Others were offended at a certain vulgarity and uncouthness of expression in those who led in prayer at the meetings. Objection was taken to an alleged uncharitableness in zealots who did not hesitate to call doubters of the reality and efficacy of the work of grace "atheists, deists, or void of religion." Some declared that the extravagant results were procured only by preaching the terrors of the law. The whole proceedings of ministers and people alike were denounced as a riot of irrational enthusiasm, whim, and fancy, asserting that fanatical delusion explained everything.

What created most questioning and aroused most hostility were the various physical effects produced on many of those who attended the meetings and were drawn under the influence of the preaching—"bodily agitations and commotions, as crying out aloud, tremblings, faintings, swoonings, falling down as dead, &c." No one alive had ever seen such manifestations and, indeed, had heard little or nothing of them before. Stewarton was too far distant in time and its tradition too vague to help to reduce the novelty of what all saw transacted before them for weeks. America was too far distant in space even if what had been happening there could be realized from mere descriptions. The commotions under John Wesley hardly seem to have been understood, while so far as can be gathered, the effects produced by Whitefield's preaching in Scotland during the preceding year had none of the extravagances of Cambuslang. It must be remembered that neither Robe nor M'Culloch were prepared to condemn or forbid bodily seizures. The former found examples of several cases in Scripture, as when Felix trembled before Paul and in the records of earlier revivals. M'Culloch considered that they did not enter into the substance of the work at all. As he wrote in 1751, "I think we may safely affirm that one cannot certainly conclude, merely from these seizures, that he himself or another is under the influences of the Holy Spirit, either in convincing, comforting, or sanctifying the soul, because it is possible these seizures may proceed from the mere power of imagination, or from some sudden fright or bodily disorder; nor yet should one suspect himself or another to be a stranger to the convincing, comforting, or sanctifying influences of the Holy Spirit merely because of his being unacquainted with these bodily seizures." This was the opinion he held during the course of the revival. Although he took, so far as we know, no active steps to restrain or end extraordinary manifestations, it is evident he would rather have been without them. "By all that I can observe or hear," he says when reviewing ultimate results, "there are more of these that were under deep concern here in 1742 that appear still to persevere in a good way, and in a gospel becoming practice that never cried out aloud in time of public worship or that were never observable under these bodily agitations above mentioned than of those that were under such outward commotions, and that make the greatest noise. There are, indeed, some of both sorts whose exercises seem to have come to a gracious issue, but many more of the former than of the latter sort." It was around this point that the thick of the battle raged. Doctrinal questions hardly entered the dispute. The discussion did eventually branch into philosophy, and Ralph Erskine addressed himself to the *vain philosophy and vile divinity* of one of Robe's pamphlets, but the argument had little bearing on the chief matter at issue.

    Although the revival found almost its entire support within the established church, it did not commend itself to all within

The Cambuslang Controversy

its bounds. Those we may call the Moderates were hostile to it from the beginning and soon made up their minds as to the true nature of the outbreak. They regarded the whole affair with scorn. Its supporters claimed the revival as a genuine work of the Holy Ghost; its opponents denounced it as an operation of Satan. The Moderates required no supernatural explanation to account for phenomena, believing it originated in the physical constitution of foolish humanity. Instantaneous conversions were an impossibility. Prostration of body and anxiety of soul were alike produced by "the influence of fear and hope, of sympathy and example, aided by peculiar circumstances," as one who sided with them afterwards put it. Excitability of temperament explained what otherwise could not be accounted for. Sir Henry Moncrieff pertinently asked if these influences of hope and fear excluded the operations of the Holy Spirit, for to be conclusive, the argument should settle the exact origin of the hope and fear. However, the Moderates were convinced that delusion underlay the whole *wark*. They even shut their eyes to the fact that the revival kept within their fold many whose evangelical sympathies were more with the seceders. Whitefield was struck with this and wrote in August 1742, "The Kirk Presbyters . . . notwithstanding I have been instrumental in God's hands in some degree in stopping the secession, begin to call some of their ministers to account for employing me."

It should be noted, however, that when the advisability of admitting itinerant preachers to the Scottish parish pulpits was discussed by the Synod of Glasgow in 1748, "there was not the most remote allusion in the course of the whole debate, either on the one side or the other, to the proceedings at Cambuslang, although that parish belongs to the Synod of Glasgow."

The most strenuous opposition came from the Dissenting Churches—the Cameronian and the Secession. It is not apparent that either group took any steps to see for themselves what was going on. As a contemporary pamphlet, in a section ostensibly written by a Seceder, pointedly puts it: "I have never heard that any of our Presbytery were at Cambuslang, or any other place where these alleged delusions prevailed, that they might converse with these people that are under them; and so be better able to judge what Spirit it is, a Good or a Bad. I humbly think the matter is of so great importance that the Presbytery should have been at all possible pains to get information before they proceeded to condemn it as a delusion." Robe has the same complaint to make. Perhaps the Churches considered themselves all the better judges because of their extreme detachment.

Had the revival stood alone, the question at issue between the Dissenters who condemned it and the Churchmen who favored it would have been comparatively simple. The whole situation, however, was complicated by the presence of Whitefield in Scotland and by the part he played in the movement. The dissenters took an uncompromising attitude of personal hostility toward the evangelist—a hostility which can be explained only when the whole history of the Scottish struggle against Episcopacy is kept in mind. Each Church had its fault to find with him, but the Seceders added to their dislike of his principles, the element of wounded vanity and chagrin. He had come to Scotland at their invitation and yet had refused to be bound by the rules they laid down for his conduct. They desired to keep him exclusively among themselves. He preferred to retain his liberty to preach the gospel how and to whom he pleased. They had arranged that he should abjure his Prelacy. He determined to remain true to it. There was neither obstinacy nor ingratitude in what he did, but the Secession did not seem able to overlook the affront they thought he had put upon them.

It was the custom of the time to provide "testimonies" when there was profound dissatisfaction with either a prevailing doctrine or practice. These statements purged sensitive consciences

The Cambuslang Controversy

from even the appearance of participation in the error denounced and, at the same time, made the position of the testifiers known to all men. The Cameronians, accordingly, issued a *Declaration, Protestation, and Testimony . . . Against Mr. George Whitefield and His Encouragers, and Against the Work at Cambuslang and Other Places.* They harshly described Whitefield as "a limb of Antichrist" and "an abjured prelatic hireling of as lax toleration principles as any that ever set up for the advancing of the kingdom of Satan." Those who countenanced him, they said, were "as far forsaken of God, and as far ensnared of Satan as the children of Israel were when, in an unsanctified fit of madness, they were dancing about the golden calf to the dishonor of God, and their own sin and shame among their enemies." The main reason assigned for this wholesale denunciation was that no repentance and turning from sin could be genuine which did not include true sorrow for national transgressions and an acknowledgment of the heinousness of having been unfaithful to Scotland's covenanted religion. Every work of grace must be "a witnessing for the Headship of Christ," and without this essential content, such ongoings as were taking place at Cambuslang were merely "the putting on a new clout of delusion upon the garment of apostasy." Minor objections included such things as, "A right law work" did not "influence the body with pain and convulsions," because Scripture warns that bodily exercise profiteth nothing. "Great and extraordinary gifts of utterance in prayer and other performances" could be accounted for on the ground that Satan sometimes appears as an angel of light. Grace humbles, whereas those who have come under the influence of Cambuslang will "not endure any who doubts the work." The final objection is that the Kingdom of God cometh not with observation, and the furor, noise, and extravagance which have been inseparable from the movement is its sufficient condemnation, and justifies the conclusion that the whole is nothing else than "a delusion of Satan."

The harsh language and absurdity of argument amaze us but we know Cameronian judgment was warped by an exclusive fidelity to an outstanding idea. They accused the adherents of Cambuslang of spiritual blindness, saying the work in which they rejoiced, instead of enlightening, only shut their eyes closer. The retort is obvious. There is some relief in knowing that the protest does not seem to have reached the ears of those who took part in the controversy—at least none of the polemical papers consulted took notice of it. In recent times their own Church Historian has repudiated their position. "It is matter of regret," he says, "that such declarations were given forth by Christian communities against a work, which, though connected with some things not to be commended, is all but universally acknowledged to have been a genuine spiritual awakening."

If the Cameronian denunciation passed without attracting much attention, it was otherwise with that of the Seceders. The country rang with their opposition and the outcry their proceedings raised. The Associate Presbytery met in Dunfermline in the middle of July and solemnly took into consideration the religious condition of the whole land. They found evidence everywhere of defection both in belief and practice. Special, though not exclusive, stress was laid upon the proceedings at Cambuslang as part of the general national declension. They objected to Whitefield on two grounds: his extreme toleration, which made for the destruction of the Church and besides, "in the account he gives of his life, he makes a plain discovery of the grossest enthusiasm, and most palpable error and delusion touching his own experience with reference to the effectual application of the redemption purchased by Christ." They also deplored "how much people are imposed upon by several ministers, who, notwithstanding of all the ordinary symptoms

The Cambuslang Controversy

of a delusion attending the present awful work upon the bodies and spirits of men, yet cry it up as a great work of God, and are at indefatigable pains, by their printed missives, attestations, and journals, to deceive, if it were possible, the very elect." "It is obvious," they add, "that bitter outcryings, faintings, severe bodily pains, convulsions, voices, visions, and revelations are the usual symptoms of a delusive spirit that have appeared in the Quakers, Sevennois, Comizars, and other enthusiasts."

The venerable Presbytery had forgotten that almost the first official act of their corporate existence had been to desire some such extensive turning to religion, for they had looked back with longing eyes to Stewarton, and Stewarton apparently saw the same phenomena as did Cambuslang. But they seemed to discover some essential difference between Stewarton and Shotts on the one side, and Cambuslang and Kilsyth on the other, and followed up their denunciatory act by threatening to excommunicate any of their people who had part or lot with the deceived. In some cases this was actually done, as by David Smyton of Kilmaurs. "When you had your Sacrament at Kilmaurs," says the pamphlet already quoted, "your preacher debarred from the Table of the Lord all such persons as were drawn away with the delusion of Cambuslang, which made many of the well-meaning people leave you."

The enemies of the Secession had no difficulty in assigning a cause for their violent opposition. They affirmed that it was due not so much to a hatred of the thing they denounced as to an improper and unworthy jealousy that such blessings should be vouchsafed to a Church they had left. There does seem to be that modicum of truth in the charge that renders it stinging.[2]

---

[2] Webster refused to believe that the Secession said "that not one soul can be converted within the pale of the Established Church of Scotland." *Divine Influence*, p. 11.

Scotland Saw His Glory

The Seceders were disposed to argue that a work could not be genuinely religious which had its origin in a community which, as a recent writer somewhat bluntly states it, "whitewashed heretics, and had driven faithful men from its pale."

An attempt was also make to fix a charge of inconsistency on Ralph Erskine in regard to his whole attitude. Three years before Cambuslang, John Wesley had written Erskine telling him of some extraordinary manifestations that had followed his preaching. "Some of them drop down as dead, having no strength nor appearance of life left in them. Some burst out into strong cries and tears, some exceedingly tremble and quake," &c.,—and asking "whether any outward appearances like these have been among you." Erskine replied in a long letter in which, in spite of the untoward commotions, he blessed God "for the good and great news" and then goes on to say such things as, "All the outward appearances of people's being affected among us in time of preaching, especially upon sacramental occasions, may be reduced to these two sorts. One is hearing with a close, silent attention, with gravity and greediness, discovered by fixed looks, weeping eyes, joyful or sorrowful countenances, evidencing tenderness in hearing. Another sort is when the word is so affecting to the congregation as to make them lift up their voice and weep aloud, some more depressedly, others more highly, and at times the whole multitude in a flood of tears, all, as it were, crying out at once, till their voices be ready to drown out the minister's, so as he can hardly be heard for the weeping noise that surrounds him." What essential difference, it was asked, was there between this and the events of the work he had condemned? Erkskine, however, did not approve of these outbursts. It is said that under the preaching of David Smyton of Kilmaurs, congregations at Orwell and Abernethy were so moved that the noise threatened to interrupt the services. The commotion was

The Cambuslang Controversy

stopped only by the rebuke of Erskine who urged that nothing extravagant or disorderly could be supposed to proceed from divine influence.

No more space need be given to accusations, defenses, and counter assertions. Sufficient has been said to indicate the nature of the opposition. The chief protagonists on the Secession side were Ralph Erskine, Adam Gib, and James Fisher; on the other side they numbered among them James Robe, John Willison, John Erskine, and Alexander Webster. All were men of ability, distinctness of view, and eminence of character, and the violence of their words is only another illustration of what good men can do when they become partisans. Adam Gib came to repent of the vehemence of an onslaught he made on Whitefield, and Whitefield, the much maligned and defamed, so far forgot the attacks made upon him that when Erskine died he spoke of him as "God's triumphant saint."

The conflict, however, did much mischief. It widened the breach the Secession had made. The language used created great bitterness and almost incited to deeds of violence. Dr. John Brown tells how he found a letter among the papers of James Fisher. In it the minister is informed that he would have been pulled out of his pulpit if, on the preceding Sabbath, he had mentioned Whitefield's name. At the same time he is told that if he does not desist from attacking Whitefield and Cambuslang for the future, both pulpit and manse would be burned over his head. Controversies which could produce such a spirit were self-condemned.

There could be no doubt of the sincerity of each side. The revivalists believed that God was indeed sending showers of blessing, however perplexing might be some of the accompaniments. They could not imagine that a work proceeding from Satan could possibly drive men to Christ—as was actually happening. They remembered the saying that a house divided against itself fell. The Seceders, on the other hand, feared that the true source of salvation was being overlooked and hope built on the insecure foundation of a man's emotion. Too much stress was laid, they argued, on outward assent, and too little on inward contrition. Bodily convulsions, even if otherwise unobjectionable, were fitted to deceive, as they had already been known historically to have done. Both sides were anxious that true religion should prevail and that the glory of the Redeemer's Kingdom should be advanced.

Sympathy for the part played by the Seceders has gradually ebbed away and even their own church historians have abandoned the cause they maintained. "We can look back on these scenes," says Dr. Brown, "with minds undisturbed with prejudice and passion, and see in them a remarkable display of the sovereignty and power of divine grace rendering the clear impressive statement of elementary gospel truth effectual to the conversion of many sinners of very various descriptions who showed the true character of the change produced by a long course of consistent Christian conduct." Describing the revival, M'Kerrow candidly says, "In the controversy to which these events gave rise, the Secession bore a prominent part, but truth and candor require me to state that the part which the leaders of it acted on this occasion was by no means creditable to their cause." "The controversy," says Professor MacEwen, perhaps the latest writer on the subject, "showed the Erskines personally at their worst. . . . They were unbridled in their resentment, and ignored the genuine and pious enthusiasm of men like MacLaurin and Robe. They wrote with a violence for which their apologists need to plead that it was usual in those days."

Chapter 10

Moulin, 1799

The story of the Revival at Moulin is inseparable from the personal history of Dr. Alexander Stewart, minister of the parish at the time when the movement took place. He himself frankly recognized the connection. "In narrating the means by which the people were brought to a more serious attention to their eternal interests," he writes, "it is necessary to say something of my own case;" or, as he expressed it on another occasion, "my own story is closely interwoven with that of my parishioners." It is therefore fitting that some account of its leader's spiritual history should precede the recital of the events of the revival itself.

Stewart, who belonged to both a Levitical and a landed family on his father's side, was born in the manse of Blair-Atholl. The scene of this first ministry was accordingly only separated from his birthplace by the Pass of Killiecrankie. He was educated at St. Andrews and on September 21, 1786, was ordained over the parish of Moulin[1] through the presentation of the Duke of Atholl.

For the first dozen years of his ministry, Stewart belonged to the school of the Moderates. Studious by inclination, he had no great interest either in his pulpit presentation or in his pastoral visitation. His people were unfortunately fashioned in

---

[1] The center of population in the parish has now shifted to Pitlochry, distant less than a mile from the village of Moulin. In the days of the revival the latter still had the supremacy. It contained 37 families while Pitlochry had only 30. *Old Statistical Account,* Vol. 68.

the same mold, and none of them discerned the note omitted from his preaching. On the whole they were rather proud of the accomplishments of their young minister. He was an honorary member of the Highland Society and was a devoted student of the Gaelic language.[2] Some may marvel at his description of himself during that early time of spiritual torpor, but this is what he wrote when in later days he discovered the manner of man he had been: "Although I was not a *despiser* of what was sacred, yet I felt nothing of the power of religion on my soul. I had no relish for its exercise, nor any enjoyment in the duties of my office, public or private. . . . I was quite well pleased when a diet of catechizing was ill-attended, because my work was the sooner over: and I was always satisfied with the reflection that, if people were not able, or did not chuse, to attend on these occasions, that was no fault of mine. I well remember that I often hurried over that exercise with a good deal of impatience, that I might get home in time to join a dancing party or to read a sentimental novel. My public addresses were for the most part cold and formal. . . . I preached against particular vices, and inculcated particular virtues. But I had no notion of the necessity of a radical change of principle: for I had not learned to know the import of those assertions of Scripture, that 'the carnal mind is enmity against God;' that 'if any man be in Christ, he is a new creature;' and that 'except a man be born of water and of the Spirit, he cannot enter into the kingdom of God.'"

Several distinct agencies were concerned in the conversion of Stewart. His sister, Margaret, who acted as his housekeeper

---

[2] While the revival was running its course under his guidance, he was busy preparing for the press a Gaelic grammar, which had a considerable vogue. It was published in 1801 and four editions were called for, the last appearing as late as 1879.

Moulin, 1799

before his marriage and continued to reside with him as long as he remained at Moulin, was a gracious influence in his life. It is doubtful whether Stewart himself or those who have written about him have given her her true place in the story of his changed life and in the revival that followed. Some of his parishioners also had their unwitting share in turning their pastor's eyes towards the light.[3] "Two persons under conviction of sin and terrors of conscience applied to me for advice," he says. "They supposed that one in the office of the ministry must of course be a man of God and skilled in administering remedies for the diseases of the soul. They were widely mistaken in their judgement of me, for I had learned less of the practice than of the theory of pastoral duty. I said something to them in the way of advice, but it afforded them no relief." That he remembered the incident long afterwards shows how his inability to help these distressed souls left its mark on him. Christian biography also lent its aid to emphasize his uneasiness and to point the difference between himself and those who lived spiritually fruitful lives and died "in composure, joy, and triumph."

It was, however, to David Black, minister first at St. Madoes near Perth, and afterwards at Edinburgh, that the minister of Moulin really owed his soul. Black was a man in whom wisdom dwelt abundantly. He became Stewart's confidential correspondent to whom he could send his sermons for criticism and before whom he could lay bare the innermost doubts and fears of his soul. Black used his opportunity with great discretion and tact. Although he early recognized Stewart's lack and need, no word of reproach fell from his lips that his friend should so long have attempted to exercise the

---

[3] It is noticeable how often the words "light" and "enlightenment" occur in the story.

functions of a ministry for which he evidently had not received the essential call. He sent Stewart, Thomas Scott's well known *Force of Truth,* a book which detailed how a man had come to the knowledge of the truth even after he had been ordained to teach it to others, and he supported the testimony of the book by further examples. "Scott's case," he wrote, "though remarkable, is not altogether singular. There have been several instances of persons entering into the office of the ministry, totally devoid of real religion, who have afterwards been brought to a happy change in their sentiments and conduct. Mr. Walker of Truro is as striking an instance of it as Mr. Scott. The means employed were of the ordinary kind too. If I recollect right, it was by means of a conversation with a pious friend that Mr. Walker received his first serious impressions of the truth. The effects produced were great. From being a dry, useless preacher to a careless, unconcerned congregation, he became a zealous and faithful minister of the gospel, and was the honored instrument of the conversion of many souls. I have likewise by me a short account of Mr. Sheriff, the first minister of Lady Glenorchy's Chapel, in Edinburgh, who experienced a like happy change, a considerable time after he was a preacher."

Personal intercourse between the two men added to the impressiveness of their correspondence. On his part, Stewart was not slow to acknowledge the great service his friend rendered him. His biographer says he "always referred to a conversation with his friend at St. Madoes as connected with the commencement of his spiritual life. Mr. Black, as they sat together in an arbour in the garden, took occasion to describe the triumphant dying scene of a deceased sister. Such a fact was not to be accounted for on Mr. Stewart's principles. Many years after this incident he writes: 'The dear name [of Mr. Black] is always associated with my first perceptions of divine truth and redeeming love. My thoughts took a long flight backwards, and

Moulin, 1799

the parlour and garden at St. Madoes appeared to me like an upper chamber in Jerusalem and like the garden of Gethsemane.'" But although Black thus sowed, another was destined to reap.

The correspondence with Black commenced in 1791, but Stewart did not enter into light until five years later. Meantime he continued preaching and his search side by side, although he felt the falseness of his position. He did not seek to hide the false position in which he stood. He openly declared to his people that he did not feel the full power of the gospel in his own heart. A pathetic story is told of him during this time of darkness. One day, when conducting public worship in his own church, he was about to give out his text when he paused, leaned over the pulpit, looked around with a sad, despairing glance and then said: "My brethren, I am bound in truth and faithfulness to tell you that I feel myself to be in great ignorance and much blindness on the subject of vital religion. I feel like one groping in the dark for light and as yet I have found none. But I think it right to tell you that if God in mercy will give me any measure of the true light, joyfully shall I impart the same to you. Do you, therefore, all of you, pray God fervently that He may be pleased to bestow upon me the true light or such portions of it as He may deem fit for me."

It was an announcement calculated to cause gossip over a whole countryside and we are told that many came to hear him, drawn either by curiosity or by sympathy. For the most part they returned disappointed. Weeks and months passed and the preacher had no declaration to make. But deliverance did come at last and that, as is often the case, in a most unexpected way.

The Rev. Charles Simeon, minister of Trinity Church, Cambridge, had already acquired fame as a successful and impassioned evangelical preacher. In 1796 he set out on a preaching tour in Scotland, although some had doubted the wisdom of such a campaign. Accompanied by James Haldane, he passed through Central Perthshire. At Dunkeld they determined to see the far-famed Pass of Killiecrankie. "Quite a random thought" had suggested to Black that he might furnish Simeon, as he passed through Edinburgh, with a note of introduction to his friend at Moulin. On Saturday, June 25, the note was presented to Stewart, and after a short interview with him, the strangers passed north. It seemed as if the golden opportunity had also passed, but Simeon could not find accommodation for the night at Blair-Atholl and had to retrace his steps to Moulin. By arrangement, the visitors were lodged in the manse.

Next day was Sacrament Sabbath and Simeon was easily persuaded to take part in the services. "The congregation," he says, "was numerous and the communicants about a thousand." He preached the "action sermon," served one of the tables, and conducted the service in the evening. It was this evening discourse that brought light to the darkened and troubled soul of Stewart. His own declaration was that about the middle of the sermon, Mr. Simeon, who had evidently studied his case and endeavored to adapt as much of the discourse as was practicable to it, uttered the sentence which to Mr. Stewart looked like a revelation from heaven. His own significant expression was that "it seemed as if the dense cloud canopy which had hitherto interposed between his soul and the vision of God in Christ reconciling a guilty world to Himself had suddenly burst asunder, and through the chink a stream of light had come down direct from heaven into his soul, displacing the darkness which had hitherto brooded over it, filling it with light, and enabling him to rejoice with exceeding joy." The impression made was confirmed by an intimate interview which Stewart and Simeon had that same evening in the solitude of the latter's bedroom. The older man prayed with and counselled

Moulin, 1799

his host as the occasion demanded, and Stewart from that moment counted Simeon his "spiritual father."[4]

We have two estimates by Stewart of the moral condition of his parishioners. One was written as part of the description of Moulin which he compiled in 1793 for Sir John Sinclair's *Statistical Accounts of the Parishes of Scotland*. Neither his own state of mind nor the purpose of the *Accounts* themselves allowed him to be particular from the religious point of view, and the best he could say about his people was that "they are humane, very obliging, well-enough contented. . . . It cannot be said that the people are addicted to drinking. Even at weddings and on holidays, instances of persons drinking to excess are few, and a drunken squabble is extremely rare." When the eyes of his mind were enlightened, he could go further. In the story of the revival which he prepared,[5] he could write: "Very few, indeed, know the way in which the gospel informs us a sinner may be reconciled to God. The opinion of their own works recommending them to the favor of God and procuring a reward from His bounty was almost universal. . . . Very few seemed to annex any meaning to their words when they said that they expected pardon for Christ's sake. . . . They were not, indeed, addicted to open vice if we except lying and swearing. They were rather distinguished for sobriety, industry, and peaceable behavior. . . . They attended church and partook of

---

[4] Alexander Haldane, the author of the *Lives of the Haldanes*, complains that James Haldane's part in the service of Stewart's enlightenment has not been sufficiently recognized.

[5] Dr. Sievewright, Stewart's biographer, says this account had an excellent reception and a wide circulation. "Letters from entire strangers, both in England and America, bore testimony how well the narrative was received; and among others we may mention the venerable Newton, who, both at the time of its appearance and several years after, expressed a most favorable judgment of the publication." It appeared in several editions.

the Sacraments and rested from their work on the Sabbath. There was little reading of the Scriptures at home; little religious instruction of children; no religious conversation; no laboring, in any manner, for the meat which endureth unto everlasting life." It was not that vital religion had altogether died out of the parish, for even while he deplored the low religious life of those to whom he ministered, he acknowledged that all along God had still preserved a seed to serve Him.

On the Sunday following the visit of Simeon, Stewart publicly proclaimed the great gift of light he had received, and forthwith began the work of dispelling the darkness in others. He immediately developed an interest in individual cases of awakening in his own parish, for Simeon's visit seems to have been blessed to more than the minister. He even wrote to several beyond its bounds who, he thought, required rousing. In his pulpit ministrations he chose texts which bore more directly on evangelical truth. Thus from August 1797 to January 1798 he followed the selection of texts in a tract entitled, "Short Sermons,"[6] and they must have given him the needed opportunity for pressing home gospel truth.

Considering Stewart's own condition in the early days of his ministry, it is no wonder that he could write, "In summer 1798, the Lord's Supper was dispensed in our congregation at the usual time of the year. For some weeks before, I endeavoured in preaching to explain more fully, and with more application to the conscience, the nature of the ordinance; and the character of those who, under the denomination of disciples, were commanded to keep it. The exhortations and warnings then

---

[6]A list of these texts is worth noting: Matthew 16:26; 1 John 3:4; Romans 3:23; Galatians 3:10; Romans 6:23; Acts 16:30; Mark 1:15; 1 Timothy 1:15; John 6:37; Romans 5:1; 1 Peter 2:7; Hebrews 12:14; Titus 2:13; Luke 11:13; Hebrews 12:27; Hebrews 2:3.

Moulin, 1799

given appeared to be accompanied with a divine blessing. Some of the ordinary communicants, judging themselves to be in an unconverted state, kept back, of their own accord, from partaking of the sacrament. Others, after conversing with me privately on the subject, took the same resolution. Many of those who might otherwise have applied for admission, forbore to apply. I inferred this from the comparatively small number of persons applying. For some years before, the number of candidates for admission each summer amounted to thirty, forty, and sometimes near fifty. In summer 1798, there were not above twelve; of whom nine were admitted. The sacrament was dispensed again in November, on which occasion there were only six more new communicants admitted.

"Although the number of communicants was thus for the time diminished, yet the number of those who were brought under concern about their eternal interests was increasing. This concern showed itself chiefly among the younger people under twenty-five or thirty. Their knowledge was yet imperfect. A natural shyness often hindered them long from discovering to others what they thought or felt. They had as yet no friend or intimate whom they judged able, from experience, to understand their situation, or to give them counsel. Some of them began to visit one of the two earlier converts . . . from whose reading and conversation they observed considerable benefit. By means of this common friend, they were brought more acquainted with each other. One might now observe at church, after divine service, two or three small groups forming themselves round our few more advanced believers, and withdrawing from the crowd into the adjacent fields, to exchange Christian salutations, and hold Christian converse together; while a little cousin, or other young relative, followed as a silent attendant on the party, and listened earnestly to their religious discourse.

Scotland Saw His Glory

"As the sacrament of the Lord's Supper had been much abused, by admitting, without strict examination or special instruction, all candidates who could give a tolerable answer to common questions, and who were free from the grosser immoralities; so it must be confessed, that the sacrament of baptism had been still more profaned. Nothing but one kind of scandal was understood to preclude a man from admission to that ordinance. Gross ignorance, or immoral behavior, only laid a man open to some admonition or reproof; or at most laid him under the necessity of procuring another sponsor; but hardly ever hindered the baptism of his child. Nothing subjects a man to greater disgrace and obloquy among us, than to have his child remain unbaptized. The dominions of custom in this matter is so despotic, that most parents would choose rather to carry their children a hundred miles to be baptized by a Popish priest, than be refused baptism when they demand it. The superstitious notions, and other abuses attending our celebration of this sacrament, called loudly for reformation. Last year, I preached a short course of sermons on baptism. At the same time, agreeable to a recent resolution and recommendation of the Presbytery to which I belong, I revived the laws of the church which had fallen into disuse, relative to this ordinance. . . . By these means many have been brought to understand better the nature of this sacrament, and to attend to it with more reverence. It had been long customary for the parent to give an entertainment, according to his station, to his neighbours and connections, immediately after the baptism; by which means the sacred ordinance, instead of being regarded as a most solemn religious service, had degenerated into an occasion of carnal mirth and festivity. The more religiously disposed amongst us have set the example of discontinuing the practice."

At about this same time that Stewart was instituting the above reforms, he discarded reading his public discourses and

Moulin, 1799

preached extempore—a thing he had not ventured to do before. This added a dimension of freedom and power to his preaching.

Much good was also done by a meeting for prayer, meditation, and fellowship that was organized in the house of a pious old woman. "It was proposed that they should come together to her house at a time appointed, and that I and some of my family should join them and spend an evening hour or two in reading, conversation, and prayer. In the process of time, different persons, who were enquiring after the one thing needful, hearing how we were employed, and believing that God was with us, were, at their own request, admitted of our party. In this poor woman's little smoky hovel, we continued to hold our weekly meetings to August 1799, when she was called away to join the general assembly of the first-born above." Stewart then arranged, that by the ringing of a bell, a general invitation was given to all who might care to join in the evening worship of his household, an exercise which was conducted either in his kitchen or at the door if the weather permitted.

All this resulted in the community taking a more serious view of their religious responsibilities. The preacher was rewarded by seeing conversions taking place under his preaching. The movement, however, did not become marked or general until after March 1799. In that month Stewart did what M'Culloch of Cambuslang had done with such effect—he began a series of discourses on regeneration, founded on the story of Nicodemus. It was then that a general personal anxiety for salvation became evident. Speaking of these sermons, Stewart says they were "attended with a more general awakening than had yet appeared among us. Seldom a week passed in which we did not see or hear of one, two, or three persons brought under deep concern about their souls, accompanied with strong convictions of sin and earnest enquiry after a Saviour." The interest was not confined to the immediate vicinity of the church. Glenbriarachan, the more detached part of the parish, Stewart says, was "blossoming as the rose." Converts were made in his native parish of Blair to the north, and visitors who came from such places as Dunkeld, a dozen miles to the south, returned blessing God for the grace given them.

The general attention continued throughout the autumn of 1799. Black visited his friend in the month of August and on his return home made this entry in his diary: "Such a revival I never witnessed before.... Had a great deal of conversation in private with many of those under religious concern, and considerably under the influence of doubts and fears.... They have a keen appetite for the Word of God and an evident love for the Saviour.... Some are more advanced and greatly enlightened in the knowledge of divine truth. These serve as guides to the rest, and are exceedingly useful by their example and conversation." Two months later Stewart wrote his friend: "O my dear brother, had you but been here with us for a week past, how your heart would have rejoiced! Such hungering and thirsting after communion with God! Such genuine humility and contrition for sin! Such devotedness to the Saviour! Old converts quickened and new ones added to the Lord! Yesterday was, I trust, a great day of the Son of Man."

Stewart took care to let it be known that the gracious work proceeded without excitement of any kind. There were no convulsions or unseemly outcries. In two cases only did emotion appear to gain the ascendancy. One woman had to leave the church during worship and another was rendered unfit for her work for some days. "Excepting these two instances I know of none whose emotions under the preaching of the Word discovered themselves in any other manner than by silent tears." But even though carried on with circumspection and without extravagance, the movement had its detractors. It was misrep-

Moulin, 1799

resented beyond the parish and exaggerated accounts were circulated regarding what was taking place. "But we only hear of such things," says Stewart. "They are hardly permitted to come nigh us. The chief opposition arises from those who possess scholarship and acquaintance with the Scriptures. These contend that there can be nothing substantial or necessary in that experimental knowledge which illiterate persons may pretend to have attained: and that it is mere arrogance in them to imagine that they can have a larger share of saving knowledge than men who are greater scholars and better versed in the Scriptures"—an objection as old as the Acts of the Apostles.

The revival had its effect, as might be expected, even among these who did not come directly under its operation. The moral tone and general behavior of the parish were distinctly bettered. "The external effects of a general concern about religion have appeared in the behavior even of those who do not seem to have experienced a change of heart. While the younger people attended a Sabbath School, those who were grown up used to spend the evening of that day in sauntering about the fields and woods, in gossiping parties, or visiting their acquaintance of a distance, without improving their time by any profitable exercise. Now there is hardly a lounger to be seen; nor any person walking abroad, except going to some house or meeting where he may hear the Scriptures read. Swearing, profane talking, foolish and indecent jesting, have in a great measure ceased. At late wakes, where people assembled to watch by the body of a deceased neighbor, the whole night used to be spent in childish, noisy sports and pastimes. Even the apartment where the corpse lay was the scene of their revelry. This unnatural custom, which is still pretty general over a great part of the Highlands, is almost wholly discontinued in this part of the country. They still assemble on such occasions, but they pass the time in reading the Bible or some religious book, and in sober conversation."

When solicited for spectacular accounts of conversions, Stewart replied, "In reply to your request of relating a few of the more remarkable cases of conversion which have occurred among this people, I must say that I have little uncommon to communicate. I have mentioned already that almost all our converts have been brought to serious concern and enquiry in a quiet, gradual manner. To an intelligent observer, the change in the conversation, temper, deportment, and the very countenance of individuals is striking; the change too, on the general aspect of the manners of the people is conspicuous. The effect is thus, on the whole, obvious; yet there are few particulars in the case of each person, which, taken singly, will appear uncommon, or worthy of being detailed in a separate narrative. We have no instances of persons remarkable for profligacy of manners or profaneness of speech, who have been reclaimed from such enormities; because there was none of that description to be found in our society. The change has been from ignorance and indifference, and disrelish of divine things, to knowledge, and concern, and spiritual enjoyment. Neither are there among us examples of persons suddenly struck and impressed by some alarming event, or singular interposition of Providence. The Word of Truth proclaimed in public, or spoken in private, has been almost the only outward mean of producing conviction of sin, and confidence in the Saviour. In every single case, the power of God is visible in the effect produced; but there is little 'diversity of operation.' Instead of endeavouring to paint the beauties of holiness in the scene around me, I rather wish to prevail with you and other friends, who know how to enjoy such a spectacle, to 'come and see.'"

The work proceeded with more or less intensity during 1800 and 1801. When Stewart wrote his account of the revival in the

Moulin, 1799

autumn of 1800 he condescended to provide some numbers: "Having lately made an enumeration of those of our congregation, whom, to the best of my judgment, I trust I can reckon truly enlightened with the saving knowledge of Christ, I find their number about seventy. The greater part of these are about thirty years of age. Several are about forty; six or seven above fifty; one sixty-six; and one above seventy. Of children under twelve or fourteen, there were a good many who seem to have a liking to religion; but we find it difficult to form a decided opinion in their case." The numbers do not seem large, and would be greatly increased if many who did not belong to the parish were included. The news of the awakening at Moulin made Stewart a desirable visitor at other places. In August 1802 he journeyed to Ross-shire on the invitation of several ministers, but we have no record of these apostolic labors.

In the autumn of 1801 the *Missionary Magazine* reported: "We rejoice in hearing that the revival of religion in Moulin . . . is still going on. The progress, we are informed, is indeed more silent and gradual, and to common observation less perceptible than at first. But it cannot be doubted there is progress." The movement, however, seems to have exhausted itself in 1802. Several years later an English clergyman, who had had similar experiences in his own congregation, wrote Stewart in regard to the Moulin work. In his reply Stewart tells his southern correspondent that after 1802 "there did not appear any accession to the number of converts. The bulk of the people appeared satisfied with lending their approbation to what they saw and heard and attending regularly to ordinances, but there was no more pressing into the kingdom of heaven. The heavens appeared to be shut up and the showers were withheld. Of those who formed our little Christian society, some were in Providence removed to a distance and others were called home by death, so that our numbers began to lessen rather than increase." In 1805 Stewart had to face the possibility of leaving Moulin, and the fact that no harm would be done to any work then in progress helped him to decide in favor of a change. "As to the state of the people here," he writes, "there has been no gross declension nor scandalous falling off among those who appear to be truly enlightened. But we cannot reckon on any accession to their number for many months past. There is, or appears to be, a diminution of liveliness and a dullness of spirit hanging over the most of us."

Stewart was transferred to Dingwall on September 26, 1805. By the appointment of a successor who had no sympathy with vital religion, all hope of the renewal of the gracious experiences of the past vanished. Communication with his old parish did not end with Stewart's removal. He continued to receive news of its condition and was able to answer the enquiries of strangers regarding it. Of the great body of the people, he could give no good report, although he could say that "the few godly keep close together for prayer and confidence, and love and cherish one another. I have visited them repeatedly since my settlement here and found them 'sorrowful and rejoicing.'"

Independent testimony as to the perseverance of the converts comes from, among others, William H. Burns of Kilsyth. In 1811 he had what he calls "a solitary ride" through the Perthshire Highlands and, in the course of his journey, stayed a night at Moulin. He found several of the parishioners in a depressed condition of mind because of the unevangelical nature of their pastor's ministrations. Some of them had been present at a service which Burns had conducted at Persie, twenty miles distant. When he arrived at Moulin, they asked him to minister there also, but Burns had regard to ecclesiastical courtesy and merely conducted family worship with them. "I had," he says, "a conversation with two very interesting men who had been elders in Mr. Stewart's time, and among the

Moulin, 1799

subjects of the gracious work there. They told me that they had paid a visit to their beloved spiritual father and former pastor, travelling the whole way on foot to Dingwall, and had a refreshing though somewhat pensive meeting with one whose removal from among them they and so many deplored." Burns adds, "I found unquestionable evidence in my short visit to Moulin of the reality of the far-famed revival in that district."

In the autumn of 1817, the well-known William M'Gavin of Glasgow visited Moulin. He had no good report to make of the condition of religion in the parish and tells how it had been represented to him that "they had been rather annoyed by too much religion. Even the ladies, it seems, could talk about it and almost preach!" But he adds, "The truth, however, has neither been starved nor driven out of the parish, having found refuge in a small society of Baptists." Twenty years later similar testimony is forthcoming. Writing in February 1839, the then minister of the parish says that "a few even of those who were in 1800 accounted subjects of conversion are still living and have uniformly through life, by the piety and consistency of their conduct, given proof of the reality of the saving change that had been effected on their heart."

William Burns of Kilsyth claimed the revival had more than a local influence and spoke of "the salutary effect" it had "on the state of religion in the Church" at the time. One of the converts in Glenbriarachan was so impressed with the low state of the spiritual life in his neighborhood that he opened a Sabbath class for adults. That class and the occasional visits of James Kennedy, Congregational minister at Aberfeldy, "resulted in producing, by the blessing of God, a most remarkable change in the life and character of many." In 1793 Stewart reported that there was one student of Divinity in the parish. He may have been John Shaw, a native of Moulin, who was ordained at Duirinish in Skye, in October 1805. If Shaw was not one of the direct fruits of the revival, he certainly breathed its spirit throughout his ministry and must accordingly have been influenced by it. He speaks of Stewart as being "ever dear" to him. At the time of his settlement, Skye was in a condition of extreme spiritual destitution. His coming was hailed as that of a sincere friend of evangelical religion, and he appears to have done his part well. His tombstone sums up his services to the island—"As a Christian minister he was well known in devotedness to God; in zeal for the salvation of souls; in humility, meekness, and longsuffering." He died January 16, 1823.

Another name more greatly celebrated and connected with more extended service is also linked with the story of the Moulin Revival. Among the converts were James Duff and Jean Rattray, then both under seventeen years of age. By and by they married and one of their sons became Dr. Alexander Duff, the famous missionary. It is interesting to think that the lives of Simeon, who in one sense made the revival possible, and of Duff, who was born of the revival's spiritual children, should have crossed at more than one point. Simeon took a foremost part in founding the Church Missionary Society and was chiefly responsible for sending Henry Martyn to India where Duff made his name. They met at least once. The common interest of the two men in India led Duff to visit the aged evangelist at Cambridge in 1836, a few months before he died. Their conversation, however, was not all on missions, for Duff was able to tell the veteran preacher many gladsome things about that providential visit of his to the north in 1796. Also, In 1859 it was proposed to build a new Free Church at Pitlochry, and Duff addressed a long letter to the editor of the *Witness* on the project. It appeared on March 10, 1860, and recalled the happy days of the revival. Among other things it stated that "some of the converts were Christians of extraordinary gifts and graces. They were for many years the light and life of the parish."

Chapter 11

Arran, 1812

During the summer of 1800, James Haldane and his fellow-worker, John Campbell, visited Arran. They do not seem to have formed a high opinion of the religious life of the island. At his Jubilee Meeting in 1849, Haldane told how "on a Sacramental occasion he had been present in a parish church (in Arran) where there was a pause, and none of the people seemed disposed to approach the Communion tables. On a sudden he heard the crack of sticks, and, looking round, saw one descend on the bald head of a Highlander behind him. It was the ruling elders driving the poor people forward to the tables much in the same manner as they were accustomed to pen their cattle at a market. Had this happened," adds Haldane's biographer, "in a remote corner of Popish Ireland it would have been less wonderful, but the Gaelic population of Presbyterian Arran seemed accustomed to submit to this rough discipline without a murmur."

Even apart from such anecdotes, there can be no doubt about the poverty of Arran's religious life at the beginning of the nineteenth century. One who loved the place applied to it the text—"Darkness shall cover the earth, and gross darkness the people" (Isaiah 60:2). Part of the responsibility for this state of affairs was due to the inadequate provision made for the spiritual needs of the island. The whole of the extensive area—at least ten by twenty miles—was divided into just two parishes, the boundary separating them traversing its greatest length. Other districts in Scotland could perhaps point to a slender ecclesiastical equipment, but the position in Arran was aggravated by the situation of the parish churches. One was placed nearly two-thirds down the eastern coast of the island, while the other was built almost at its southern extremity. To make up somewhat for the derelict condition of the northern end, a mission church, with a catechist in charge, had been planted at Lochranza by private enterprise, but an unfortunate clause in the deed of endowment prevented the ordination of the missionary. With the exception of a chapel at Shisken, where the minister of Kilmorie, the western parish, sometimes officiated, this was the total provision made for the wants of the island. The population at the time must have exceeded 5,000.

A foretaste of coming revival was given in 1804. "In that year and the year following," says Angus M'Millan, to whom almost alone we are indebted for our knowledge of the religious history of Arran at the time, "many were awakened at the north end of the island, especially about the farms of Sannox and their neighborhood. Although this awakening, as to its power and progress, was not of long continuance, yet a considerable number of the subjects of it testified by their after lives and conversation that they had undergone a gracious change." This is all that M'Millan says, but there seems to be good reason for concluding that a proper modesty prevented him from indicating that he himself was the means used in the movement.

According to the *Glasgow Revival Tracts, No. 5,* this day of small things was the commencement of the revival which followed. From this time, a change for the better was observable in the religious sentiments and conduct of many among the people. Numbers seemed now to be awakened from the slumber of spiritual death and disposed to attend to the things which belonged to their everlasting peace. Their eyes were now opened to see the evil of their former wicked ways, their perishing condition as sinners, and their need of Christ as a Saviour. They began also to distinguish between truth and error, to relish evangelical doctrine, to attend with diligence on the

Arran, 1812

means of grace, and to set up the worship of God, morning and evening, in their families. Religious meetings were also set up in many places. In the course of a few years, a kind of reformation was thus visible throughout many parts of the island.

Angus M'Millan was a native of North Sannox. He was converted in Kilmarnock where he had gone to learn a trade. He entered Glasgow University in 1803. It is recorded of him that "at the end of every session he went back to his native village and opened a Sabbath school and a weekly prayer meeting, both of which were well attended and highly valued by the inhabitants of the surrounding district; and which there is every reason to believe were owned of the Lord for much good." Other workers were probably engaged in the glen about the same time, for in 1806 a congregation of Independents was formed there under the pastorate of Alexander Mackay, and the statement is made that the Church was organized for some time before his settlement.

But it was the ministry of Neil M'Bride which produced the most striking as well as the most lasting results for Arran. He was inducted to the parish of Kilmorie on November 18, 1802. Almost immediately, the power of his preaching began to be felt. His nephew states that "so eager were his parishioners to wait on his ministry that he was seldom able to conduct divine worship in the church, and even in winter crowds were obliged to stand outside the doors." In 1810 the church, which was "a long, narrow building," had to be enlarged by the erection of "an aisle or outshot with gallery." The worshippers came long distances. There are interesting accounts of how the difficulties of trying journeys were overcome. Some lived so far off that they had to start before dawn. When the sun rose, they hid their lanterns among the heather or left them at some convenient farm house and recovered them on their way home. M'Millan indicates that this earnestness in spiritual things was but part of

Scotland Saw His Glory

a general movement that was forming itself over the whole island as a result of the work done in Glen Sannox in 1804. While true, it detracts nothing from the prominent place which M'Bride occupied in the awakening which in 1812 roused Arran from its long lethargy.

Tradition and record agree concerning the qualities of M'Bride's preaching. His sermons were not "sensational." They dealt with great New Testament topics and are usually described as having been "close and searching." "He dwelt," says M'Millan, "more on the consolations of the gospel than on the terrors of the Law. The excitement seemed to be generally greater under the sermons in which the riches of divine grace and the consolations of the gospel were exhibited than under such as were more awful and seemingly better fitted to awaken. M'Bride's preaching was distinguished for seriousness, fervor, and great zeal for the salvation of sinners. This often led him to make very close appeals to the conscience." M'Bride himself was fully aware of the convicting power of his message, as is apparent from a traditional saying of his which has come down: "If you are of the true gold," he would say at the end of a discourse, "you will be none the worse for this rubbing."

Unfortunately, few details of the origin and progress of the Revival of 1812 are available. No special date can be set for its commencement. It is agreed that months before pronounced effects were visible, a silent special preparation had been going on, some of the people showing a gradual deepening of their spiritual life and more earnestness in their search for God. Many, on the other hand, were developing a greater callousness of indifference. "In 1810 and 1811," says M'Millan, "many were bolder in sin and more abandoned to wickedness than they had been at any former period." The religious were accordingly driven to prayer, and for a year previous to the manifest commencement of the revival, frequent gatherings for united

Arran, 1812

supplication were held. Fast days were also kept, both in public and in private. This silent preparation corresponded in a measure to the chief characteristic of the actual movement itself when it came, for M'Millan observes that it was "not of a sudden: it was gradual and spread from place to place."

After twelve months of these special exercises, results began to be seen. "About the beginning of March 1812 the Lord began to work in an unusual way among them, in a way of which they had not until this time any expectation, and which accordingly caused some surprise. It was at this time that the outcrying commenced which was afterwards so common for a considerable time. It began at first in some private meetings, but afterwards extended to the public assembly under Mr. M'Bride's ministry. What made the thing the more remarkable was that it made its first appearance among the people of God." Tradition has preserved the name of the man who first allowed his feelings to overcome him in this way. It is stated that "his cry was so powerful that he alarmed the whole meeting so that a portion of the people went out." It is agreed that the physical effects produced did not proceed to the extremes which had appeared elsewhere. Alexander M'Bride, of North Bute, declared the revival was "free from the extravagances which form so marked a feature in those of America, yet there was much bodily agitation and loud outcrying. . . . Mr. M'Bride was disposed to lay little stress on these outward manifestations and rather discouraged than countenanced them, but, though he generally disapproved of them, yet when he had occasion, as frequently was the case, to check them, he did so with all tenderness and love." In spite, however, of their objectionable features—and there were such things as "panting, trembling, and other convulsive appearances"—it is acknowledged that the outcries did much to spread the revival over the island.

Scotland Saw His Glory

After continuing for about three months, the interest died down somewhat, only to be renewed the following December for another three months. This revival impulse corresponded in time with the settlement of M'Millan over the station at Lochranza. It is likely that the two events were related to each other as effect and cause. M'Millan was a man of like sympathies with M'Bride. His biographer tells how he was greatly exercised over the lost estate of many among whom his lot had been cast. "He has been known at this period, to spend whole nights in a favorite and retired spot at the foot of one of the lofty mountains . . . wrestling with God on behalf of sinners." M'Millan himself gives us one picture of the kind of work he carried on at the time. "In the spring of 1813, I was catechizing one day at a particular farm . . . and when speaking of the character of Christ as the Redeemer of God's elect and attempting to describe the preciousness of His blood and the riches of His grace, an excellent Christian, who is now in the world of spirits, cried out in an elevated tone of voice, 'O the infinite virtue of the blood of Christ—the preciousness of His Blood! What am I, what am I, that He should ever spend one thought concerning me! O my nothingness, my nothingness, my nothingness!' And soon after she exclaimed, 'I shall soon be with Thee, I shall soon be with Thee—be forever with the Lord!' I have seen others also, on various occasions, affected much in the same way." It is apparent, therefore, that M'Millan, at least, was speedily brought into contact with the movement and had energetically thrown himself into the work.

Several interesting details are supplied as to the immediate effects produced by the revival. It was not confined to the parish of Kilmorie but spread to Kilbride also. M'Millan was diffident in giving numbers but says the awakened "must have amounted to two or three hundred persons, old and young together. . . . A marked change was for the time produced in

Arran, 1812

the life of the community. There was scarcely a family but had worship in their houses both morning and evening." As befitted the time, Psalms alone were sung in the public assemblies, and it is said that "Coleshill" was almost the only tune used. Barns were frequently employed both for public and private prayer. "When the reapers," says Alexander M'Bride, "sat down on the harvest field to sharpen their sickles, instead of the jest and the song, they joined in prayer or praise. In every farm—and at that time each farm was a hamlet containing from eight to twelve families—there was in the evening a weekly prayer meeting, which was attended, not by the inhabitants of the farm itself merely, but by those of the surrounding ones. The very children partook of the general awakening. They had prayer meetings of their own, and in going to and from them, they might be heard in little bands singing together the praises of God in the way." Attendance on public ordinances was greatly increased, worshippers frequently travelling the whole length of the island to be present. Sometimes meetings were continued the whole night through, and "almost every sermon seemed to be effective in awakening, quickening, or refreshing."

During the press of the work, M'Bride was helped by several ministers from the mainland. Notable among these were Dr. Love of Glasgow and Dr. Balfour of the same city. Perhaps his most constant helper was Kenneth Bayne of Greenock, a man of evangelical fervor who was not afraid to break ecclesiastical law in his desire to aid those who felt the pressure of the dark days that followed the revival. On his death in April 1821, Dr. Love preached his funeral sermon, and in the course of his address said of Bayne, "his zeal and benevolence were of a very expansive character. They led him to take a deep interest in the work of God in neighboring places. This was remarkably manifest for a series of years respecting the great awakening which appeared in the island of Arran."

Scotland Saw His Glory

As was true of so many revival movements about this time, the end of the Annan awakening was somewhat sad. There is evidence that its effects were felt beyond the shores of the island on which it arose and that Bute and other western isles shared in the blessing it brought. But all the same, M'Millan speaks of the revival as "degenerating latterly through the weakness and folly of men" in the place of its origin. A fatal blow was dealt the cause by the death of M'Bride on July 8, 1814. He had journeyed north to Lochranza to dispense the Sacrament at his friend M'Millan's station, took ill on the day of his arrival, and soon breathed his last. It is told how the dying evangelist dreaded what might happen on his removal. He accordingly called M'Millan to his bedside and made him promise that he would not leave the island "until the gospel was preached in some of its pulpits—a charge which he cheerfully undertook and faithfully observed," although he had more than one opportunity to accept a more lucrative appointment. M'Bride had evidently more than suspicion to go upon. He must have discovered opposition to the revival movement in high places, for his fears were more than justified. Like Stewart's successor at Moulin, the man presented to the vacant charge proved unfriendly to the revival. Extraordinary as it may appear, he took occasion from the pulpit to flout the whole experience of these parishioners. He "did not hesitate to deny the doctrine of regeneration, and to declare in the face of the congregation that he had never experienced such a change—that it was fanaticism to desire or expect it, and yet that he did not fear to stand before the judgment seat of God and be received into the kingdom of heaven." The faithful seceded from such a ministry and, under the pastoral care of a layman named William M'Kinnon, worshipped in a cave until M'Millan himself became pastor of the parish in 1821.

Arran, 1812

It must not be supposed, however, that the whole effects of the revival disappeared when its immediate operations died down. Many converts remained faithful to the call given them and their consistent lives left their mark upon the community. For a time sacraments continued to be more largely attended. M'Gavin tells how in the year 1813 he met several who had come under the influence of the revival. In 1821 Dr. Love said that "the fruits are still clearly to be traced though under great and various disadvantages." As late as 1836, Mrs. Lundie Duncan reports that "having conversed with those who have recently passed summer weeks in the Isle of Arran, it is very comforting to learn from them that the savor of its blessed days has not yet, at the end of twenty-three years, expired. Some aged people still live to tell of what the Lord did for their souls at that happy time; and the descendants are made partakers of like precious faith." Several ministers of the gospel, all natives of Arran, dated their conversion as well as their call to the ministry from that moving time. Four of them, especially, prolonged the Arran evangelical tradition in various parts of Scotland. Peter M'Bride was his namesake's nephew and was brought up under his care. He discharged a well-known and fruitful ministry at Rothesay. John Macalister did good service first at Tain and then for a short time at Brodick. Archibald Cook of Bruan, and afterwards of Inverness, showed a like evangelical energy in the spheres in which he labored. Of his brother, the redoubtable Finlay Cook of Reay, it is written that he was "one of the most thoughtless, lightheaded young men in the island; indeed he was in the act of jibing and mocking the venerable servant of God [M'Bride] in his pew in the church when the arrows of divine truth smote him." So changed did he become that a friend could say of him: "That his first religious exercises, in respect both of convictions and deliverances, were unusually deep and thorough, might be gathered from hints

Scotland Saw His Glory

occasionally dropped by himself in after life; but indeed the character of his personal religion and of his ministry of the gospel abundantly manifest this." The harvest of the Arran revival must accordingly be gathered from broad Scotland.

A most commendable Arran custom is said to have grown out of the experiences of that gracious time. "When the fishermen are out for the night, they engage in the duty of family worship with as much regularity and composure as they do at home." Dr. Landsborough of Kilmarnock, who knew Arran well, gave poetic expression to this interesting tradition:

"And now the nets are set. For little space
Silence ensues; but silence broken soon
By what the choirs seraphic might regale
And what is worth acceptance heard by God.
It is the praises of redeeming love,
Raised from the tranquil bosom of the sea
In dulcet strains, by distance softer made.
The gladdened waves prolong the joyful sound,
The zephyrs bear it on their balmy wings
To the curved shore. The hills re-echo it,
As if unwilling it should ever die."

For many years after the revival, the religious life of Arran ran on common levels. M'Bride of Rothesay had to write the statistical account of Kilmorie in 1840. Having passed through the revival, he could refer to it sympathetically, but he had sorrowfully to add: "A spirit of indifference prevails among the rising generation that painfully contrasts with that which animated their fathers in regard to the means of grace. Still, the attendance at public worship, though far from what it once was, is as good as in most parishes of the same population." Arran, however, has not been left altogether to itself for a whole century, and more than once it has been visited since with blessings from on high.

Chapter 12

Skye, 1812

The misty Isle of Skye has long been famous for its magnificent mountain scenery, its lonely lochs and moorlands, and its unrivalled coast line. Its inhabitants still linger kindly in the memory because of their associations with Prince Charlie and for the stalwart breed of men which for many years the island gave to serve in the national wars. More recently it has been looked upon as the home of a strongly religious people.

Its reputation for piety dates only from the introduction of evangelical Christianity within its bounds in the nineteenth century. Before that time "the ignorance that pervaded the minds of the inhabitants is almost incredible." Public morality was not far removed from that of heathenism.[1] Nominally Protestant, the people polluted even their sacred offices with unseemly orgies. The Reformation in this area of Scotland was nothing more than a change from the profession of one creed to that of another according to the views of the proprietors of the soil. It was purely political and partook of none of the intelligence and preference of truth in opposition to papal ignorance and superstition which distinguished that blessed era in the southern and northeastern counties. Had a pious clergy succeeded their ghostly predecessors, the knowledge of the *letter* of the truth would, no doubt, have been imparted to the population of the districts in question; and although they might, notwithstanding, have been left without any remarkable revivals

---

[1] See the heavy indictment in *An Account of the Present State of Religion throughout the Highlands of Scotland,* pages 49-59.

of religion, the *gross darkness* which for so long prevailed would in part at least, have been done away. This, however, was not the case. There are parishes which even into the nineteenth century had never had the benefit of the pure preaching of the *glad tidings* of salvation.

Not only was Bible truth unknown, but Bibles themselves were hardly to be found within the island. "The only one in the parish of Sleat, as an old man informed me," said the late Rev. John S. Macphail, long a minister in the island, "was a copy in the pulpit out of which the minister read a single verse as his text on Sabbath. It was the same in Kilmuir." Even when better days had dawned, there was still room for further Bible distribution. In 1826 the Inverness Society for Educating the Poor of the Highlands reported that "in Skye 1,243 families possessed Bibles, while 2,379 had none. Of the latter number, 901 families had those who could read them." In such circumstances it is no wonder that evangelical faith had almost perished out of the land. "As far as can now be ascertained," says the author of the *Present State,* "there were only two persons at that time within the Presbytery of Skye to whom the language of the apostle could with certainty be applied, 'You who were dead in trespasses and sins hath He quickened.'"

As a specimen of the doctrines taught, it may be mentioned that two ministers once went in company to visit a dying man whose conscience was awakened. He told them in great alarm that he was mightily afraid he was going to hell. His guides told him they knew him from his youth and saw nothing in his life deserving hell; that in fact there were many good things in him and done by him that (besides God's mercy) would obtain heaven for him; and that if he went to hell, many had cause to fear. The dying man replied, with a deep sigh. "Is there no word of Christ? Is there no word of Christ?"

Skye, 1812

Many years ago, long before any awakening took place in Skye, a young girl of little more than childish years, resided in a glen which during the revival was distinguished by much of divine power. She became deeply impressed with the idea that God was not in her native isle. At the same time, she was overcome by the feeling that she must go in pursuit of Him where He was to be found. She accordingly stole away from her parents and travelled across the island to the ferry which she took to the mainland. As she proceeded, she made no secret of the errand on which she had departed. Because her relations had decided she had become unsound in her mind, little attempt was made to recall her. As soon as she was out of Skye, she began to ask every passenger she met where she might find God, for He was not in her country. She also called at houses along the way, asking direction in her uncommon inquiry. Pity and kind treatment marked the conduct of all towards her. Her question excited surprise; but as her manner expressed sincerity and deep earnestness, every one answered her soothingly, as if unwilling to interfere with the hallucination under which they conceived she labored.

In this way, she journeyed for days and weeks; but though disappointed in every application for the knowledge which she sought, she did not desist. At length, she reached the town of Inverness which she had often heard of and which, in her youthful imagination, she had long pictured the center of all that was good and valuable as well as great. The first person whom she met there on the street was a pious lady. She stopped her and said in Gaelic: "I am come from Skye, where God is not—can you tell me where I shall find Him?" The lady was struck both with the unusual nature of the statement and with the deep-toned earnestness and solemnity of her manner. Her first impression was that of all the others to whom the poor child had spoken by the way; but after engaging in conversation with her she became satisfied as to her sanity. At last she said, "Come with me, perhaps I can bring you to where you shall find God." She took her to her home. Next day was Sabbath. The wanderer accompanied her kind protector to the house of God. For the first time, the gospel was proclaimed in her hearing—it came "in demonstration of the Spirit and of power" to her soul. She was an awakened sinner, and soon became a happy convert—lived for many years in the lady's family—never again returned to Skye—married and settled in the parish of Croy, near Inverness, and was one of the most eminent Christians of her day. She lived long and was greatly distinguished for her devotedness and fervency as a follower of the Lamb. Often have the pious in Skye said to each other: "Who can tell but the prayers of her who was led by a way which she knew not, to the knowledge of the God of Abraham, may be receiving their answer in the great work which, in this dark place, He has been pleased to produce?"

It was in the year 1805 that the Island saw the beginning of better things. The western parish of Duirinish fell under the drop of a gospel ministry for, as has already been stated, John Shaw, a native of Moulin, was settled over it in October of that year. He was a man who had a proper sense of the responsibilities of his office. To one who asked his advice on receiving license to preach, he wrote on December 2, 1807, "A circumstance, or rather quality of the office to which my attention is directed as much as to any is the solemn tenure on which we hold it, 'Woe unto us, if we preach not the gospel.' The sinner must receive warning else his blood will be required at our hand. By faithful dealing with all we must deliver our own souls." Shaw, however, did not stand alone long. A few months after his settlement, the Rev. Donald Martin, who since 1785 had been minister of Kilmuir, the most northerly parish in the island, was converted.

Skye, 1812

The influence of these two men on the religious fortunes of Skye was great, still it was as nothing in comparison to that of a man who came as a sojourner to the island, preached in it for a few weeks, and then disappeared from it forever. In the story of the Breadalbane Revival of 1816, there is no more interesting figure than that of John Farquharson. His chief Scottish work was done on Lochtayside, but nowhere is his memory greener than in Skye.

Why he came to the western island is now unknown. He may have been sent as one of the Haldane "missionaries," or his own love of the work may have constrained him.[2] Whatever may have been the cause, he appeared in Portree in 1805 and began preaching. An air of novelty surrounded his efforts, for he broke away from the whole ecclesiastical conventions of the island. He held no communication with any of the settled ministers, and his zeal made weekday and Sabbath alike suitable for his message. The whole style and matter of his discourses were utterly different from what the people were accustomed. His sermons, we read, "were very pointed and justly severe against the sins that overspread the island, especially against self-righteousness; and in all his discourses he prominently held forth the righteousness of Jesus Christ as the only ground for a sinner's justification before God"—a new message for Skye.

---

[2] The account given in M'Cowan's *Men of Skye* is attractive, but it is in conflict with tradition and with what direct testimony is available. He writes: "It is said that Mr. Farquharson did not intentionally go to Skye, but that he was a passenger on board a ship bound for America, when, owing to wind or some other cause, they put into Uig Bay. It was the end of the week, and intimation was given to the people of the surrounding districts that on the following Sabbath he would preach at Uig. . . ."

Scotland Saw His Glory

From Portree, Farquharson proceeded to the parishes that lie to the north and west—Kilmuir, Bracadale, and Snizort—preaching as he went. He was followed everywhere by Donald Munro, in many ways a most remarkable man, who was destined to carry on the evangelical labors of Farquharson. He had lost his sight in early youth and earned his livelihood by the mixed occupation of fiddler and parish catechist. Early in the mission, he professed conversion and to the end ascribed the change to the evangelist—"To me," he said "he was a messenger from God." Had the stranger done nothing more by his tour than turn the eyes of the blind catechist to the light, he accomplished a great work.

One of the immediate outcomes of Farquharson's mission was the establishment of a prayer meeting in the parish of Snizort. It was held monthly and its novelty caused the usual amount of suspicion and speculation. For two years it prospered and converts were made through it. Its usefulness, however, was marred by the advent of a sectarian preacher who prevailed upon some of its members to join him. The others withdrew discouraged, and the gathering ended. But if one door closed, another soon opened. The conversion of Martin of Kilmuir caused him to call Donald Munro to his help as catechist and to invite a like-minded schoolmaster to take duty in the parish as well as to set about procuring a wider circulation of the Scriptures among his people. The parish soon became a center of light for the whole island.

A temporary check came to the forward movement in 1808, for in that year Martin accepted a call to Inverness and his successor was, unfortunately, a man of different sympathies. Accustomed as the people had now become to evangelical preaching, they refused to wait on his ministry and unofficially set Munro over them as their spiritual teacher. The catechist continued to conduct meetings which drew multitudes. Not

Skye, 1812

unnaturally, the new minister became angry, and through a rigid application of the rules of the Society for Propagating Christian Knowledge which prohibited their agents from preaching, Munro was dismissed from office. This did not, however, shut the evangelist's mouth. In the end it greatly aided his work, for the people flocked to him more than ever.

Munro's method was simplicity itself. He was careful never to encroach on the stated functions of the ministry and never attempted to conduct formal services. "So much, indeed, did he keep within the bounds of lay order that he never was heard to have taken one passage of truth to preach from. He invariably lectured, and the burden of his doctrine consisted in exhortations." He moved from house to house and from farm to farm, gathered as large an audience as was possible, taught the Shorter Catechism, and furnished what explanations he could. Being blind, he had committed long portions of the Bible to memory. These he recited with great animation. Various societies for improving the religious condition of the Highlands had provided Gaelic translations of well-known English classics, and to aid in the instruction of the people, Munro caused sections of these books to be read and commented on them. His own skill as a musician was of service, and the joyful singing of the Psalms made his meetings glad. "In many instances he conducted that part of solemn praise with great unction, specially on winter nights when candles or oil were scarce." In all these exercises, Munro was helped by others like-minded with himself.

As was to be expected, the effect of this constant, consecrated labor was very great. "It was a common thing," says the Rev. John S. Macphail, himself one of the most acceptable of Gaelic preachers, "after the opening services when the Bible was read, that great meltings came upon the hearers; the deepest attention was given to every word as verse after verse was solemnly repeated, tears flowed down, half suppressed sighs come next, then sobbings that could not be restrained, and sometimes those affected cried aloud or threw themselves upon the grass weeping bitterly. When the service was concluded, the people were to be seen in all directions calling upon the name of the Lord. Such was the thirst for the Word of God that it was difficult to get the people to go to their homes for necessary nourishment, and to attend to household duties."

Part of this description applies to the revival that spread over Skye about the end of the year 1812. It began in the north where the labors of Munro had been most abundant and extended quickly to the neighboring parishes of Snizort, Bracadale, and Duirinish. It was fortunate that the awakening was most pronounced during the winter months "when manual labor is at an end in the Highlands." Bodily agitations and crying out were not uncommon. As has been so often observed in other revivals, the flame of awakened life broke out spontaneously in certain districts: no connection could be traced between them and places where the work was actually going on. "These emotions were like summer showers which move about, when the rain falls on one field, without a drop on another. They were here today, and in another place tomorrow. Some persons came under conviction when attending the meetings—others when they came in contact with awakened persons who attended them. The leaders of the meetings were deeply sensible of their own insufficiency, and felt that their strength could only come from God. This led them to cry to God day and night for His gracious presence and support; and with gratitude they had to acknowledge, that at sundry times they were furnished with strength, which enabled them to testify of Him in public; and often they felt much life and refreshment communicated to them by the reading of a chapter without note or comment. These were days of power and of

Skye, 1812

sweetness to as many as had spiritual taste and discernment,—so that, when they met, they were reluctant to part. Very little sleep was sufficient to serve them. They were much devoted to prayer, public and private. 'Verily,' says one, 'there was here then such power with the Word of God as can scarcely be believed by Christians who did not witness it or feel it experimentally.'" Conspicuous results were obtained among young people, and even boys are said to have held separate prayer meetings for themselves. Altogether, the movement continued for two and a half years during which time "several hundreds professed to have turned to the Lord."

Unfortunately, the revival had one or two painful accompaniments. Marked fanaticism, finding a more than usually favorable soil in the Celtic temperament, appeared especially among some women. "They pretended to have dreams and visions, and to have received a spirit of penetration which enabled them to foretell who should be saved and who not. A few of these were at this time so positive, in their conceit, of the certainty of what they affirmed, that they neither could be advised nor reasoned out of it by the most intelligent Christians among them." What was perhaps more deplorable was the active opposition against the movement engendered in unexpected quarters. The minister of Kilmuir became incensed at the meetings which he believed were being held irregularly in his parish. He received the support of the local gentry in complaining to the proprietor, Lord Macdonald, and in asking the suppression of the gatherings on the ground that they were an infringement of his privileges as well as subversive of all public authority. The ejection of the offenders from their holdings seems to have been suggested. Timely intervention, however, saved the situation. The absurdity of interfering with those who were proving themselves of the best character was pointed out and the whole attempt failed.

Scotland Saw His Glory

The warmness of the converts' evangelical faith naturally raised the question whether they could continue attendance at churches where seemingly unconverted ministers were in control. Unfortunately, the church of the one evangelical minister in the island—John Shaw of Duirinish and later of Bracadale—was so awkwardly situated that many had the opportunity of resorting to him only on rare occasions. Hence field meetings were frequently held. A few years afterwards a meeting-house capable of holding two hundred was built near Snizort, and there services were conducted by Munro and others whom the people trusted. The methods used continued to be the same as those which had proved so effective already. "Two or three of acknowledged superior knowledge and experience preside alternately. Besides this principal meeting, there are three others of a similar description held in farm houses. Two of these are in different parts of the parish of Kilmuir, and the remaining one, which is but small, is held in the parish of Portree. These meetings are held on Sabbath days, but on week days there are more than three meetings held."

Before Shaw died, a great evangelical successor had been raised up to him, both as a preacher and ultimately as an occupant of his pulpit—the redoubtable Roderick Macleod of Snizort, affectionately known as "Mr. Rory" by his people. It was from Shaw's library that Macleod obtained Bellamy's *Christian Religion Delineated,* which first opened his mind to the truth—an impression which was deepened by the perusal of Dr. Chalmers' *Lectures on Romans.* At the time of his conversion, Macleod was serving as ordained missionary at Lyndale (a few miles from his father's church at Snizort) where he had been settled in 1819, and the change in his views was speedily seen in the new way he performed his duties. "His fervour burned. Week-day lectures and meetings were continuously superadded to Sabbath services. His whole conversation was

Skye, 1812

new. His labors were multiplied." The result, says his biographer, was that "a time of revival came; and every meeting—and frequent were they—was crowded; and many a soul still living, and spiritually living, dates his first and deep impressions to those meetings and lectures and the very frequent conferences that increased in number between minister and people."

Under such ministrations the parish of Duirinish was again stirred. The movement followed the lines of the earlier revival and its consequence were much the same. "It was often a stirring sight to witness the multitudes assembling during the dark, winter evenings—to trace their progress, as they came in all directions across moors and mountains, by the blazing torches which they carried to light their way to the places of meeting." Old and young alike participated in the results. Mention is even made of a man who began his life anew when he was above one hundred years old.

It is impossible to exaggerate the importance for Skye of these early religious movements. They found the island in a state of practical heathenism and so aroused the people that evangelical religion has never since been displaced within its bounds.

Preaching at the Sea-side.

Chapter 13

Breadalbane, 1816, 1817

In spite of such an encouraging history as that of the Moulin Revival, it would be easy to paint a startling picture of the religious condition of Perthshire at the beginning of the nineteenth century. There is abundant testimony that the beautiful district of Breadalbane shared in the prevailing ignorance. "The district was destitute of evangelical preaching. There were actually no Bibles, scarcely any Testaments, and the people lived without prayer," says the biographer of the Haldanes. "The doctrines of salvation by grace and of the second birth," says another, "were as great novelties to the people . . . as if they had never read their Bibles, and as if their Church had been Popish and not Protestant and Calvinistic."

John Farquharson came to this region of spiritual destitution in 1800 as catechist and preacher. He was a native of Glen Tilt. At first sight he seemed the most unlikely man to produce a religious impression on such a neighborhood. He had few or none of the gifts usually associated with the ministry. On account of his zeal and godliness he had been recommended for training for the Church and had entered one of the newly-formed independent classes. After six months' trial he was rejected because his "capacity of learning seemed hardly to warrant his persevering in academic studies." He was sent by the recently-founded Society for the Propagation of the Gospel at Home to Breadalbane "with the view of trying whether he might not be of use as a Scripture reader amongst the poor and uneducated Highlanders." Farquharson, however, was of that type who do not need the imprimatur of any school of the prophets and whose call comes directly from God Himself. His sincerity, zeal, and devotion overcame all obstacles, and he was successful from the first.

Writing long afterwards, Principal Daniel Dewar of Aberdeen described Farquharson as "the most wonderful man he had ever known" and says, that while he preached almost every day, "he was remarkable in this respect, that he seldom preached without someone being awakened. . . . I think," he continues, "I see him still on his black pony, riding round Loch Tay and from farm to farm, carrying the message of salvation to the people. Divine power accompanied his ministry. There was an awakening all round the loch. Many were brought to Christ and continued steadfast and immovable in the gospel." Further testimony to this good man's zeal and success is equally emphatic. "From the accounts of him which still linger in the traditions of the people, we learn that he was continually going from house to house, from hamlet to hamlet, to make known the Saviour. Of Him he spoke on the road, in the house, in the assembly, wherever he could find listeners. He seemed as if there was no room in his mind for any other object."

It is hardly believable that such labors should have been rewarded with envy and opposition, but thus it was. "So strong was the opposition of the Established Church ministers and the landed proprietors . . . that only three families in the wide Breadalbane district would receive Mr. Farquharson into their homes." No inn would shelter him for a night, and all this unkind opposition occurred almost from the beginning of his labors. He started work at Killin, a village at the western extremity of Loch Tay, but his place of meeting was soon taken from him. A new start was made at Ardeonaig, several miles along the south shore of the lake. It was there and at Ardtalnaig and Acharn, still farther to the east, that the chief events of his ministry took place.

Breadalbane

By the autumn of 1802, the results were of such importance that they could be spoken of as a *revival.* Farquharson was aided by two of his converts—John Campbell, a native of Ardeonaig, who afterwards became pastor of the Congregational Chapel at Oban, and James Dewar, afterwards minister at Nairn, whose father was a farmer on the north side of Loch Tay. The movement began unostentatiously enough at Ardeonaig. It is said that those who were awakened endeavored to conceal their state from Farquharson and met in secret to support and encourage each other by prayer. But one day, while crossing the loch, a boatman informed the evangelist of what was happening in his absence. This seems to have brought the movement to the surface, and a corresponding increase of interest was shown. Men who were engaged in the work or who saw it for themselves, made such reports as the following: "The manner in which many of them [the converts] were impressed was to be at first surprising—they were suddenly struck during the time of prayer; they fell to the ground, and many of them, both young and old, continued speechless for twenty minutes or half an hour." "From this place it spread to———and———a space of about nine miles.[1] They all flocked together and continued to go from house to house, praying and praising God, for eight or ten days and nights, with only two hours' sleep each morning; and many of them were several nights without any sleep, busily employed conversing and comforting those who were impressed."

"It was at meetings for social prayer that the most considerable awakening took place, April 1802. At one of them, at

---

[1] In many of the accounts of these revivals, writers adapted the irritating plan of concealing names of persons and places under initials or dashes—most frequently for no discoverable reason whatever. Here the dashes probably stand for Ardeonaig and Ardtalnaig.

Scotland Saw His Glory

Cartlechan, a most extraordinary influence was felt. Fourteen persons fell down to the ground crying for mercy. Worldly business was wholly neglected, and whole nights spent in prayer and exhorting one another."

One of the immediate results of this attention to religion was the formation of a congregation of seventy members at Acharn in 1802, a number which was increased in the following year to one hundred. Farquharson was ordained over them as their pastor, and members were drawn from all the neighboring glens. Everything seemed prepared for a fruitful ministry, but unfortunately dissension broke out in the congregation in 1804. It is impossible now to discover the cause, but however extraordinary it may appear, it seems to have been connected with dissatisfaction with Farquharson's preaching. Farquharson resigned and after ministering for a time at Killin, ultimately emigrated to America, where he shortly afterwards died.

A revival could hardly survive such an experience, the more especially as petty disputes also arose in the district over unimportant points in ritual and church government. The final blow was administered when the Haldanite discussion on baptism threw everything into confusion, and those whom the revival had called into spiritual life became the fiercest of sectarians. "Thus the interesting churches at Acharn and Killin were diminished in number and weakened in influence, and shortly afterwards . . . they became as sheep without a shepherd. Four Baptist Churches subsequently emerged from the general confusion." However sad though this result was, it would be a mistake to suppose that the work was made totally without effect. It was the first rough ploughing of unbroken land. When the next sowing took place, the harvest was plentiful.

The set time to favor the district came during the ministry of Robert Findlater whose name is still remembered with

Breadalbane

reverence on Lochtayside after the lapse of nearly a century. This movement took place within the Established Church.

Like many Highland parishes, those of Breadalbane are of great extent. Fortingall includes the long stretch of twenty miles which forms the secluded valley of Glenlyon, as well as large tracts beyond its mountainous walls. Kenmore runs westward from the village of that name and almost encloses Loch Tay. It is beyond the power of the most energetic minister to do justice to territories of such extent, and special efforts were accordingly made in many cases to accomplish their spiritual purposes by planting extra stations. The Royal Bounty Fund and the Society for Propagating Christian Knowledge stepped in to help with resources of men and money. The pious Lady Glenorchy placed a chapel in Strathfillan and gave financial assistance in other cases. Since the beginning of the eighteenth century, the part of Kenmore parish near the western extremity of Loch Tay had been provided for in this special way. Both sides of the loch were put under the charge of a mission minister whose stipend was drawn from the funds available for the purpose. Each side had its own place of meeting: the church on the north side being at the Milton of Lawers, and that on the south side at Ardeonaig. The manse stood near the latter building.

In 1810 Robert Findlater came to take charge of the double station. He was a native of Kiltearn, in Ross-shire, and had been licensed by the Presbytery of Dingwall in October 1807 when he was only 21 years of age.[2] He was not a man of careful scholarship, but he was especially adapted for the work that lay before him. He was evangelical, devoted, prayerful, and diligent, and accordingly well fitted to carry on the tradition of

---

[2] He was not ordained until July 2, 1811, more than a year after his settlement at Ardeonaig. The Presbytery allowed him to serve his own convenience as to the date.

Scotland Saw His Glory

Farquharson's work. The field, he discovered, sadly needed cultivation. The roll of communicants was large and out of proportion to the number of the population; yet Findlater had to say: "I have cause to fear I cannot make up so many as would form a society in this place for prayer and Christian converse." An earnest of his ministry, however, was soon given. "It is said that the very first sermon he preached at Ardeonaig resulted in the awakening of a young woman."[3]

Findlater began and carried on his work in the most systematic manner. Soon after he entered on his duties, he started a regular house-to-house visitation of his people for the purpose of catechizing them. He used the Shorter Catechism as the basis of his instruction. "My plan," he said, "is to cause them to say over the Question first, which I generally illustrate two at a meeting . . . I can, in public catechizing, talk from my own experience and observation and I have found that without knowing the individual, I have hit the peculiar character whom I was addressing. I find as yet the people are willing to follow my plans, and many are busy at present learning the Questions. It is a new thing to them, and I am told there are some who have not been catechized for about fourteen years." Within a twelve-month period, he had personally examined and taught 1,600 persons. Public worship was conducted on each side of the loch on alternate Sabbaths. Although Lock Tay is regarded as a dangerously stormy place, Findlater was prevented crossing on only one Sabbath during his eleven year ministry.

He also tried other methods of creating an interest in religious things. In the summer of 1812, he began a Sabbath

---

[3] *Memoir of Findlater,* 1840, p.136. This volume is the chief source for the facts of the Breadalbane Revival. Unfortunately its author had not the faculty of orderly narrative. The book is consequently a strange welter of dates and repetitions.

Breadalbane

school at Ardeonaig. A year afterwards, he testifies to its success saying that he found "more pleasure in it than with the old people." A prayer meeting was also started, but it cannot have been a hopeful undertaking at the beginning, for, while he tells of its existence, he had to add, "We are very destitute of spiritual life." Indeed, during the first half-dozen years of his ministry, his letters are full of his sorrow over the hardness of his people's hearts. "I desire to be thankful," he writes on Christmas Day 1812, "that matters are on the whole not worse, some say there is an alteration to the better, but I fear the whole is from an open unconcern to formality, and though knowledge is acquiring, it would grieve a feeling mind to observe the vanity and want of concern of a rising generation."

In spite of these drawbacks, Findlater's ministry was not without its results. Interesting stories could be told of how persons, even at a distance, came under his influence. Perhaps the most important event was the appearance of the people of Glenlyon at his services. About 1813 a young man from the glen got into the habit of crossing the eastern shoulder of Ben Lawers to attend his church. Next year he succeeded in inducing others to accompany him. "In spring 1816 the group increased to the number of perhaps twelve or fourteen, and during the whole of that summer a goodly number went regularly every Sabbath." There can be no doubt that the evident earnestness underlying that weary trudge over the dreary moorland did much to prepare the way for the revival.

It is said that, as the summer of 1816 advanced, a more than ordinary interest was observed, especially among the men and women from Glenlyon. A largely-attended sacrament at Killin helped to deepen the impression. The same ordinance was to be observed at Ardeonaig in the month of September. Findlater, as if anticipating the event, secured the best preachers then to be had. The celebrated Macdonald of Ferintosh had

Scotland Saw His Glory

assisted him several years before, but the Apostle's fame had increased since that time. News had also come of wonderful awakenings under his ministry in the north. Now Findlater had secured his services again, and information about his coming was spread far and wide.

The whole preliminary services of that memorial sacramental season were impressive. On Friday evening, a special time of worship was held at Lawers. Dr. Macdonald preached until the light failed. "Owing to the darkness of the night," says Campbell of Kiltearn, himself a native of the glen and living in it at the time, "the poor people of Glenlyon could not return home, and some of them were quite unfit for the journey, a sense of sin pressing so heavily upon their hearts. Those who were able to go home next morning brought with them the tidings of Mr. Macdonald's arrival and of the effects of his preaching—news which excited an ardent desire to hear the extraordinary preacher and to witness scenes before unheard of in Breadalbane; while some desired to experience such influences themselves as were felt by others. The result was that the most of the Glenlyon people were at Ardeonaig on Sabbath."

That Sunday the size of the concourse that met at Ardeonaig Church was unusual. Findlater estimates the number at between 4,000 and 5,000, a number all the more remarkable in that there was no large center of population nearer than Perth. The multitude was accommodated on the green braes of the hillside just above the present manse. Macdonald preached the action sermon. The discourse took nearly two hours and a half to deliver. The text was Isaiah 54:5, "For thy Maker is thine husband." The sermon was not only one which Macdonald frequently preached, but it was also one of his most famous efforts. Its effects on this occasion were notable. The whole multitude was moved. "The most hardened in the congregation," says Findlater, "seemed to bend as one man; and I believe if

Breadalbane

ever the Holy Ghost was present in a solemn assembly it was there. Mr. Macdonald himself seemed to be in raptures. There were several people who cried aloud, but the general impression seemed to be a universal melting under the Word. The people of God themselves were as deeply affected as others, and many have confessed they never witnessed such a scene." A number dated their entrance on a new life from that afternoon. "A Gaelic teacher who was accounted a godly man by all who knew him, and who took a leading part in every good work in the district where he lived and taught, declared that 'he knew fifty persons who were awakened by that sermon at Ardeonaig, and that he was one of them himself.'"

Next day, room was made for Macdonald to preach again. His text was Luke 16:2. Findlater states that the sermon "was in no way inferior to the last, though there were not so many who cried out. Several were pierced to the heart, and some came to speak to him after the sermon. I have seen and conversed with some of them myself, and have every reason to believe that they are under the gracious operations of the Holy Ghost."

This was the beginning of a work which continued for the next three years with more or less intensity and fruitfulness. The sacrament took its place as part of the history of the district, and today is still remembered as "The Great Sacrament." The following Sabbath, Findlater preached at Lawers, and the agitation among several of his hearers showed that the impressions made had not been evanescent. The interest spread far and wide. Parishioners from Kenmore, Killin, and Fortingall, flocked to Lochtayside in large numbers, attending either at Ardeonaig or Lawers, according as the services were held on the north or on the south side of the lake. So universal was the movement that Findlater could report, "there were few families without one, and some families two or three, professing deep concern about the salvation of their souls."

The men of Glenlyon were particularly assiduous in their attendance, for the revival had its stronghold among them for as long as it lasted. When the fervor had to some extent passed away, it was reckoned that only five or six families in the whole glen had been left untouched. "These families were looked upon as objects of pity." During September and October of 1816, few remained at home who could face the rough road between them and Loch Tay. "One hundred persons might be seen in one company, climbing the hill separating these two districts of country, having to travel a distance of from nine to fifteen miles, and some even farther."

About that time, however, the glen secured an evangelist for itself. In 1806 the Rev. James Kennedy had been ordained as Independent minister at Aberfeldy. He had done much to keep alive gospel truth in the whole surrounding district. Hardly knowing the full extent of what had taken place, he came in the course of his work to Glenlyon in October 1816. He found the valley aflame. So eager were the people that three weeks passed before he returned home, driven away by sheer exhaustion. During that time, he preached sometimes as often as three times a day, and hardly a service was held but "some new case of awakening occurred." As opportunity offered, he returned again and again to the glen and proved an able and anxious coadjutor of the work. Several picturesque descriptions are given of his services. No adequate place of meeting was possible, and the crowded congregations had to seek what accommodation was to be found on the hillsides or in the woods. One wood in particular was used. In later days it was spoken of as "a place which the divine presence had rendered venerable." We read of the people listening eagerly to the gospel message, "sometimes amid bleak winds and drifting snows, with their lamps suspend-

Breadalbane

ed fairy-like from the fir trees." Writing to Kennedy's son, the Rev. David Campbell of Lawers, a native of Glenlyon and one of the fruits of the revival, said, "I have seen your father stand almost knee-deep in a wreath of snow, while at the same time it was snowing and drifting in his face all the time he was preaching, and the people gathered round him, patiently and eagerly listening to the fervent truths that proceeded from his lips."

During the winter of 1816 and the whole of 1817, the general attention to religion continued. The people still resorted in large numbers to Ardeonaig and Lawers. A temporary difficulty sprang up with the minister of Glenlyon who thought that his brethren, Findlater and M'Gillivray of Strathfillan, a man of like evangelical spirit, were too zealously interested in his parish and too little concerned with what was due to himself as its religious overseer. The difference, however, was of short duration, and soon after Findlater was assisting him at his sacrament. Dr. Macdonald preached at Loch Tay in April 1817 and helped at the sacrament in September, each time with manifest seals to his ministry. One discourse which he delivered on the Monday of the sacrament is still remembered, and the Hog's Park near the present pier of Lawers where the service was held is still pointed out because of its fame. "This appeared," says the record, "to be one of the most powerful and effective sermons he ever preached in Breadalbane. The fervent eloquence and the pathetic appeals near its conclusion seemed to move and constrain even the most careless. Many were deeply affected and agitated both in mind and body." "I have heard old people speak of his sermon," says Mr. Macgregor of Dundee, a native of the district. "One man who was present told me that the weeping towards the end reminded him of the bleating when lambs are being weaned—loud, general, as if the whole hillside were bleating!"

Scotland Saw His Glory

In October, a preacher who does not give his name, visited Glenlyon and conducted a service at Invervar. His report is interesting. "As we could not," he says, "like Mr. Kennedy once before, preach at night by candle light in the open air, the people applied for a large flour mill which was near, and though busy at work, it was instantly stopped to give place to the bread of immortal life. When the broad two-leaved door was thrown open by the eagerness of the people to gain admittance, the press was so violent that we feared what might be the consequences; a vast number for want of room stood contentedly before the door, beaten by the high wind and pierced by the cold. . . . I was so wedged in where I stood that some of those behind had their chins placed almost on my shoulders. . . . It was ten o'clock when we dismissed." By this time about a hundred persons in Glenlyon alone professed conversion since the preceding harvest.

One episode of November of that same year stands out by itself. Macdonald had promised to preach at Ardeonaig on Sabbath, November 23. As usual, the news of his coming had been spread far and wide. Saturday, however, passed and the preacher did not arrive. An immense congregation gathered on the following day, but still there was no word of him. Findlater had made no preparation for preaching himself. As the hour of worship approached, he was almost overwhelmed at the prospect of having to take the place of the great preacher. Compelled at last to start the service, he was so agitated that he could hardly stand. He began by giving out the Psalm:

"My flesh and heart doth faint and fail"—

when, overcome, he had to sit down. Recovering somewhat, he rose to his feet again with the cry:

"But God doth fail me never!"

In saying this he received such strength that he was able to go on with the service. His text was "Behold the Lamb of God,"

Breadalbane

and he began by saying, "He taketh away the sin of the world, and He taketh away a world of sin!" From that moment, he held the congregation in his hand. One who was present said: "Such was the holy unction with which he spoke and the deep interest manifested by the congregation . . . that I never witnessed a more affecting scene. There was not so much of that crying aloud and agitation of the bodily frame as had been sometimes felt and seen under Mr. Macdonald's preaching, but the greater part of the congregation seemed to be melted into tears, a gentle, sweet mourning in every corner." Findlater's himself remarked, "The Lord was with us indeed. The scene was melting: it was Bochim, for I never witnessed such a scene under my own poor preaching."

And so the work went on into 1818.

By this time much interest had arisen over the country regarding the spiritual condition of the Highlands. For the first time, the more favored Lowlands seem generally to have realized the religious poverty of their fellow-countrymen in the north. Several societies had been instituted whose main object it was to carry gospel ordinances and evangelical influences into these waste places. This anxiety was greatly intensified by the meager accounts that slowly reached the south country regarding the good work that had been done in Breadalbane, and especially in Glenlyon. Among others, the Associate (Burgher) Synod awoke to its responsibilities and resolved to send deputies to the Highlands whose duty it was to bring back first-hand reports of the religious condition of the districts they visited and to preach when opportunity offered.

The first of these deputies was the venerable Rev. John Brown of Whitburn who made a journey through the Perthshire Highlands in the autumn of 1818. On his return he published a short account of what he had seen. He has much to say of the Breadalbane Revival and particularly of what had taken place in Glenlyon. Speaking of the latter, he says, "Everything about it wore the impress of divine influence, and its consequences have been of the most satisfactory kind. As one of them, it may be mentioned that an intimation of sermon, which a few years ago would with difficulty have drawn together a dozen or two, will now collect the inhabitants by hundreds." Brown, however, saw that the people as a whole needed instruction and strongly recommended the institution of libraries of evangelical literature in their midst.

The Rev. Samuel Gilfillan of Comrie, the father of the more famous George Gilfillan, visited the glen in the following year in company with Young of Logiealmond and Kennedy of Aberfeldy. They actually had the happiness of starting the library for Glenlyon. "Upwards of sixty persons gave their names as befriending and supporting the institution. The ministers (who were visiting) promised a donation of books as a commencement." Associations with a like purpose were formed at about the same time at Killin, Lochtayside, and Fortingall.

As is apparent from the foregoing narrative, the earlier stages of the movement, both on Loch Tayside and in Glenlyon, had been marked by cryings out and even more pronounced bodily agitations. It is generally acknowledged, however, that they never rose to excess or continued long. In January 1818, Findlater writes that he had been reading Jonathan Edwards' sermon on the marks of a true and saving work of the Spirit, and adds: "There was a number of things in his congregation which we have not had, as effects on the body, &c. It is a mercy to us that nothing has yet appeared like delusion or enthusiastic fanatical feelings."

William M'Gavin, the well-known champion of Protestantism, twice passed through Glenlyon in the latter half of 1817. His testimony on this point is equally clear: "It is one pleasing feature of this revival, that it is in a great measure free

Breadalbane

from the extravagance which is said to have accompanied a revival in some other places. When the work began indeed under the preaching of Mr. MacDonald, it was attended by something of a similar nature. Some were under violent agitation when first awakened to a sense of their guilt and danger; and I am far from saying this is either extravagant or unnatural. There was, however, so little of this, as scarcely to be remembered. It was, in general, rather a silent melting under the preaching of the Word; and those who did appear under violent agitation at first, never exhibited such symptoms after they believed and received the comforts of the gospel. I made particular enquiry, but did not hear of one instance of periodical or mechanical agitation, or any sort of indecorous behavior during divine worship, by those who made a credible profession of the faith. It is not uncommon indeed to see a large congregation melted into tears. This is not only consistent with a sober reception of the truth, but it may be considered as a pleasing accompaniment of the tenderness and ardour of first love; and such has been the effect upon the preacher himself, that he has had to stop and weep with them."

Kennedy noted that the people of Breadalbane showed themselves most accessible to the sweeter influences of the gospel—the love of Jesus Christ—whereas the men of Strathardle, among whom he also did a notable work, were mostly moved by the terrors of the law. The visitors were, in fact, struck with the eager quietness and the profound attention with which the people listened. "It was truly a delightful spectacle," say Gilfillan and Young, "to those who are favored to behold and enjoy it, to see a people once so indifferent to religion, now so earnest in hearing the news of salvation by Jesus Christ. There were no commotions, no bodily agitations apparent among them, as had happened formerly in some instances, but a quiet fixed attention to God speaking in His Word."

Scotland Saw His Glory

As was to be expected, such a general and widespread attention to religion soon had its effect on the common conduct of the neighborhood. M'Gavin reported: "The character of those who appear to be under the influence of the truth (and there are many such) is that of affectionate earnestness with regard to their eternal interests. So far as I could learn, there is not one, of whose conversion there was satisfactory evidence, who has fallen from his profession, or done dishonour to the cause of truth. A visible change has taken place in the temper and conduct of great numbers. As an instance, there is a man who was so quarrelsome and so noted a fighter that he was called the Lion of Glenlyon. He is now quiet as a lamb; and an acquaintance whom we met with at Aberfeldy told us that she had seen him a few days before driving along in his peat cart reading the Bible."

One of Findlater's correspondents, writing after Findlater had left the district in 1821, says that "the low and debasing sins of drunkenness; rioting, especially at fairs and other pubic meetings; swearing, and irreligious and profane talking were not for a considerable time so much as seen or named among them." It was left to Major-General Stewart of Garth, who took his territorial title from an estate in Glenlyon, to deplore the events that had wrought such a change. In his description of the Highlands, he speaks at length of the state of religion as it then was, and doubtless referring to what had taken place at his own doors, continues: "In this respect, their (i.e. the people's) character and habits have undergone a considerable alteration since they began to be visited by itinerant missionaries and since the gloom spread over their minds has tended to depress their spirit. The missionaries, indeed, after having ventured within the barrier of the Grampians, found a harvest which they little expected and, amongst the ignorant and unhappy, made numerous proselytes to their opinions. These converts, losing by

Breadalbane

their recent civilization—as the changes which have taken place in their opinions are called—a great portion of their belief in fairies, ghosts, and second-sight, though retaining their appetite for strong impressions, have readily supplied the void with the visions and inspirations of the 'new light,' and in this mystic lore have shown themselves such adepts as even to astonish their new instructors." He adds in a footnote: "Thus have been extirpated the innocent, attractive, and often sublime superstitions of the Highlanders." Possibly a devotion to antiquities and folklore could go no farther!

During 1819 there were signs that the revival had spent its force. In the preceding year, Glenlyon had the unhappy experience of seeing some go back on their profession. As 1819 opened, evidence of decline in interest around Loch Tay was convincing. In April, Findlater had to write: "It is to be feared that the Lord's work is at a stand as to new instances of persons brought under concern." The dying fire did occasionally thereafter show expiring flickerings, but 1820 apparently saw the end of this special dispensation of grace.

There was something sad about the closing days of this memorable movement. It is generally acknowledged that as in the case of its forerunner, sectarianism and embittered controversy on ecclesiastical and doctrinal questions helped to bring the movement to a close. The work attracted at least one fanatical preacher to Glenlyon, but he does not seem to have done much damage and his stay was short. Opposition, however, came from quarters that should have been more friendly. A member of Presbytery preached and wrote against the movement,[4] and distorted accounts of what had taken place at one of

---

[4]*Substance of a Speech Delivered Before the Commission of the General Assembly of the Church of Scotland* by Dr. Alexander Irvine, of Dunkeld (Edinburgh, 1819), was a savage and unrestrained attack upon the Revivals

Scotland Saw His Glory

the communions reached the ears of the Presbytery itself. An inquiry was made into the allegations in March 1819, but Findlater seems to have had no difficulty in convincing his brethren that the irregularities complained of had no foundation in fact. All these things, however, tended to pain and sorrow, and prevented the movement from spreading and continuing.

The results achieved by the revival were more than local. The year 1816 was one of great physical scarcity. That and other circumstances increased the stream of emigration towards America. The good seed was accordingly carried to that distant land, and in numerous townships its fruit was gathered after many days.

Among the converts was a notable trio of brothers belonging to Glenlyon: Patrick Campbell was brought to Christ on the Monday after the "Great Sacrament" and did good service in his native glen as schoolmaster and voluntary evangelist. Duncan entered the Church and was successively minister of Lawers, Glenlyon, and Kiltearn. He dated his conversion from one of the sermons on Jeremiah 8:22 which Findlater preached during January and February 1817. The third brother, David, also entered the Church and succeeded Duncan as minister at Lawers. Twenty years later the religious awakening which began at Kilsyth found prepared soil for it in Breadalbane.

---

of 1804 and 1816. He was minister of Fortingall from February 1805 to May 1806. Apparently he thought no charge too gross to bring against the "independents."

Chapter 14

Lewis, 1824-1833

"Upon perusing the ecclesiastical records," said the Rev. Lachlan Shaw in 1775 in his *History of the Province of Moray,* "it is apparent that true, rational Christian knowledge made very slow progress after the Reformation. It was long before ministers could be had to plant[1] the several corners and particularly the Highlands. In the year 1650, the country of Lochaber was totally desolate, and no Protestant minister had before that time been planted there. And when the number of ministers increased, very few of them understood the Gaelic language, and teachers were settled in the Highlands who were mere barbarians to the people. Through want of schools few had any literary education, and those who had would not dedicate themselves to the ministry when livings were so poor as not to afford bread. Hence ignorance prevailed in every quarter." The General Assembly did indeed, now and again, cast its eye beyond the Highland line and made fitful attempts to cope with its duty to these remote districts. The Assembly of 1646, for example, resolved that churches should be placed throughout the bounds of the Highland area "as other Kirks in this Kingdom;" that the eldest sons of gentlemen should be sent south to be educated in order that "the knowledge of God in Christ may be spread throughout the Highlands and Islands;" and that "Scots schools be erected in all parishes there according to the Act of Parliament where conveniently they may be

---

[1] The usual word for setting up congregations and placing ministers over them.

had." The unsettled times, however, prevented much being done.

The late appearance of books in the Gaelic language also greatly retarded progress, for there were no manuals of instruction available except such as were in an alien tongue. As early as 1567, a translation of John Knox's Liturgy—a book which is now among the rarest of bibliographical rarities—was published at Edinburgh by Bishop Carswell, but it required another century before even a portion of Scripture could be placed in the hands of the people. In 1659 the Synod of Argyle published the Shorter Catechism and a rendering of fifty of the Psalms. In 1684 a private translation of the whole Psalter appeared, and the Synod completed theirs in 1694. In 1690 the General Assembly issued 3,000 copies of an Irish translation of the Bible, but it was not until 1767 that even the New Testament could be obtained by Highlanders in their native dialect.[2] The Old Testament took longer to appear, being published in four parts, dated respectively 1783, 1787, 1801, and 1786. For many years, however, the cost of these books rendered their extensive use impossible, the prohibitive price of the New Testament being sixteen shillings in its cheapest form.

A real forward step in relieving the darkness of the Highlands was taken in 1704 when the Society for Propagating Christian Knowledge was formed. In 1725 the Government made a grant of 1,000 pounds—a sum afterwards doubled—to provide preachers for the more destitute districts. It was, however, at the opening of the nineteenth century that the conscience of the people seems to have been awakened to the need of their Gaelic neighbors. The formation of several societies was the result. In 1811 the Gaelic School Society of

---

[2] The translation was by Rev. James Stewart of Killin and was published by the Scottish S.P.C.K. with aid from the London S.P.C.K.

Lewis, 1824-1833

Edinburgh was begun, to be followed the next year by a similar society in Glasgow. The year 1818 saw the start of the Inverness Society for Educating the Poor of the Highlands, which made the reading of the Gaelic Scriptures its primary object. This undenominational effort was followed up by the Church of Scotland, whose General Assembly instituted a Committee to further the planting of schools in needy districts.

The Edinburgh Gaelic School Society, with which this chapter has mainly to do, put in the forefront of its constitution that its "sole object" was "to teach the inhabitants of the Highlands and Islands to read the Sacred Scriptures in their native tongue." In order that its limited resources might be used to the greatest possible advantage, it was arranged that the schools should be ambulatory and that no school should remain in one place for more than two or three years at a time. This rule led to a perpetual stream of petitions to the Society from isolated districts asking that a school should be settled in their midst. They make pathetic reading. Modern missionary biography has accustomed readers to the simple, eager requests made by heathen communities that have realized the benefits of a Christian teacher working among them. These moving, pleading cries for help were received from districts no further off than the Highlands. Here is a sample. From one of the townships of the parish of Uig in Lewis, where the work of the Society was most blessed towards religious awakening, the following petition reached its office: "We have been lamentably neglected as to the concerns of eternity and our immortal souls; no people can be more ignorant than we are, and no people can be more needful of the means of instruction: we never had a catechist or a schoolmaster and we have hitherto been grossly ignorant of everything that is good, and still, though we feel a desire, there are but few among us (and some of them at a considerable distance) who can read a word to us out of the Bible or any good book." When a school was planted in any district, it was eagerly taken advantage of. The minister of Uig reported that he had visited the school at Callernish in his parish and found "110 in attendance of whom 35 are from 20 to 40 years of age, and 5 who exceed 50 years." For aged readers, the Society provided spectacles as far as possible.

The sole textbook used was the Bible, and its study proceeded in the direction the Society most desired, for the people passed from its letter to its spirit. A correspondent wrote to the Society that "the effect produced on the poor and uncultured by being enabled to peruse the sacred volume was in many instances a frantic consternation, similar to that felt by a person on discovering himself on the brink of destruction. But the frantic fever soon subsided; and in that infallible mirror in which they discovered their disease, they also discovered the consolatory efficacy of the Divine Physician's prescription." Reviewing the Society's whole operations in 1830, the Secretary said: "In broad and plain terms, we say a mighty work of the Spirit had been and now is carried on by means of the men who teach your schools." The Rev. Robert Finlayson of Lochs, Lewis, in his own flowery way, wrote on February 26, 1833, "The Gaelic Bible found its way to Lewis as the cake of barley bread fell into the camp of Midian, which smote their tents and overturned their camp. . . . In the same manner, the Bible, the sword of God's mouth, found its way to this remote island and did smite the mighty host of the Prince of darkness and overturned the strongholds of ignorance and superstition and Sabbath breaking."

Two of the lay teachers deserve special mention. One was an agent of the Gaelic School Society named John Macleod. He was a singularly devoted man. His heart mourned over the deplorable darkness of the land. Besides teaching to read, he explained the Scriptures to all who came to him. The minister

Lewis, 1824-1833

of the parish said of him that he had "all along been made eminently useful in several districts of this island, not only in the capacity of a teacher of youth, but for rousing sinners to, and convincing them of, their fallen state, both by nature and practice, and was at unremitting pains to instruct his fellowmen in the whole doctrines of inspiration, with an understanding and feeling which evidently gave satisfaction that these doctrines were made spirit and life to his own soul." So earnest was he in his desire for conversions that he transgressed the regulations of the Society in regard to preaching and had to relinquish his post under it. A salary was, however, supplied by an interested friend and he continued his labors. Despite their treatment of him, the ex-teacher was so convinced of the good work done by the Society that on his death he left half his possessions—which altogether amounted to 150 pounds—for its benefit, a tribute alike to the teacher and to the Society. He died in Uig, October 8, 1832.

The other name is of some consequence in the religious history of the time. It is that of John Morison, the poet-blacksmith of Harris, and "a direct descendant of the hereditary armorers of Macleod of Harris." He owed his conversion to Dr. John Macdonald who had been forced by stress of weather, while on his way to St. Kilda in September, 1822, to wait at Rodel where Morison resided. The evangelist conducted service and "an evening meeting having been announced, John Morison having listened once was anxious to listen again." For the poet, it was the turning point in his life. He was confirmed in his course by the friendship and instruction of Donald Munro, the blind catechist of Skye. In 1828, he was appointed an agent of the Society for the Propagation of Christian Knowledge. The appointment conferred no greater opportunity on him than he had formerly enjoyed and was merely an acknowledgement of the work he had already done unofficially. When the revival came, Morison rendered notable service.

The preparatory and foundational work of such men made the task of the ministry all the easier when the time came for the upbuilding of the Holy Spirit. The first evangelical minister to be settled in Lewis was the Rev. Alexander Macleod, a native of Assynt, who was admitted to the parish of Uig in April, 1824. His settlement was brought about through the influence of a Christian lady, the Hon. Mrs. Stuart Mackenzie of Brahan, daughter and heiress of the last Earl of Seaforth, who desired to see all the pulpits of the island filled by men who would preach a full and a free gospel. It is said that in selecting suitable preachers, she relied on the advice of Dr. Macdonald of Ferintosh. In the case of Macleod, no happier choice could have been made, and his fame as a preacher soon extended far beyond his own district.

Macleod found his parish in as backward a condition as any part of the Highlands. The story is told that at his first prayer meeting one of his elders petitioned that a wreck might be cast ashore, and another spoke of the death of Christ as a misfortune which should have been averted. The people obviously required education as well as spiritual stimulus. Macleod accordingly threw himself with ardor into the work of enlightening them. He plied the Gaelic School Society with requests for teachers, and it is noteworthy that none of the plans he suggested was set aside. Some of his descriptions of the spiritual destitution of the people are eloquent. Six months after his settlement at Uig, he wrote, "I labour alone without a catechist or a useful teacher within the bounds of the parish." About the same time he says to the officials of the Gaelic School Society: "I am sorry to say that among a population of 3,000 there is no school in the parish at present but this one (Capadale), and another taught by one Morrison, another of your teachers. In a part of the parish

Lewis, 1824-1833

called Kneep and Riff there are eighty-five families without a teacher and still laboring under gross ignorance owing to the want of Bible education. Another district of the parish called Loch Roag, consisting of forty-two families who never had a teacher and who are twelve miles from Church, are still in deplorable ignorance. Another district of the parish called Callernish, consisting of fifty-two families and within three miles of each other, are now anxiously seeking after knowledge as it is in Jesus and begin sadly to deplore that they never had a teacher among them. In the Island of Bernera there are fifty-two families where Mr. Morrison is at present, but they are so scattered that they would require another teacher." Most of the teachers sent in answer to Macleod's pleading proved of immense service in the way of preparing the people for the awakening that afterwards took place. The names of some—Angus M'Iver, Angus Mathieson, Kenneth Ross, and Hector Morrison—are still held in affectionate remembrance in the district; while others—John MacRae, Robert Finlayson, Peter Maclean, Alexander M'Coll—afterwards made their fame known over the whole Highlands as preachers of the gospel.

In the purely religious exercise of his ministry, Macleod was equally energetic. "In addition to the Sabbath services, a lecture was held on Thursdays and prayer meetings were regularly conducted." The people had been in the habit, as elsewhere, of crowding unthinkingly to the Lord's Supper, but he made admittance to it stricter. He delayed the feast until such times as communicants were better instructed. The result was that only five out of a total membership of over 800 sat down at his first spreading of the table. This was probably the celebration at which Macdonald of Ferintosh was present, and concerning which he wrote: "Mr. Macleod, the minister of Uig, gave me a pressing invitation to assist him at the Sacrament of our Lord's Supper on the 24th (June, 1826). . . . I preached on

Scotland Saw His Glory

Saturday, Sabbath forenoon, and yesterday. The crowd which assembled on the occasion was immense. I suppose the number on Sabbath day was not under 7,000. The occasion, I trust, was a season of awakening to some and of refreshing to others, and to myself among the rest. The Lord seemed to have favoured us with a shower of divine influences which had been evidently felt both by saint and sinner."[3]

Within two months of his settlement in Uig, a difference was observable in the attitude of his parishioners towards the gospel. There is evidence that a religious movement happened in his neighborhood immediately prior to his settlement. "Before 1824, during the ministrations of some itinerant preachers, there had been great and unreasonable excitement and violent agitations amongst multitudes who, after the excitement subsided, brought forth no fruit, but settled down into their former stupor."[4] The work inaugurated by Macleod was, however, of a more solid and enduring nature. Soon after his settlement, he wrote to his friend, Sage of Resolis, that "the appearance throughout the island furnishes very cheering evidence that there is plainly a revival exhibiting itself under the preaching of the gospel, and a marked and almost incredible change in the morals of the people." "He justly observes," continues Sage, summarizing the letter, "that there is danger of underrating revivals on the one hand and that he feels considerable delicacy in saying anything with confidence, lest he should

---

[3] A week later Macdonald addressed a much smaller gathering in Harris. "Something of the shower with which the Lord favored us at Uig," he says, "seemed to have fallen upon them. Many were in tears and there was much weeping on the occasion. Oh! it is not difficult to preach to people in these circumstances." Similar emotion was shown at Scalpay and Tarbet.

[4] This is perhaps the time which is still referred to as "the year of swooning."

Lewis, 1824-1833

speak prematurely or inaccurately. He earnestly invites me to come over and witness for myself the heart-cheering prospects of that benighted land, now gladdened with the beams of the Son of Righteousness and rendered fruitful unto God." In 1826, two years after he began work, Macleod could write: "I desire to praise the Lord for the wonderful things he has brought about for this parish in His providence, since I came among them." Year by year the tide of interest arose until between 1828 and 1830 the awakening seemed to be at its fullest strength. "The Gaelic Scriptures began to be circulated. Boston's *Fourfold State,* then newly translated, began to be read to groups of weeping and wondering hearers." The impressions made were oftentimes deepened by visits from Dr. Macdonald.

Although the movement spread to the whole island, Uig continued to be its center. Several interesting descriptions remain as to the eager interest of the people. "Incredible efforts were made by earnest souls in all parts of the island to be present at the preaching of the Word, even on ordinary Sabbaths. Men and even women travelled from Ness, Back, and Knock, distances of twenty to forty miles to Uig Ferry, from Saturday till Sabbath morning, to overtake the boats for church, which often required to leave very early on account of head winds and the distance to be travelled by sea which could not have been less than ten or twelve miles." At communions, numbers were largest. It is said that 9,000 assembled at Uig in 1828—a multitude which was rivalled by a vast concourse which gathered at the same place in 1833. Little wonder that Macleod was constrained to say in 1834: "Ten winters have I passed here, all wonderfully short, pleasant, and delightful."

As has been already said, the awakening impulses were felt over all Lewis, Harris, and even in the long chain of islands that stretch from them southward. In 1829, two ministers were settled in Lewis, both of whom shared the evangelical sympa-

Scotland Saw His Glory

thies of Macleod. Finlay Cook, a convert of the Arran Revival, was placed at Cross in the north. He remained five years and it is reported that he did "a solid and prolonged work in his parish." Robert Finlayson, who had acted as a teacher in Uig, was in the same year ordained at Knock and, after two years there was transferred to the same neighborhood in Lochs. The help Finlayson gave was of longer duration and was therefore probably more effective. "Such was the eagerness to hear him that not only was his Church [at Knock] crowded on the Sabbath, but every night the parlour and lobby and stair and every available inch of space within the manse was filled at the hour of prayer. Many walked every night from Stornoway, a distance of four of five miles, to be present. These parlour preachings were blessed to many."

An interesting account is given of how the more immediate work of awakening began in Harris. John Morison, the poet, had undertaken the charge of a continuation of the meeting at which he had been converted. As its influence spread, he secured as associates in the work several like-minded men belonging to the Gaelic School Society. They began open-air prayer meetings. One is specially mentioned, attendance at which was reckoned to be above 2,000. Some time in the year 1830, Morison was being assisted at one of his meetings by a catechist who had just come from the revival area. At first Morison could hardly officiate because of the strength of his own emotion—"many of the people also were during the reading of the chapter silently melted and overcome." In his turn, the catechist "exhorted the meeting during which more were deeply melted and others cried out in deep distress. John Morison recovered so as to be able to address the meeting when the impressions were heightened and rendered more general so that there was a mighty shaking among the dry bones on this occasion." It was the beginning of a special outpouring of the Spirit and for some time meetings were held daily.

Among the deeply touching accounts of this revival is that of its effect on the youngest child known to have been turned to God. "Catharine Smith was a native of Pabay, a small island in Loch Roag, where dwell seven families. From their insular situation and poverty, it has not been in the power of the parents to educate their children; but little Kitty is an example of the truth that all God's children are taught of Him, for when only two years old she was observed to lay aside her playthings, and clasp her little hands with reverence during family worship; and at the age of three she was in the habit of repeating the 23d Psalm, with such relish and fervour as showed that she looked to the Good Shepherd in the character of a lamb of His flock. Her parents taught her also the Lord's Prayer, which she repeated duly, not only at her stated times, but often in the silence of the night. She frequently pressed the duty of prayer, not only on the other children, but on her parents, and she told her father that, in their absence, when she would ask a blessing on the food left for the children, her brothers and sisters would mock at and beat her for doing so. At another time, when she was probably six years old, she was out with her companions herding cattle, when she spoke to them of the comeliness of Christ. They, probably to tempt her, said He was black. She left them and returned home much cast down and said, 'The children vexed me very much to-day. I will not go with them for they said that Christ was black, and that grieved my spirit.' Her parents asked her what she replied to that. 'I told them,' she said, 'that Christ is white and glorious in his apparel.'

"The Rev. J. Macdonald of Farintosh, having preached in the parish of Uig, Kitty's parents were among the many who went to hear him. On their return, they mentioned what he had said about the formality of much that is called prayer, and the ignorance of many as to its spirituality; they stated, according to their recollection of the sermon, that many had old, useless prayers, and greatly needed to learn to pray with the Spirit. The child observed this, and two days after, said to her mother, 'It is time for me to give over my old form of prayer.' Her mother replied, 'Neither you nor your prayers are old;' but she rejoined, 'I must give them over and use the prayers which the Lord will teach me.' After this she withdrew to retired spots for prayer. At one time her younger sister returned without her, and on being asked where she had left Kitty, she said, 'I left her praying.' Her father says that he has often sat upon his bed listening to her sweet young voice, presenting this petition with heartfelt earnestness, 'Oh, redeem me from spiritual and eternal death.'

"From the remoteness of her dwelling, Kitty had never attended any place of public worship—but the Sabbath was her delight—and often would she call in her brothers and sisters from the play in which they were thoughtlessly engaged, asking them to join in prayer and other devout exercises, and warning them that if they profaned the day and disliked God's worship, they must perish. Her mother, observing the intent gaze with which she looked on a large fire, enquired what she saw in that fire? She replied, 'I am seeing that my state would be awful if I were to fall into that fire, even though I should be immediately taken out; but woe is me, those who are cast into hell fire will never come out thence.' Another day, when walking by the side of a precipice, and looking down, she exclaimed to her mother, 'How fearful would our state be if we were to fall down this rock, even though we should be lifted up again; but they who are cast into the depths of hell will never be raised therefrom.'[5]

"One day her mother found her lying on a bench with a sad countenance, and addressed some jocular words to her with a view to cheer her. But the child's heart was occupied with solemn thoughts of eternity; and instead of smiling, she answered gravely, 'O, mother, you are vexing my spirit, I would rather hear you praying.' In truth, eternity was very near to her, and the Spirit of God was preparing her for entering it.

"As she got up one morning, she said, 'O, are we not wicked creatures who have put Christ to death.' Her mother, curious to hear what one so young could say on such a subject, replied, 'Christ was put to death, Kitty, long before we were born.' The child, speaking with an understanding heart, said, 'Mother, I am younger than you, but my sins were crucifying Him.' After a pause she added, 'What a wonder that Christ could be put to death when He Himself was God, and had the power to kill every one; indeed, they only put Him to death as man, for it is impossible to kill God.'

"Soon after she had completed her seventh year she was attacked by that sickness which opened her way to the Kingdom of Heaven. When her father asked who she pitied most of those she would leave behind, she replied that she pitied every one whom she left in a Christless state. She suffered much from thirst during her illness, and her mother, reluctant to give her so much cold water as she longed for, fell upon the evil expedient of telling her that the well was dried up. The following day, when she saw water brought in for household purposes, poor Kitty's heart was grieved, and she said, 'O, mother dear, was it not you who told the great lie yesterday,

---

[5] The reader is reminded that the child's words are translated from the Gaelic and thus have lost something of their childish expression.

when you said the well was dry—O, never do so again, for it angers God.' During her illness, she was enabled almost literally to obey the command, 'pray without ceasing,' and was often interceding with the Lord to look down and visit her native place. On the morning of her last day on earth, her father said, 'There is reason for thanksgiving that we see another day.' Kitty opened her eyes and said, 'O, Holy one of Israel, save me from death. . . .' In her last moments she was heard to say, 'O, redeem me from death.' Her father, leaning over her, said, 'Kitty, where are you now?' To which the reply was, 'I am on the shore;' and immediately her soul was launched into the great ocean of eternity." This was in December of 1829.

The revival continued with more or less intensity for several years. In the statistical account of his parish written in 1833, Macleod, in a matter-of-fact way, stated that the people's "improvement of late years in religious knowledge has been very perceptible and has taught them to be contented with their circumstances and situation in life and to enjoy and value the invaluable privileges of the gospel dispensation. . . . The attendance at the public ordinances of religion is probably as punctual and full as in any parish in Scotland." It was left to others to speak with more enthusiasm, if not with more thankfulness. The well-known Rev. John MacRae said that "the finest moral spectacle he had ever beheld during his whole course was presented by the congregation of Uig under the pastorate of the Rev. Alexander Macleod." Mrs. Lundie Duncan was "disposed to rejoice over it more than over any other Scottish revival" and speaks of its "calm and deep and prolonged flow." It sent many laborers into the field—ministers, evangelists, and teachers—and its fruit is still to be found in the way that large sections of the Outer Islands continue to welcome gospel preaching and a gospel ministry.

Chapter 15

Kilsyth, 1839

During the century which succeeded its great experiences of 1742, the town and parish of Kilsyth had no outstanding events in its religious history. Gospel ordinances continued to be observed with commonplace regularity during the whole time. In 1839, however, the parish awoke as from "a dream of a hundred years."

The Rev. W. H. Burns was admitted to the charge of Kilsyth on April 19, 1821. The state in which he found the parish was deplorable. A few weeks after the outbreak of the revival, he described its condition when he came. The account he gives curiously resembles what Robe had to say of its state before 1742. "I saw a beautiful valley before me, like that of Sodom, rich and well-watered, but, alas! it bore too close a resemblance to it also in its spiritual and moral aspect. Yet there were several Lots, yea, Jacobs among them, who prayed and wrestled for the return of the time of revival. This was often referred to in the prayers of my predecessor, and familiar to the ears of our people, who seemed to think it an honor to have their fathers' names and sepulchers thus built up and honored, while they, alas! followed not their example.

"A visitation of every family in a parish, after a minister's induction, is generally an important event in its history. Nothing could have been more kind than the reception I received from all classes and denominations, and which has met me ever since in my annual rounds. The appearance, too, at church, and the solemnity and prayers at funerals, struck me as indicative of more of a spirit of religion than I had anticipated: but these good symptoms were overbalanced by the appalling number who attended no place of worship, and by the woeful prevalence of intemperance and the lightness with which that vice seemed to be regarded, even by religious professors. I was struck with the meaning of our Saviour's words, 'Because iniquity shall abound, the love of many shall wax cold.'"

Owing chiefly to the custom of frequenting sacraments in distant parishes, regular attendance at public worship was exceptional, even in the most devoted. Public morality "generally was low. Intemperance was fearfully prevalent." Scourges fell upon the place, but these seem to have made no permanent impression.

In 1830, in consequence of some unusual outbreaks of sin in connection with drunken brawls, a parochial day of fasting and prayer, in the view of prevailing sins and backsliding, was appointed by the Kirk Session and observed with marked seriousness and solemnity. In 1832, the near approach of the cholera which fell heavily on the neighboring village of Kirkintilloch but never actually entered Kilsyth . . . summoned the pastor to lift up his voice in another earnest call to repentance and newness of life.

Both by experience and by personal training, Burns was decidedly the man required for such a situation. Throughout his whole ministry, he showed an absorbing interest in the subject of revivals. As has already been noted, he visited the scene of Stewart's labors at Moulin and was a diligent student of the stirring times of 1742 in his own district. In 1836 he lectured on the topic before a clerical society in Glasgow. He was consequently never without the hope of an outpouring of grace on his own parish and was constantly directing the attention of his people to its possibility.

The unconscious preparation of the parish for the coming revival can now be easily traced. Prayer meetings—"the

Kilsyth, 1839

smoldering embers of a great fire"—had been carried on continually from the days of Robe. One of them was mainly composed of members of session. The number of these meetings was augmented in 1832 when the cholera scare touched the consciences of the parishioners. "A weekly meeting," says Dr. Burns in a lecture he delivered in 1840 on the mode of conducting a revival, "was commenced in the year of the cholera, 1832, with us, as it had been in many places. It was often thinly attended, but never given up. Not a few have obtained saving impressions when they dropped in to these meetings. . . . Besides, there were weekly meetings held in two rural districts." These regular gatherings reached only a small proportion of the people, the larger body, however, was not neglected. "In March, 1836, after the communion, a prayer meeting held in the church, especially for revival, was addressed by the Rev. Mr. Walker of Muthil, who had preached on the subject on the Friday before, after which the prayer meetings in dwelling-houses were considerably increased in number and in attendance—all in connection with the church."

The dissenting Churches, the Relief and the Methodists, took an honorable part in this work of preparation, especially the latter, which had the joy of revival foretaste. As early as 1827, preachers belonging to this community had begun to visit the town, but it was not until 1833 that they appear to have effected a permanent footing. In that year those who adhered to them numbered "fifteen steady members." In 1835 the little circle was surprised with an unusual experience. On the last Sabbath of February, while the teacher was addressing the Sabbath School, "it appeared as if an overpowering light broke in upon their minds; an unusual solemnity pervaded the school, and soon there were heard in all directions sighs and sobbings. . . . The business of the school was stopped, and for a considerable time nothing could be heard but mingled lamentations and prayer for mercy. Meantime the hour arrived for the adult congregation to assemble for the public preaching, but the hall was pre-occupied by the young people, who could neither be removed nor restrained from crying aloud to God with groans and tears for the salvation of their souls. The congregation was, therefore, obliged to take their places in the midst of the agitated and agonizing youths." This movement is spoken of as the "Revival of 1835," and although on a small scale, did indeed open up the way for greater events. "The concern about eternal things was diffused among all classes of the population, and in the course of a week about a hundred persons found peace with God." At intervals thereafter, converts continued to be made throughout the town among all the denominations.

During the year 1838, several circumstances hastened on the revival, chief among which was the growth of an interest in foreign missions. To increase and conserve this interest, a meeting was started about the beginning of the year.

Some time before, Robe's old church had proved too small for the increasing population, and a new one had been built in the village on a site that better served the needs of the people. The old building was demolished and the vacant space left in the old churchyard suggested to Burns that he might utilize the cemetery for open-air gatherings. Accordingly, during the summer of that same year, services were held there, conducted chiefly by the minister and by the Rev. A. N. Sommerville, a young Glasgow probationer whose name was to become better known in the church later as a "modern apostle." One of these services was especially memorable. It was held on the anniversary of Robe's death.[1] The sermon was preached by Burns who stood at his predecessor's grave. He took as his text the words

---

[1] The date of the sermon is August 12, 1838. There is some difficulty in ascertaining the exact date of Robe's death.

Kilsyth, 1839

inscribed in Hebrew on Robe's tombstone[2]—"Thy dead men shall live, together with my dead body shall they arise. Awake and sing, ye that dwell in dust, for thy dew is as the dew of herbs and the earth shall cast out the dead."[3] The impression made by the whole service was very great. "Many afterwards spoke of this season as one by them never to be forgotten; and but for the strong restraint with which the feelings of the hour were repressed, it has been thought that the outward manifestations of awakened life which arrested all eyes in the summer following might have dated from this day."

Meantime, religious interest was gathering in several places throughout the country. The *Home and Foreign Missionary Magazine* for September, 1839, spoke of "manifest symptoms of a general religious awakening." It pointed to what was going on at Kilsyth and Dundee as well as to the south where, "beginning near Cavers and extending towards other places, through the instrumentality of that devoted servant of God, Mr. Douglas of Cavers,[4] assisted by pastors of different denominations," a good work was being done. There can be no doubt that the first motion which showed that a revival was imminent took place at Kilsyth on Tuesday, July 23, 1839.

As in the earlier Kilsyth Revival, one name has become prominently attached to the story of the movement. This time, however, it is not that of the minister of the parish but of his son—The Rev. William Chalmers Burns. He had just passed his twenty-fourth birthday and only a few months before had been

---

[2] This stone has been replaced by another which does not bear the text.
[3] Isaiah 26:19. The discourse is printed in the Appendix to *The Pastor of Kilsyth*.
[4] Douglas, the owner of Cavers, wrote a treatise entitled *Revival of Religion*.

licensed as a preacher of the gospel.[5] He had already definitely committed himself to the career of a foreign missionary, in which afterwards he did such splendid service. At the moment, he was waiting until his appointment to the field should be made. During his University course, he had distinguished himself as a student. It is noteworthy that he kept up his studies when the academic necessity for doing so had passed away. Many who could not understand the fervor and enthusiasm he displayed thought him a fanatic. It is recorded, however, that "he was observed in order to retain due calmness in his mind, when driving in the coach from Edinburgh to preach, to be busily engaged in reading one of Aeschylus' Greek plays."

Young Burns had been appointed to take charge of St. Peter's, Dundee, the congregation of the saintly Robert Murray M'Cheyne, while its pastor was absent on his famous missionary journey to the Jewish stations of the Church. On Thursday, July 18, Burns attended the funeral of a relative in Paisley and on the way home to Dundee remained at Kilsyth for the communion which was to be observed on the following Sabbath. In the course of the celebration, he conducted several services with great acceptance, On Monday, it was announced that if the weather permitted, the young preacher would address an open-air meeting in the public square of the town next morning before he left for his work in Dundee. To the people of Kilsyth he was an interesting personality on various grounds: he was one of themselves, his power as a preacher delighted them, and they knew of his missionary intentions. A great crowd was accordingly expected. The day, however, proved

---

[5]"There was another ground of prejudice against the whole work, arising from the circumstance that the Lord had employed in it young men not long engaged in the work of the ministry, rather than the fathers of Israel." *M'Cheyne's Memories.*

Kilsyth, 1839

unfavorable, and the service had to be held in the church. Burns saw in this arrangement a wise providence of God, "for, while on the one hand it was necessary that our meeting should be intimated for the open-air in order to collect the great multitudes, on the other it was very needful in order to the right management of so glorious a work as that which followed, that we should be assembled within doors." The building was crowded in every part and Burns preached from Psalm 110:3: "Thy people shall be willing in the day of Thy power." Toward the close of the discourse, the preacher spoke of the wondrous outpouring of the Spirit at Kirk of Shotts on that ever-memorable Monday when five hundred were saved. What immediately took place is best described in his own words: "Just as I was speaking of the occasion and the nature of this wonderful address, I felt my own soul moved in a manner so remarkable that I was led, like Mr. Livingston, to plead with the unconverted before me instantly to close with God's offer of mercy, and continued to do so until the power of the Lord's Spirit became so mighty upon their souls as to carry all before it, like the rushing mighty wind of Pentecost. During the whole of the time that I was speaking, the people listened with the most rivetted and solemn attention, and with many silent tears and inward groanings of the spirit; but at the last their feelings became too strong for all ordinary restraints and broke forth simultaneously in weeping and wailing, tears and groans, intermingled with shouts of joy and praise from some of the people of God." The commotion necessarily was great. "For a time," says his father, "the preacher's voice was quite inaudible; a Psalm was sung tremulously by the precentor and by a portion of the audience, most of whom were in tears. I was called by one of the elders to come to a woman who was praying in deep distress; several individuals were removed to the session-house, and a prayer-meeting was immediately commenced. Dr. Burns of Paisley spoke to the people in church, in the way of caution and of direction, that the genuine, deep, inward, working of the Spirit might go on, not encouraging animal excitement."

The work thus begun continued for many weeks. Daily services were held, most often in the church, but sometimes in the public square and at the graveyard. The people showed an intense eagerness to hear the gospel. "The web," says an eye-witness, "became nothing to the weaver, nor the forge to the blacksmith, nor his bench to the carpenter, nor his furrow to the ploughman. They forsook all to crowd the churches and the prayer-meetings. There were nightly sermons in every church, household meetings for prayer in every street, twos and threes in earnest conversation on every road, and single wrestlers with God in the solitary places of the field and glen." The various denominations worked in complete harmony. Sir Archibald Edmonstone, the local proprietor, a pious man of distinctly High Church opinions, greatly favored the movement. Under the date of October 12, 1839, he wrote to the people of Kilsyth saying he felt "justified in acknowledging that the hand of God was at work, and in thankfully believing that in the mysteries of His providence, it had pleased Him to visit your highly favored locality in peculiar and marked manner." In the old Relief Church, Dr. Anderson of Glasgow delivered a series of addresses on *Regeneration,* afterwards published in treatise form. Dr. Heugh preached, visited, and taught. The Methodists and Independents joined hands in the work. The people themselves were easily prevailed upon to attend public worship whether it was early in the morning or late at night.

The immediate change in the condition of the town was great. Writing on September 16, Mr. Burns, senior, says: "The state of society is completely changed. Politics are quite over with us. Religion is the only topic of interest. They who passed each other before are now seen shaking hands and conversing

Kilsyth, 1839

about the all-engrossing subject. The influence is so generally diffused that a stranger going at hazard into any house would find himself in the midst of it."

Following the custom of earlier revivals, the Session determined to hold a second communion on September 22. By this time, news of what was going on in the town had spread over Scotland, and on the Sabbath appointed, numbers came from all parts of the country. The town must have witnessed many extraordinary spectacles during the five days over which the meetings were spread. It was calculated that no fewer than twelve to fifteen thousand people flocked to the town and that at least ten thousand were present at the celebration of the sacrament either as communicants or as onlookers. Thursday night "was a remarkable night of prayer, secret and social; probably there was not an hour or watch of the night altogether silent." The Sabbath services did not end until five o'clock on Monday morning. Preaching services were held at street corners, and in several of the meetings there was much excitement. As has so often been the case, controversialists busily tried to reap a harvest for their own particular tenets. But many professed conversion, and even after the occasion was passed, Burns could write, "We are daily hearing of good done to strangers who came Zaccheus-like to see what it was, who have been pierced in heart and have gone away new men."

Dundee

The movement thus begun at Kilsyth soon broke bounds and spread over the greater part of Scotland. Young Burns had intended to return to Dundee for Sunday, July 28, but events at Kilsyth compelled him to remain and he did not reach Dundee until Tuesday, August 8. The news of what had taken place in the west had preceded him and he found the soil prepared for

Scotland Saw His Glory

sowing. "On Thursday, the second day after his return," says Dr. Andrew Bonar, "at the close of the usual evening prayer-meeting in St. Peter's, and when the minds of many were deeply solemnized by the tidings which had reached them, he spoke a few words about what had for some days detained him from them, and invited those to remain who felt the need of an outpouring of the Spirit to convert them. About a hundred remained, and at the conclusion of a solemn address to these anxious souls, suddenly the power of God seemed to descend and all were bathed in tears." On the following evening similar scenes were enacted, the impression being even greater. "It was like a pent-up flood breaking forth; tears were streaming from the eyes of many, and some fell on the ground, groaning and weeping, and crying for mercy."

During the next three months, Dundee saw many an unaccustomed sight. Crowded meetings were held night after night and numerous inquirers remained after the ordinary meetings were over. Many sought private interviews with the ministers engaged in the work. "During the autumn of 1839," wrote M'Cheyne, "not fewer than from six to seven hundred come to converse with the ministers about their souls; and there were many more, equally concerned, who never came forward in this way." Meetings were often held in the open-air. Many flocked into the town from the surrounding country, and ministers came from all directions, either to see or to help in the movement. Among those who gave their services were Macdonald of Ferintosh and Flyster of Alness from the far north; the Bonars of Larbert and Kelso; Somerville of Glasgow; and Cumming of Dunbarney. The venerable Caesar Malan of Geneva and Robert Haldane also visited the town.

M'Cheyne returned to Dundee on Thursday, November 23. The fervent season of the revival had by this time somewhat passed, but there was still enough glory to indicate something

Kilsyth, 1839

of the greatness of what had been taking place. "At the time of my return from the Mission of the Jews." he says, "I found thirty-nine such meetings [prayer and fellowship] held weekly in connection with the congregation, and five of these were conducted and attended entirely by little children." As was to be expected, M'Cheyne threw himself with characteristic energy into the work. Many anxious souls sought conversation with him. Altogether he records four hundred such interviews in the months following his return. The high tide of the revival, however, had passed and things religious continued to tend towards their normal condition. By October 5, 1841, M'Cheyne could write, "The glory is greatly departed but the number of saved souls is far beyond my knowledge."

Released from his Dundee engagement, Burns began an apostolic ministry, preaching wherever an opportunity offered. The fame of the service he had rendered spread over the English-speaking world, and he had invitations which he accepted from England, Ireland, and Canada. He continued in these labors until he sailed to take up his life's task in China in the beginning of 1847. The best part of his evangelical work, however, was done in his native Scotland. After he left Dundee, he spent some time in St. Andrews as well as in Kilsyth and the districts surrounding his father's parish. Everywhere, he had marked success accompanying his preaching.

Perth

The next important town where great results were obtained was the ancient city of Perth. The Rev. John Milne had been settled in St. Leonard's there as recently as November 7, 1839. His ministry soon began to create special interest. He found among his people a longing for revival, and their expectations were made keener by the news of what had taken place at

Scotland Saw His Glory

Kilsyth and elsewhere. On the last Sabbath of December, Burns came to assist Milne with one service. He was received with such favor that the visit extended to several months. As long as he was in Perth, "daily double meetings continued without interruption, the evening ones always densely, oppressively crowded and continuing usually for three or four hours." The surrounding districts were also moved, and many came in to Perth to attend the services, returning home during the night

While in the midst of the work, Milne wrote, "I have been busy, very busy, almost unceasingly, night and day for the last three weeks, and the result is, I trust, one of the most hopeful and widest revivals that has as yet taken place in Scotland. The person chiefly instrumental in beginning and carrying on this is Mr. Burns. . . . We are in a great degree alone, having only got help from Mr. Cumming of Dunbarney, and Mr. Bonar of Collace. . . . We have much opposition, and it is getting more violent as the work goes on. Mr. Gray is the only town minister that stands by us, though he takes no active part in the services." Unfortunately, part of the opposition came from some of the managers of Milne's own church, but it was not carried to extremes, and the good done more than compensated for all the trials that had to be endured. At the first communion (April, 1840) no fewer than 140 were admitted to membership for the first time in St. Leonard's alone. Mr. Gray afterwards reported that "never had I so interesting and delightful a class of catechumens as on that occasion." Nor were the permanent effects in the town less notable. St. Leonard's became synonymous with "great life and warmth" in congregational activities, and a prayer meeting started at the time was still in existence a quarter of a century later.

Kilsyth, 1839

Aberdeen

After leaving Perth, Burns went to Aberdeen, where he continued until the end of April. The response, however, was not so great as might have been expected, and he determined to return in October of the same year. The results were now such that the whole work roused the keenest opposition from those who looked upon such movements with suspicion, if not hatred. One of the city's newspapers—T*he Herald*—took the lead in denouncing not only Burns himself, but his preaching, his method of conducting the meetings, the effects produced upon the people, and all who aided him in any way. It printed descriptions of the services in lurid colors and generally looked upon Burns and his helpers as wild, misdirected enthusiasts. "They dwell almost continually on the mysteries of the gospel and neglect to preach up its practical injunctions; they are at more pains to exaggerate the wickedness of human nature than to teach their hearers to correct such vices as they really indulge. If they would but enforce on their hearers the plain truths of the gospel, without leading their minds perpetually to the contemplation of abstract questions which cannot be solved, they would have a better chance of promoting virtue and would be in less danger of bringing up a large number of their female hearers to be either fools or hypocrites."

Such an outburst would not, perhaps, merit notice after the lapse of eighty years, were it not for the fact that the attack performed one signal service. The Aberdeen Presbytery did not look upon the work with an altogether favorable eye. They could not, however, pass by the strictures of the newspaper in silence, and they appointed a special committee of their number to investigate the allegations made, to take evidence in regard to what was happening in Aberdeen, and so to help the Presbytery to determine its attitude toward the whole movement. The committee did its work thoroughly. It examined witnesses within its own bounds and procured written testimonies from various parts of the country. In due course a report was presented and ordered to be printed.[6] In adopting it on May 11, 1841, the Presbytery came to the conclusion that the evidence "bears out the fact that an extensive and delightful work of revival has commenced and is in hopeful progress in various districts in Scotland—the origin of which, instrumentally, is to be traced to a more widely diffused spirit of prayer on the part of ministers and people, and to the simple, earnest, and affectionate preaching of the gospel of the grace of God."

The evidence set before the committee showed that, during 1840, revival blessing had descended on various parts of the country besides those already referred to and that this had happened in places which Burns had not personally visited.[7] Thus at Kelso, Horatius Bonar reported that while the movement had not been very pronounced, yet of persons converted he could "safely say there have been upwards of one hundred." At other places in the same neighborhood there had been awakening. At Ancrum, the charge to which John Livingston had formerly ministered, the incumbent "thought it right to meet the growing demand for spiritual instruction by the establishment of numerous week-night services, conducted by myself and others of the neighboring brethren, all of which meetings continued to be attended, night after night, by

---

[6]The full title is *Evidence on the Subject of Revivals Taken Before a Committee of the Presbytery of Aberdeen*. A similar enquiry was undertaken by the Synod of Teviotdale, but the proceedings were not printed. See, however, Bonar's *Life of Milne*, pp. 55-65.

[7]No mention is made of a work of grace that took place in Stirling in February, 1840, the instruments used being the Congregationalists of the town. See: *Narrative of Revival Meetings at Stirling*.

Kilsyth, 1839

crowded and deeply-interested audiences." At Jedburgh, the town-hall was used on week-nights, and there the minister "did not preach sermons but spoke to the people about their souls and the great truths of the gospel," with the result that "the cause of Christ has been more advanced among us in one twelve-month than in the previous ten years of my ministry here."

The Rev. Robert Macdonald of Blairgowrie, wrote that he had been assisted by his neighbor, Mr. Francis Gillies of Rattray, and two probationers; that there had been little or no physical excitement; and that, whereas there had not been a single meeting for social prayer before the revival, there were "now, I believe, about thirty prayer meetings in the parish." Concerning the favored district of Easter Ross, the minister of Tain reported that the "work commenced in this district, in the parish of Tarbat, and on the Communion Monday, being the 6th of July last [1840], under the ministry of one whose praise is in the churches, Rev. John Macdonald of Urquhart. It commenced in this parish, under the ministry of the same highly-honored individual, on the following Monday, being also the communion here. In the course of a few weeks it appeared, in a great measure, under similar circumstances, in many other parishes within the bounds of the Synod, particularly Alness and Urquhart; and it has been advancing since, to a greater or less extent, throughout the district." At the time of writing, May 6, 1841, the work was still in progress.

Although this northern region was accustomed to evangelical religion, the movement aroused no small opposition. What was even stranger was that *The Aberdeen Herald* thought it its duty to make a special attack upon it—a course in which it was followed by at least one English newspaper. The outcry brought Hugh Miller into the field and his testimony to the work done is valuable. He twice spent some time among the people and

Scotland Saw His Glory

then wrote: "We have oftener than once expressed our thorough confidence in the work of Revival in Ross-shire. We are acquainted with the ministers engaged in it, the style and manner of their preaching and the doctrines which have been rendered effectual in its production; and we are assured a time is yet coming when many of its present enemies will be content to speak of it in a different tone."

Skye

All the movements now detailed can be connected together either through identity of preachers or because intelligence of what was going on elsewhere reached the various districts. Contemporary[8] with them, however, but so far as can be ascertained, independent of them, a work of grace took place in Skye. It appears that the Gaelic Schools Society had settled a teacher named Norman Macleod at the remote hamlet of Unish, near the extremity of Waternish Point. He was an old soldier and had seen active service in Egypt during the Napoleonic Wars. In May, 1840, he was to be removed to another station. On the afternoon of his last Sabbath, he called his people together for a farewell service. So impressive was the meeting that the congregation again assembled for worship between nine and ten o'clock the same evening. Macleod "read the eleventh chapter of Mark and made some remarks on the parable of the barren fig tree. In conclusion, he reverted to his three years' residence among them and asked what fruit they had brought forth, at which the most extraordinary emotion appeared among the people. They continued together the whole night, and

---

[8]There is some question about the exact year. *The Annals of the Disruption* places it "about the month of April, 1843."

Kilsyth, 1839

instead of the teacher going away on the morrow as he intended, such was the awakening that he remained for sixteen days reading, praying, and exhorting. The people continued to assemble with so little intermission day or night that the teacher could only get about two hours' sleep every morning."

As was natural, the movement captured the attention of the whole island. The Rev. Roderick M'Leod of Snizort, whose interest in revival work has already been referred to, and who was ultimately called to the Moderator's chair of the Free Church, was asked to preach to the people and without waiting for the consent of the incumbent of the parish readily undertook to do so. Unish was somewhat inaccessible, and a more central place of meeting was found at Stein some miles distant. M'Leod has left on record his impressions of the anxiety that prevailed during this whole time. He speaks of the "dense mass of people" that waited on the preaching of the Word. On one occasion "there were fifty boats at the least on the shore that had come from distant parts of the coast opposite and around." A crowded weekly service, attended by many from all parts of Skye except the distant parishes of Strath and Sleat, was held at Fairy Bridge for two months until the start of harvest operations made its continuance inconvenient. Dr. MacDonald of Ferintosh came in September and the preaching tour he made throughout the island greatly helped the work. Special movements took place in particular districts, and soon the whole of Skye, from the extreme north to the extreme south, participated in the awakening. It even broke bounds and spread to the islands of Rum and Eigg. Dr. MacDonald was no mean authority on gracious visitations. He asserted that this Skye awakening "exceeded in intensity and extent anything of the kind in modern times."

Scotland Saw His Glory

Breadalbane and Strathtay

One of the most interesting episodes of William C. Burns's own evangelistic labors was his visit to Breadalbane and Strathtay. The minister at Lawers was the Rev. Dugald Campbell, himself the fruit of a West Highland Revival. When he heard of the awakening in the south, he "did not rest" until he had obtained a promise that the evangelist would come to his parish, for he knew his people were ripe for such work. Burns consented and, approaching Loch Tay from the west, preached his way eastward for thirty miles along the banks of the loch and of the river. His opening service was at Lawers on Sabbath, August 16, 1840. It was conducted in the open-air. One who was present says: "There was an indescribable awe over the assembly. Mr. Burns' look, voice, tone; the opening Psalm, the comment, the prayer, the text (it was the parable of the Great Supper in Luke 14); the lines of thought, even the minutest; the preacher's incandescent earnestness; the stifled sobs of the hearers on this side, the faces lit up with joy on that; the death-like silence of the crowd, as they reluctantly dispersed in the gold-red evening—the whole scene is ineffaceably daguerreotyped on my memory. It was the birthplace of many for eternity."

Burns remained a fortnight in the strath, preaching at various places where the Revival of 1816-9 had been most prominent—Lawers, Ardeonaig, Glenlyon, and Fortingall. Everywhere he was met by crowded and attentive congregations. After a few days of the work, Burns wrote, "I could have supposed that I had been in Breadalbane for a month instead of a week; the events that had passed before me were so remarkable and so rapid in succession. It had been indeed a resurrection of the dead, sudden and momentous as the resurrection of the last day." Equally large and impressive gatherings took

Kilsyth, 1839

place after Burns left the loch behind him. One of the greatest was held on the green braes of Grandtully, and another filled the Church-yard at Logierait. At a few minutes' call the people left their harvesting operations at Balnaguard and crowded into the schoolhouse until it could hold no more. It was a memorable time for the whole district, and the fruits of it remain to this day.

When the Aberdeen Presbytery issued their report in May 1841, they spoke of the revival as being still "in hopeful progress in various districts of Scotland." Burns continued his evangelistic tours and everywhere met with willing response. During the winter of 1841-2, Leith was so visited with revival fervor that someone said the people seemed to be going mad. As compared with any of its predecessors, the whole movement, in fact, covered a wider area and its fruits were correspondingly greater. It came, too, at an opportune time, for the religious community was stirred over the conflict between the church and the state which ended in the Disruption. Partly the effect of this struggle, it also greatly influenced it in its turn. The question between the contending parties was prevented from becoming one of mere ecclesiastical legalism, and much of the spiritual enthusiasm which accompanied the Disruption itself can be traced to it. As a matter of fact, the Revival of 1839 merged into the religious awakening that spread over the land in 1843.

It is impossible to adequately sum up the results of such a widespread movement. Its influence was maintained perhaps longer than usual by the personal letters which Burns wrote and had printed for several of the communities among whom he had worked. It was accompanied by some regrettable things, both in regard to the extravagances on the side of those who favored the movement and as to the opposition which it stirred up. But there can be no doubt about the blessing it proved to Scotland.

Scotland Saw His Glory

"I can scarcely look around me in this city of Dundee or walk its streets," writes the Rev. John MacPherson, "without seeing in living embodiment or other palpable form the genuine and well-tested fruits of that revival. Many of the converts of the Burns and M'Cheyne period are worthy office-bearers in the churches. Of the converts in St. Peter's alone, some sixteen became ministers of the gospel at home and abroad, some of whom are now the spiritual fathers of hundreds. In short, if we may judge men by their fruits and if the fruit of the Spirit ever appears in the lives of men, the revival of that period was a great work of the Holy Ghost."

Chapter 16

The Revival of 1859-60

The Revival of 1859-1860, as it is usually named, had certain peculiarities which mark it off from similar times of blessing in Scotland. Hitherto it has been possible to associate the beginning of each revival with a distinct place, and even with a special person, while its development outward from the place of origin could be traced with more or less minuteness. Ministers have been the chief agents in each successive awakening, and the ordinary means employed have been the usual exercises of public worship.

The Revival of '59 changed these things. No particular place in Scotland can be claimed as its starting point. Laymen for the first time took the most prominent share in the work, and "singing the gospel," that method which in later days was used so effectively by Sankey, was first brought into use. Hymns sung with great fervor, for the first time furnished the people with the means of confession, decision, and thanksgiving;[1] and aggressive work in the shape of large open-air

---

[1] Two favorites were: "What's the news?" and "I can, I will, I do believe." The following is the opening verse of the first:
   His work's reviving all around—
   That's the news! That's the news!
   And many have Salvation found—
   That's the news! That's the news!
   And since their souls have caught the flame,
   They shout "Hosannah" to His Name,
   And all around they spread His fame—
   That's the news! That's the news!

meetings at places of public resort were for the first time made a regular feature of a movement.

The Revival of '59 easily takes first place among such movements in Scotland because of the extensive nature of its operations. It covered practically the whole land. Parts of Highlands were indeed shut against it because the people in these districts were not yet prepared for the ministrations of laymen, but all Scotland nevertheless shared in the movement from John o' Groat's to Maidenkirk and from the Butt of Lewis to Berwick-on-Tweed. As early as May 1860, Dr. Buchanan, in closing the Free Church Assembly of that year, spoke of the reports of the work that had reached them from all quarters. "From East Lothian," he said, "to the Outer Hebrides, from the shores of the Moray Firth to those of the Solway— and all through the central mining and manufacturing districts of the Kingdom, we heard of scenes which carried us back to the days of the Lord at Shotts and Stewartson and Cambuslang. Unless we greatly deceive ourselves, no former revival of religion which our Church and country have witnessed has ever spread over so wide a field."

At the Assembly of the following year, that is, in less than two years from the commencement of the movement, Dr. Julius Wood reported that in forty-two out of the sixty-six Free Church Presbyteries, there had been "decided awakening and revival" and that in most of the remainder, "whilst there is no decided awakening or revival, there is in almost every instance without exception, increased attention to, and interest in, spiritual things." "The revival," he concluded, "with which God has been pleased to bless us, extends over the length and breadth of the land."

It has been remarked that about the close of the sixth decade of the century there was a "mysterious spiritual susceptibility" abroad in various parts of the world. It showed itself in

The Revival of 1859-1860

countries differing widely from each other, both in creed and in custom. So far as English-speaking peoples were concerned, it first appeared in America. In the year 1857 revival began in New York and rapidly extended over the whole of the United States. Ultimately more than a million converts were added to the membership of the Church. News of what had been taking place reached Ireland which was sitting patiently waiting for such an inspiration. When and where the Irish work began cannot now be discovered, but "in more than one locality in Ulster" during 1857-58, "notwithstanding the general deadness, symptoms of awakening began to indicate the approach of a better era. Public attention, however, was soon concentrated on a rural district in County Antrim (Ballymena) which more than any other has been identified with the early history of the movement and from which, as a common center, it spread with unprecedented rapidity over the entire north of Ireland." Striking results did not begin to appear until the month of December, 1858, but by midsummer of the following year the revival was in full force.

The news of what was taking place across the Irish Channel naturally attracted great attention in Scotland. In several places there had been minor revival movements earlier in the year, as in Thurso and Aberdeen, and special prayer meetings had already been in existence for some time in several parts of the country, the object of which was to plead for an outpouring of the Spirit over the land and to prepare the community for it when it came. The awakening in Ulster lent additional zest to these supplications and the whole country was in expectation. Numbers of the Scottish clergy, as well as of the laity, personally visited the scenes of the revival. "There is scarcely a district in Scotland," said the *Witness* newspaper on September 7, 1859, "in which addresses are not delivered by parties who have returned from Ireland." The story they had to tell everywhere quickened the desire for a similar visitation.

It is impossible now to determine exactly at what precise time and place the revival movement reached the Scottish coasts. A newspaper of July 27, 1859, announced that there had been some "striking down" in Glasgow. This probably refers to what had been taking place in the famous Wynds. On July 4, the foundation stone of the new Bridgegate Church had been laid and its pastor, the Rev. D. MacColl, left immediately for the north of Ireland. Of his return ten days later, he writes: "It was Thursday before I got home. On that Sabbath while I was away, about seventy persons had been obliged to remain till after ten o'clock in the evening dealing with souls in deep distress; and when I got home I found that our hall had been crowded spontaneously every night thereafter, a few men and women being awakened on each occasion. On the Thursday evening I found myself in the midst of a revival. For many months thereafter the Wynd Church was open every night in the week but Saturday, and was kept closed with difficulty even on that night."

Naturally, as being nearest the Irish coast, the south-west of Scotland was the first to feel the gracious influence. In the first fortnight of August, several conversions were reported to have taken place in Port Glasgow, and the *Glasgow Bulletin* about the middle of the month could say, "There are various reasons for believing that we are about to be visited with a similar revival to that at present going on in Ireland." On August 13, a "strong movement" began at Adrossan and spread rapidly along the coast.[2] The *Ayrshire Express* reported that at Saltcoats

---

[2] The revival was "begun in Ayrshire through the preaching of Mr. Sellars, a Free Church student, and within a few weeks made itself felt in every part of the country. Guthrie's *Robertson of Irvine,* page 155.

The Revival of 1859-1860

"multitudes have suddenly and simultaneously become anxious about their state. . . . Meetings are held in the town every evening and are filled to overflowing. All sectarianism is forgotten." At the beginning of the following month, crowds of fifteen thousand persons assembled in the fields at Dreghorn to hear the gospel preached.

By the middle of September, it was clear that the revival had fairly extended itself to Scotland. On the first Sabbath of October, the United Presbyterian ministers of Glasgow called the special attention of their congregations to it. On October 25, the Established Church Presbytery of the same city conferred on the matter. The report laid before them said that "an unprecedented interest has of late been awakened with reference to divine things—that the Word of God has been read and heard preached, meetings for prayer and other ordinances of religion attended, with remarkable earnestness—and that in very many cases the results are apparent of hopefully changed minds and decidedly changed conduct," and concluded that "God is visiting His people." On November 1, the Free Church Synod of Lothian and Tweedale gave thanks "for the gracious outpouring of His Spirit in various parts of His church. All were agreed that the revival had come.

The month of November found the movement spreading to remote districts of the country. In the Island of Lewis and Harris, for example, the awakening was great. The Gaelic school teacher at Steinish reported that he had "commenced an evening class for adults about the beginning of November, but owing to the awakening in this place and the people attending sermons or prayer meetings every night in the week (except Saturday), I was obliged to discontinue it." The same thing could be said of other places in the same neighborhood. At Lionel there was "an extraordinary movement, especially among

Scotland Saw His Glory

the young," and in Harris "we have here in the Parish of Tarbert of late the appearance of a great awakening."

At the same time, Aberdeen, a place differing as widely as possible from Lewis in character and social conditions, was similarly moved. During the preceding summer much good work had been done, but the visit of Reginald Radcliffe, the evangelist, seemed to focus the whole effort. He arrived on November 27, and at once the city welcomed his ministrations. "In looking at him and listening to him," says Dr. Stark, "it was at first difficult to account for his power, it was so quiet and unobtrusive. There was no oratorical display, not even what could be called eloquence;[3] he had not the intellectual robustness of some of his coadjutors, such as Brownlow North. Yet no man in such a short time ever so drew and stirred Aberdeen and was the instrument of leading so many to cry out, 'What must we do to be saved?' The man's power lay to a large extent in his entire self-effacement and in the circumstance that he happened to come to Aberdeen at a time when the people were prepared to receive and profit by simple statements of gospel truth." This whole corner of Scotland had a somewhat unenviable reputation for indifference toward evangelical truth. The movement at this time as well as that which later swept over the neighborhood of the city did much to modify any unfavorable impression.

Mention of the name of Reginald Radcliffe recalls the prominent place which lay evangelists took in the entire revival. The part which certain ministers played in the work deserved

---

[3] A different opinion has, however, been held. Rev. H. W. Williamson of Huntley, who was a prominent worker of the time, wrote: "Held by the truth, he poured it forth like a torrent of lava, blistering the conscience, awakening the sleeper, terrifying the careless, and in the bright light of the Spirit, revealing the Lamb of God."

The Revival of 1859-1860

grateful recognition, but the honors remained with unordained agents. These laymen presented great diversity both as to their social standing and as to the manner and matter of their preaching. They included "a man of the world like Brownlow North, a lawyer like Reginald Radcliffe, a lord of the soil like Hay M. Grant of Arndilly, a stone-hewer like Duncan Matheson, a fish-curer like James Turner, a run-away soldier like Robert Annan, and a prize-fighting butcher like Robert Cunningham. . . . With tremendous earnestness and force, Brownlow North proclaimed in those days the most awful and glorious of all fundamental truths—God is. With singular tenderness and persuasive power, Reginald Radcliffe preached 'God is love.' Hay M. Grant of Arndilly, with uncommon clearness, set forth salvation as a gift. Duncan Matheson thundered out death, judgment, and eternity; never forgetting, however, the great doctrines of grace. James Turner of Peterhead reiterated, with consuming fervor and never-wearying frequency, the Saviour's announcement to Nicodemus: 'Except a man be born again he cannot see the Kingdom of God,' while such men as Robert Annan and Robert Cunningham gave testimony to the grace of God from their own experience, saying with the Psalmist, 'Come and hear all ye that fear God and I will declare what He hath done for my soul.'"

Other names might be added to this list, but while all of them did notable service, perhaps the preacher who acquired the widest reputation was Brownlow North. Converted in 1854 after a life of gaiety and pleasure, he almost immediately devoted himself to the work of preaching the gospel. Before 1859 he was already known as an evangelical orator of the first order. In May of that year he was given the right hand of fellowship by the Free Church Assembly and sent forth to preach with their approval—surely a bold and significant act when the

Scotland Saw His Glory

whole country was divided in opinion as to the advisability of lay ministrations.

Numberless stories are told of North's impressiveness and devotion. He was instant in season and out of season. When crossing from Belfast to Glasgow, while the Irish movement was at its height, he conducted services on board the steamer with such effect that impressive revival scenes took place. The results of his labors were to be found all over Scotland. Associated with him in much of his work were Gordon Forlong, an Aberdeen lawyer, and John Gordon of Parkhill.

The north and northeast of Scotland were favored with a series of preachers whose names are still held in affectionate remembrance in many households there. Reginald Radcliffe's work was mainly confined to that quarter. The third of "the three gentlemen preachers," Grant Arndilly, did good service in the extreme north. In the autumn of 1859, he and his nephew, now known as Canon Aitken, made an evangelistic tour throughout these northern parts and had special success at Thurso. "So great was the stir," says Canon Aitken, "that by the following Sunday a crowd computed at four thousand gathered in the open air to hear addresses from us. There were many enquiries and some clear cases of conversion." In the neighborhood of Elgin he was similarly owned, and the work at Ferryden was chiefly his.

James Turner confined his attention almost exclusively to Aberdeenshire and the southern shores of the Moray Firth. Radcliffe said of him that "he appeared to pass along the villages of that fishing coast like a flame of fire." Duncan Matheson served the same district and extended his labors to Dundee. In the markets of Aberdeenshire, in the country fairs, and in the open-air generally, Matheson did signal service and has left behind a reputation as an evangelist that is second to none of that stirring time. Describing one evening's labors,

The Revival of 1859-1860

Matheson wrote, "At eight o'clock Mr. Campbell and I preached to thousands in the open air. What a night! We had over and over to preach. The crowds had to be divided, for they were too large. We could not till nearly eleven o'clock get away from the awakened. Pray for us. The Lord is doing great things."

Robert Annan was converted during the course of the revival and became an effective preacher in his own town of Dundee. Robert Cunningham, the Glasgow butcher, also one of the revival's trophies, took part in the work done in Glasgow, as well as addressing meetings up and down the country.[4]

One of the most interesting figures in the devoted band of evangelists is that of Edward Payson Hammond, an American forerunner of Moody and Sankey. Arriving in this country as a student who had personal experience of revival on the other side of the Atlantic, he preached with great power in several centers in Scotland. He was particularly successful with the young: "When he did not seem to interest them by talking, he began to sing to them." At Musselburgh he addressed crowded meetings, and he aroused new life on the Border in January and February, 1861, when the movement seemed to have run its course in other places. The town of Annan was greatly stirred by his discourses and several notable conversions were recorded. "Many a drunkard has deserted the public-house in horror of his previous life; the artisans of the town have abandoned the corners where they lounged in the evenings and have betaken themselves to prayer; and even the 'arabs' of the burgh—the boys who were forever shouting and yelling about the streets—have every evening been engaged in singing Psalms and hymns." The movement spread to Dumfries and the neighboring

---

[4]His pathetic appeal at the close of many of his addresses is still remembered: "Oh, men, what ails ye at Christ?"

villages, and for three weeks, Hammond labored in the district with extraordinary success. Huge meetings followed in Glasgow and elsewhere, and it was only a breakdown in health caused by the severe strain of the heavy work that ended for a time his triumphant career as an evangelist.

Among the fishing communities, the revival movement was received with particular fervor and gratitude. The east coast broke at one time or another into evangelical flame along almost its entire length. Now, the divine influence would fall without warning and apparently without cause, and the little community would be turned upside down; again, a company of fishermen from a different part of the coast would bring the news in the ordinary operations of their calling and set the place of their sojourn on fire. Sometimes the chance visit of an evangelist would stir up the people. Each place as it was touched became a center from which the fervor spread along the shore on either hand.

The fishing village which first felt the impulse was Ferryden, on the opposite side of the river from Montrose. It is not a large place, but the entire community was moved as one man. "There were two remarkable weeks in the history of this work of the Lord at Ferryden," wrote Dr. Dixon of Montrose, "the first from Monday, 7th to Saturday, 12th of last November (1859); the second from Saturday, 12th to Sabbath, 20th November. The first of these weeks was one of deep widespread conviction of sin and misery, during which they were, in their restlessness, constantly going into each other's houses, speaking of their burdened and intolerable state, declaring that they could not live if they did not get Christ and salvation in Him." On Saturday evening, a young woman entered into the light. The effect of her conversion was extraordinary. Those less favored came "in crowds to her house," and their distress became greater "as they gazed on her emancipated state and

The Revival of 1859-1860

contrasted it with their own continued and terrible bondage." It was, however, the beginning of great things for the community, and the second week was "a week of deliverance as the other had been one of conviction." Even when the whole country was being awakened, the work at Ferryden attracted unusual notice. Ministers and others from various places came to assist at it, and it has been declared by one who was no mean judge that its results have "set it in the forefront of the religious movements that have taken place in Scotland within the last half-century."

Simultaneously with the work at Ferryden, a revival began at Eyemouth, on the Berwickshire coast. As in so many cases, interest was brought to a head by the recital of what had taken place elsewhere. The minister had visited Ireland and Glasgow and had also brought others who had seen the work in these places for themselves. "The last of these addresses," says the ministers, "was delivered on the 20th of November; and on the following Tuesday an individual was struck down at my ordinary prayer meeting. During the week, the report of what had happened got abroad, and on the following Tuesday more than a hundred persons attended." All denominations joined in the effort and the whole community was moved. Young and old alike were affected. "In the dark and stormy nights of December our boys held prayer meetings in the boats which were laid up at the end of town; in unoccupied houses where they had neither fire nor light. . . . Our young girls have a meeting in a place which has been provided for them in the town."

Perhaps the most interesting of these coast movements was that which spread along the southern shore of the Moray Firth. George MacDonald made effective use of what happened there in his story of Malcolm, and says: "It was supposed by the folk of Portlossie (Cullen) to have begun in the village of Scaurnose (Portknockie); but by the time it was recognized as existent, no one could tell whence it had come, any more that he could predict whither it was going. Of its spiritual origin it may also be predicted with confidence that its roots lay deeper than human insight could reach and were far more interwoven than human analysis could disentangle."

Starting somewhere in the western part of Banffshire, about the beginning of February 1860, it spread rapidly along the shore on either side, Banff, Portsoy, Cullen, Portnockie, Findochty, Portessie, Buckie, and Portgordon being soon embraced in its sweep. "In most of the villages that stud the Banffshire coast, a stranger in those days had but to signify his willingness to preach the gospel, when suddenly, as if by magic, the whole population—men, women and children—would assemble to hear the Word of God." The whole coast line, from Aberdeen to Inverness, became affected.

For a time, unseemly physical manifestations occurred. These, however, passed away and much gracious work of the best description was done. Thomas Davidson, the "Scottish Probationer," was teaching at Forres when the revival reached his neighborhood. "The movement," he wrote a correspondent, "has reached our Port—Findhorn, a village of one thousand inhabitants, among whom there are already one hundred seventy to two hundred cases of deep conviction of sin. For some days the work of the school there . . . could not be carried on. The excitement broke out among the boys, and that still more remarkably than among the adults—forty cases among them. The teacher . . . has been very active in the work and has aided the minister very much. I thoroughly believe in the genuineness of it all; it is the most remarkable event in the history of Christianity since Pentecost."

The inland towns—Huntley, Keith, Marnock, Grange, and other places—soon shared in the work. The Rev. H. W. Williamson of Huntley was one of the chief agents. By the end

The Revival of 1859-1860

of February he could say: "The awakening in the villages and towns I have named seems very extensive. In some of them there is scarcely a house in which at least some members of the family are not deeply moved. . . . The work seems as extensive and as deep as it was in Ireland when I had opportunity of visiting it last summer."

The Morayshire fishermen were accustomed to pursue their calling off the coast of Caithness. Instead of returning home each day while the fishing lasted, they were in the habit of landing and passing the time in the local harbors. In former days their presence was not always thought desirable because of their drunken propensities, but a great change had been wrought. The *John o' Groat Journal* of Wick, a few months later, noted that "some of the Portnockie crews on their way to Lewis the other day engaged in worship in their open boats in early morning. The singing of hymns and Psalms could be heard distinctly around the quays, rather novel sounds in our harbor and presenting a striking contrast to the bacchanalian orgies which used to be indulged in on like occasions."

In these earlier days of February and March, a like impression was made on the more southerly seaboard of Caithness. The inhabitants of the fishing villages there had heard tidings of the awakenings in the south with great expectation, but though there had been deep impressions, nothing unusual had taken place. The coming of the Buckie and Portessie men precipitated the blessing.

"By and by," says the Rev. George Davidson of Latheron, "they found their way to our meetings and took part in them. Hitherto there had been no violent demonstrations, though a good deal of subdued feeling was manifested by tears and sighs, but soon several became so affected as to relieve their pent-up feelings in loud cries and fervent prayers for mercy and pardon, and this, too, from night to night, for now the meetings had become nightly and often continued till morning. Many of both sexes were wont to stand up in rapid succession as if under an irresistible impulse and to utter the most earnest and fervent supplications, both for themselves and others, so that it was with difficulty that order could be maintained. The violent agitation only lasted for a few nights during which there were some cases of prostration and fainting. Afterwards matters assumed a more quiet and edifying appearance and the work went on calmly and agreeably." The movement soon embraced the villages of Lybster, Dunbeath, and Berriedale.

It is unnecessary to follow this aspect of the great revival further. Important work was done in Pulteneytown, the suburb of Wick. Later in the spring the flame was carried to the shores of the Fifth of Forth. In March and April it was burning brightly in the fishing villages of Cellardyke and Pittenweem, and had extended to Kirkcaldy. On the opposite coast, Newhaven was embraced in March, and the Eyemouth fishermen lit the torch at Dunbar whence the light spread to North Berwick and Cockenzie.

During 1860 much notable work was done in the larger towns. The summer lent itself to open-air services and they were fully utilized. Perhaps the most outstanding of these was the Huntley Gathering, a meeting due to the suggestion of Duncan Matheson. Over ten thousand people assembled in the Castle Park belonging to the venerated Duchess of Gordon during the two days of July the assembly lasted. It was productive of many conversions. "Thousands live to praise God for the open-air meetings in the Castle Park and similar meetings elsewhere, of which the gathering at Huntley was at once the parent and the broad distinct pattern." Dundee had been quietly moved for many months. The Burns-MacCheyne Revival of 1839 had been partial in that it affected only a section of the

The Revival of 1859-1860

town. "Now the prayer meetings are over the whole town and connected more or less with all the Christian denominations."

At Perth, large open-air meetings were held on the Inch[5] with tents, where inquirers might be dealt with. "Immense multitudes assembled each night," reported the Presbytery. "Multitudes were awakened to a sense of sin. Similar effects were produced in adjacent districts." Later on in the year, a renewal of the interest took place in the Fair City, when "for ten weeks the large City Hall has been crowded night after night." Glasgow Green saw several huge meetings, conducted by men like Richard Weaver. An endeavor was made in Edinburgh to carry on the movement on territorial lines. Open-air services were conducted at Crieff, Greenock, Montrose, and elsewhere. The people were hungering for the Bread of Life all over the land, and it is safe to say that Scotland never saw such a summer for preaching and religious anxiety.

The movement embraced all classes of the community. The greatest harvest was perhaps reaped from the middle classes among whom most revivals, it is said, take their rise. But rich and poor alike participated in the benefits. Special appeal was made to students and meetings were conducted on their behalf in the University centers. Edinburgh and Aberdeen were prominently noted for the response made. It cannot, however, be said that one class was moved more than another. Just as all parts of the country were visited, so every rank of society came under the power of the Spirit's work.[6]

---

[5] A meadow by the river.

[6] "The time of this visitation may be said to have extended from the autumn of 1859 to the spring of 1861. . . . With the wearing away of 1861 there had been a gradual subsidence of the tide which has not, happily, brought back things to their former state again, but which has, to a great extent, eliminated that element of susceptibility to spiritual impression which

Scotland Saw His Glory

The lasting effects of the revival must be looked for in many directions. The results of such a movement cannot be reckoned through the number of conversions alone, or even by the apparently permanent impressions made on individual lives. In former revivals this appears to have been the only method used in appraising the benefits rendered to the church or to the community; perhaps it was then the only possible plan. In no Scottish revival, however, could such a method be more arbitrary and injudicious than in this. The conversions were numerous, and that the converts themselves became in turn the means of bringing others into the kingdom is splendidly true. Many of them became occupants of pulpits or went as missionaries to the foreign field. James Chalmers and the heroic work he did in New Guinea, for example, can be reckoned as one of the direct fruits of the movement in this direction. But the revival had other effects, effects that were religious, social and philanthropic. In estimating the service it did for its day and generation, these must be emphasized.

The question of lay preaching had frequently been the cause of ecclesiastical disturbance in the past; the revival did much to settle the vexed question permanently in favor of the right of all to proclaim the gospel message if they themselves knew it. While nothing was consciously done to displace or weaken the regular ministry, it was everywhere recognized that each man, whether ordained or not, is his brother's keeper. "A new emphasis was given to the obligation which lies upon all who have heard for themselves to invite others to come to the Saviour; and thus, there can be no doubt, the evangelistic force in the country has undergone a great practical expansion." It

---

formed one of the most precious and important features of the peculiar period defined." *British and Foreign Evangelical Review,* Vol. 11, (1872), page 99.

The Revival of 1859-1860

was no small gain that the religious welfare of the community was freed from the taint of possible professionalism.

Many are accustomed to lay stress on what the revival did to create a social and civic conscience. In Glasgow, the movement was followed by much laborious effort on behalf of the lapsed and lost. In Aberdeen its effects are still widely discernable. "Much of the Christian philanthropy that has been in our city for the last thirty years," says Dr. Stark, "owes a great deal to the impulse received at that time. Institutions that flourish amongst us today, having for their object the uplifting of our fellows, have their roots in that movement." Other towns have the same tale to tell. No one who travels today along the southern shore of the Moray Firth can avoid being struck with the apparent material comfort of the fishing communities. The housing accommodations are excellent and there is an air of thriving plenty which is too often conspicuously absent in similar townships elsewhere. The prosperity has been traced directly to the revival. "Revival is a reality here. You can see it, you can touch it, you can measure it, you can go into it and be sheltered by it, and taste some of its material sweets." And these are but samples of the leaven which the Revival of 1859-1860 hid in the national life of Scotland.

Farewell meeting at Glasgow

The interest at the Glasgow meetings was so great that toward the close no hall large enough to hold the people could be had, and Mr. Moody spoke in the open air.

Chapter 17

Moody and Sankey, 1873-1874

What distinguishes the Revival of 1873-1874 from all other Scottish revivals is that it was so distinctly linked to the labors of the evangelists with whose names it is associated. Moody and Sankey were not the first foreigners to put Scotland in their debt. Whitefield's work in the northern kingdom was historic. Wesley paid no fewer than twenty-two visits to Scotland, although it is acknowledged that the impression he made could not be compared with that of Whitefield. Charles Simeon's flying visit was a notable factor in preparing the way for the Moulin Revival, and during 1859-1860, several Englishmen aided the work of preaching. But this was the first time that the main movement was the result of the efforts of two comparative strangers—men who although speaking the common tongue, were almost unacquainted with Scottish religious history and unversed in the nation's religious peculiarities.

The Revival of 1859-1860 had its way prepared for it. The sound of its coming had been heard for many months before it actually reached the shores of Scotland—first as a far away murmur across the Atlantic and then as the falling of many waters on the neighboring island of Ireland. It was otherwise in 1873-1874. There were no particular indications that the land was to be specially visited. Doubtless there were many anxious souls upon the watchtowers and the cry was continually going up—"Watchman, what of the Night?" Several places did have preliminary meetings when once the work was begun and before its influence reached them, but on the whole, there were no general preparations, no special desire over the country, and no special expectancy among the people. Moody and Sankey

Scotland Saw His Glory

came to Scotland almost as Whitefield had come long before, unheralded and unknown and with the same result. The people were in the midst of a revival almost before they knew it.[1]

This work was more fully organized than at any former time. As a systematic part of their plan of campaign, the Americans employed many methods which, if they had been tried before, had been used only tentatively or accidently. The ordinary services were always followed by what were called *inquiry meetings* where those awakened by the message were personally dealt with by experienced Christians. Elaborate precautions were taken to assure that only suitable persons were employed in this delicate work. During the principal meetings, an opportunity was usually given for those who were already followers of Christ to make open profession of that fact. Care was taken to arouse as little publicity as possible while the *anxious* were invited to indicate, by some sign, their state of mind so that concerted prayer might be offered for them. Written requests of prayer, either on behalf of the writers themselves or of careless relatives and friends, were also handed in to the preachers. After being read they were gladly responded to by the people. Every care was taken that undue excitement and hysteria of all kinds should be immediately suppressed. It is notable that phenomena which had disfigured

---

[1] "It did not altogether take us by surprise. Though it seemed to burst suddenly upon the public, to some it was not unexpected"—*Scottish Congregational Magazine,* February, 1874. In a not altogether friendly lead article, the *Glasgow Herald* said, "It is worthwhile noting a new feature connected with the movement in this country. The revival wave cannot be said to have arisen spontaneously. It was announced that a couple of men gifted in a certain way were coming, singularly enough, from America—the birthplace of so many sensations. Curiosity was roused: the men arrived, and their performances struck in some sense a prepared chord."

Moody and Sankey

former revivals were altogether absent from the whole movement. *Decision for Christ* was the watchword of the work.

Perhaps the greatest innovation was the solo-singing of Sankey who accompanied himself on a small American organ. As has already been noted, singing the gospel was not altogether new in revival work. It had been used effectively during 1859-1860. It was not unknown during American revivals and in 1872 one of its exponents, Philip Phillips of the United States, had shown its possibilities in Scotland itself. But for the first time, Sankey made it an integral part of the service. The advertisement in the public press calling attention to the meetings declared—"Mr. Moody will (D.V.) preach the gospel, and Mr. Sankey will sing the gospel." The evangelists were well aware of the opposition they were likely to encounter on this particular point. "Much had been said and written in Scotland against the use of *human hymns* in public worship," says Sankey, "and even more had been uttered against the employment of the *Kist o' Whistles*, the term by which they designated the small cabinet organ I employed as an accompaniment to my voice." The suspicion, however, was not of long duration. Dr. Andrew Thompson of Edinburgh put the matter thus—"We might quote, in commendation of this somewhat novel manner of preaching the gospel, the words of good George Herbert—

'A verse may win him who the gospel flies,
And turn delight into a sacrifice.'"

At his first Scottish meeting, the soloist sang *Jesus of Nazareth Passeth By* and the reception it met with was all that could be desired. "The intense silence that pervaded that quiet audience during the singing of this song at once assured me that even 'human hymns' sung in a prayerful spirit, were indeed likely to be used of God to arrest attention and convey gospel truth to the hearts of men in bonnie Scotland, even as they had in other

Scotland Saw His Glory

places." Subsequent events proved that Sankey was right. Many conversions were directly traceable to his singing. The simplicity both of music and words made the hymns easy for the common people to learn and they spread rapidly over the whole country. In many places they prepared the way for the revival.

Dwight L. Moody and Ira D. Sankey landed at Liverpool on June 17, 1873, two practically unknown men. They had come on the strength of some rather indefinite promises that a way would be opened up for them, but the unexpected death of those who had given the invitation seemed to shut out every possibility of usefulness. A beginning, however, was made at York, and although the mission was not highly successful, it showed the stuff of which the evangelists were made. Engagements followed at Sunderland, Newcastle, and other places in the north of England. The meetings in Newcastle were crowded and the fame of the American preachers steadily advanced.

The Rev. John Kelman of Leith heard from his brother in Sunderland of the good work done in that town. He went to England to see it for himself and was so impressed with the power the evangelists displayed and the manifest results that followed that he personally invited them to visit Scotland. Requests for services also reached them from Edinburgh and Dundee. Such invitations could not be set aside and Moody agreed to come and begin work at Edinburgh as the best center.

Only six weeks were allowed for preparation. A daily prayer meeting was immediately begun, to which ministers and others were invited. It grew in interest and numbers. "The meeting was to some extent thrown open, the prayers were brief, pointed, earnest supplications for the outpouring of the Holy Spirit and were alternated with frequent singing of sweet songs which are now so much prized as the tender utterance of faith and joy and spiritual affection." The form of the meeting achieved a double result—it accustomed the public to the

Moody and Sankey

expectation of blessing, and it initiated them into the peculiar methods to be employed during the mission. Great care was also bestowed upon outward organization. A large committee, representative of all the churches, with Dr. J. H. Wilson at its head, was formed to make the necessary arrangements.

The first service was held on the Sabbath, November 23. Edinburgh had in the past stood aloof in a somewhat marked way from revival work. It seemed to have received Whitefield with open arms, but never betrayed much enthusiasm for any of the other movements that approached its walls. Although special meetings were held in the city in 1839, the bulk of the population was unmoved. The Revival of 1859-1860 was scarcely felt. But now all was changed. The proud city capitulated to the gospel. The largest available hall was crowded, and although Moody himself was unable to be present because of illness, there never was, from that first day, any doubt as to the success of the effort to be made.

A week or two after the beginning of the mission, a circular was sent to all the ministers in Scotland calling attention to the great and hopeful work that was going on in the capital and asking for united prayer that it should continue and spread over the whole country. It was a remarkable document in many ways. It was signed by thirty-eight of the chief ministers and laymen of the city, representative of every denomination and even of every learned rank and profession. Besides suggesting a special week—January four to eleven—for this combined prayer, it sketched the progress of the work already underway. "Edinburgh," it says, "is now enjoying signal manifestations of grace . . . God is so affecting the hearts of men that the Free Assembly Hall, the largest public building in Edinburgh, is crowded every day at noon with a meeting for prayer; and that building, along with the Established Church Assembly Hall, overflows every evening when the gospel is preached. But the

Scotland Saw His Glory

numbers that attend are not the most remarkable feature. It is the presence and the power of the Holy Spirit, the solemn awe, the prayerful, believing, expectant spirit, the anxious inquiry of united souls, and the longing of believers to grow more like Christ—their hungering and thirsting after holiness. The hall of the Tolbooth Church and the Free High Church are nightly attended by anxious inquirers. All denominational and social distinctions are entirely merged. All this is of the God of Grace." The description is not exaggerated; the whole city had indeed been moved to its foundations.

Every day except Saturday the work went on without intermission. The services were usually conducted in local churches, with larger gatherings in the Assembly Halls on Sabbaths. Several meetings were frequently carried on at the same hour. Moody did his best to be present at as many as possible. Everywhere, Sankey's singing was welcomed. The noon prayer meeting so increased in attendance that at last the large hall alone sufficed for it. Special week-day evening meetings crowded places that were never intended for such work: the Corn Exchange provided accommodation on one occasion for 5,000 men. Two meetings stand out with notable prominence. One was the crowded Watch-Night service that filled the Free Assembly Hall on the closing evening of the year. For five hours the huge congregation waited the advent of 1874. Moody announced that "anything that is worship will be in order, and when I am speaking, if any one has an illustration to give, or would like to sing a hymn or offer prayer, let him do so." Five minutes before midnight, "kneeling or with bowed heads, the whole great meeting, with one accord, prayed in silence, and while they did so the city clocks successively struck the hour. The hushed silence continued five minutes more. Mr. Moody then gave out the last two verses of the hymn, *Jesus Lover of My Soul,* and all stood and sang. . . . There probably never was

Moody and Sankey

a New Year brought in at Edinburgh with more solemn gladness and hope of spiritual good."

The other was the Convention held on January fourteenth—an American institution which proved useful in spreading the influence of the work done in Edinburgh to other parts of the country. The Assembly Hall was inadequate for the multitude that desired entrance and the gates had ultimately to be locked. Ministers and others came from long distances both to hear at firsthand of the good work done in the capital and to ask questions. Reports of further progress made were received from the English towns where the evangelists had been laboring, and Scottish ministers told how in their own towns and parishes evidence of awakening was showing itself on all hands. The Convention had a double effect: it focused the work that was being done, and it provided a means by which the glad news could be carried to distant parts of the country.

And so the good work went on. Never had Edinburgh experienced such a Christmas and New Year. A General Election was pending, but it provided no counter-attraction to the gospel. One or two things marred the perfect happiness of the time. Several stories discrediting the evangelists were spread by enemies of the movement, but in every case, investigation cleared away the calumnies. By the whole movement, Edinburgh vindicated its right to be the capital. It became the religious center of the country in a way it had not been since the days of Knox and of the Covenant. When the evangelists left the city on Wednesday, January twenty-first, they had earned, by God's providence, the privilege of entrance to every town and village in Scotland.

Toward the end of January they paid a short visit of one day to Berwick where Principal Cairns was laboring. During the course of the entire mission, it was frequently noticed that the greatest results were often achieved after Moody and Sankey

Scotland Saw His Glory

left the place where they had been working. It was so at Edinburgh where the revival seemed to grow in intensity after their departure. This same thing proved true at Berwick where the movement they inaugurated lasted for the next two years. In November 1874, Dr. Cairns wrote, "Our work here survives though it is quieter. Some blessed fruits remain and I have seen no evil." Meetings were held nightly as well as a noon prayer meeting, in all of which there was cooperation between the ministers and laymen of the town. Much more was done than what was apparent at the public services. Cairns realized that many did not have the courage required to face the inquiry-room so followed them to their own homes. He wrote, "My chief labour has lain in going to people's houses and entering on serious dealing with them." The results were conspicuously seen in the numbers of young people gathered into the membership of the church.

After a fortnight in Dundee where the same means were adopted with similar results to those at Edinburgh, the evangelists reached Glasgow in time to start work on Sunday, February eighth, 1875. Several meetings were successfully held throughout that day. The first, entirely reserved for Sabbath School teachers, filled the largest hall in the city to its utmost capacity. The interest displayed at the beginning of the mission never flagged as long as the evangelists remained in the western metropolis. The *Glasgow Herald* began by giving a weekly report of the various meetings but was soon compelled by the force of circumstances to allot space daily to an account of the progress of the work. A storm of opposition was created in some quarters and newspaper controversy raged high. The Rev. George Gilfillan of Dundee saw fit to enter the strife with letters that were most bitter and contemptuous in their denunciation of everything—doctrine, methods, and results. But in spite of all hostility, the movement spread in Glasgow and its

Moody and Sankey

neighborhood with an enthusiasm and earnestness which exceeded even that in Edinburgh.

The noon prayer meeting held at Wellington Street United Presbyterian Church grew in numbers and interest. Buildings that were chosen for special meetings proved too small, and neighboring churches had to be opened for the crowds that desired to hear the gospel. The local ministers as well as celebrated preachers from a distance, Brownlow North among the rest, and students from Edinburgh aided in the work, and every district of the city was overtaken. Results equally satisfactory were obtained in both the east and the west ends. So great was the impression made that the accommodations provided for the final meetings conducted by Moody and Sankey were totally inadequate for the numbers of persons wishing to be present. A hugh structure of glass, then called the Kibble Palace, in the Botanical Gardens, could hold thousands, but hundreds were turned away from its doors every time it was opened. The usual Monday evening meeting was attended by 3,500 who professed to have been converted during the mission. Seven thousand men crowded it on Wednesday evening. At the final meeting, April seventeenth, it could accommodate only a small part of the multitude that flocked toward it. "The Palace was immediately filled but the afternoon sun was so hot there, that soon the whole had to turn out on the green; there a crowd, variously estimated at from twenty to thirty thousand, was soon gathered." Little wonder that many thought of the enormous congregations that assembled to hear Whitefield more than a century and a quarter before in the same city. Moody preached on "Immediate Salvation" with such power that two thousand persons adjourned to the inquiry-meeting held in the Palace.

It is impossible, in a brief compass, to follow the evangelists in detail as they carried the gospel over the country. They only ventured within the Highland line—along the southern shore of the Moray Firth and in Caithness, where the revivals of former days had accustomed the people to lay-preaching, and on the eastern seaboard of Ross-shire, where an evangelical ministry was welcomed. They also preached at such places as Oban, Campbeltown, and Rothesay with great success, but as a whole, the Highlands were closed against them. The language may have been a difficulty, but the greater problem was the men themselves and their methods. The influence did indeed reach some places within the Gaelic-speaking area, but it came without the direct aid of the evangelists. Lowland Scotland, however, was deeply moved throughout its length and breadth. "The quietest schools were stirred, the dullest churches were moved. Every sermon had its reference to the work, every prayer its special burden. Every newspaper had its paragraph, in which for the most part criticism was somewhat disarmed. Every traveller had his story. In the train, in the busy mart, on 'Change, no place was too secular, no business too pressing, no company too gay, to exclude all reference to the topic of the day. Everywhere the new songs of Zion fell upon your ear. The streets and highways were full of earnest conversation on the work of grace and the way of life."

From Glasgow as a center, short visits were paid to Paisley, Greenock, and the towns of Ayrshire. At no place did the evangelists remain more than a few days, but in each case they did enough to give a new impetus to work already proceeding or to awaken to life and energy those who were slumbering. The opening days of June were spent in Perth. In the following week, a second visit was paid to Dundee, and on June fourteenth they began work in Aberdeen. In that northern city, great gatherings were held both in churches and in the open-air, one of the most interesting of the latter taking place in the quadrangle of Marischal College. Thereafter towns scattered along the whole east coast, from Arbroath to John o' Grout's were visit-

Moody and Sankey

ed—Peterhead, Elgin, Nairn, Inverness, Tain, Wick. Everywhere, the preachers were met with eager, expectant crowds, and everywhere the same scenes and results followed. No place they visited was satisfied with the length of their stay, but they could do little more than touch at centers to which they had been invited. The shortness of their visits seemed in no wise to hinder the work. In fact, as already noted, it usually increased in volume and effectiveness after their departure. The long Scottish series was brought to a close at the beginning of September when Moody and Sankey crossed the channel to Belfast to begin there a similar work for Ireland.

Perhaps the most striking feature of the whole mission was the way it seized upon young men—confessedly a difficult class to reach in a work of this kind. In the specific accounts of events in particular localities, prominent notice is frequently taken of the numbers that attended the meetings and the remarkable results achieved among them. It is even said that in mixed congregations men sometimes outnumbered women.

The divinity halls were particularly moved. Some of Moody's most active assistants were students from the New College, Edinburgh. Henry Drummond was very active in the campaign and in some respects became Moody's right-hand man. "Mr. Moody was feeling the need of a young man to take charge of the meetings for young men, and it is a tribute to his insight that he chose one whose style and tastes were so different from his own." The choice was amply justified, and Drummond was soon addressing meetings for young men and children who attended in thousands. As news of the work proceeding in Edinburgh spread over the country, demands came pouring into the city from all quarters for information regarding it. This gave further opportunity for the student-volunteers, and the young men were dispatched in all directions to carry the news to those who longed for it.

Scotland Saw His Glory

This particular branch of the work was strikingly successful in Glasgow. Dr. Stalker gave an account of a meeting held in Ewing Place Church, known from its results as the Hundred and One Night. "The large church was packed from floor to ceiling. After Dr. Wilson's address, five students of the New College spoke in succession—Henry Drummond, James Brown, Frank Gordon, James Miller, and James Stalker. At this point, Mr. Moody, who had been at another meeting, came in accompanied by Principal Cairns, who delivered a brief address. Seeing how deep the impression was, Mr. Moody ordered the front seats to be cleared and then invited those who wished to decide for Christ to come forward and occupy the vacant pews. Thereupon from every part of the building a stream began to flow along the passages until a hundred and one young men took their places in front; and Mr. Moody proceeded to deal with them solemnly and tenderly." On the following evening the number who took their stand was even larger. The work continued for many months thereafter.

It is always interesting to have a personal account of such a movement from one who was influenced by it. Principal Sir George Adam Smith provided one. He tells how he came to one of Moody's meetings somewhat out of sympathy with the way in which the gospel was usually presented by the revival preachers. "The crowd was enormous. The sight of two thousand men, all of them serious, most of them anxious, plunged him into real life again. The words of the hymns he heard were poor and the music little better, but the mystical power came back with them, and he found himself worshipping. Mr. Moody began to speak with that Yankee accent, in which, except when it is boasting of its country, you seldom fail to feel the edge of the real. There was an occasional exaggeration, but some humor fell and swept the address clean of every appearance of unreality. Mr. Moody spoke of the peril of life, of the ghastly

Moody and Sankey

hunger of the soul without God, of conscience and of guilt; then with passion and with tenderness of God's love and of the Savior Christ, who is among us today as surely as on the shores of Galilee or by the Pool of Bethesda. Hundreds of men stood up in silent witness that they had found salvation, and the young men knew what they had found. He did not stay behind with them, but he went away feeling that God was in the meeting, very clear what Christ could save him from, and conscious that it was at the peril of his manhood if he refused to follow him." Never before in the history of Scotland has such a work of grace been done among its young men.

When the blessing wrought throughout Scotland is considered, the instrumentality used stands out conspicuously in its weakness and apparent insufficiency. "There came to England two men, one with a Bible, and the other with a hymn-book; one speaks and the other sings, while both pray in secret to God. The truth spoken makes an impression. It is then clothed with the melody of song and the impression is deepened." Neither preacher nor singer possessed powers of the first order. Sankey's music could not please the more refined. Moody's gift of speech sometimes failed. Sir George Adam Smith bluntly says, "Mr. Moody said some rash things, as a foreigner could not help doing, and many crude ones, as an uneducated man must. While some of his addresses were powerful, others were very poor." Prof. W. G. Blaikie, with whom Moody resided while in Edinburgh, more graciously says, "Moody's sermons were certainly not intellectual and those who went to his meetings in hopes of hearing something original and brilliant were doomed to disappointment. They were plain, honest, somewhat blunt appeals, but wonderfully brightened and made telling by a copious supply of illustrations, anecdotes, and personal reminiscences."

Scotland Saw His Glory

How then did the evangelists succeed so well? Both were men who knew the needs of the people. Their apprenticeship in Christian work in Chicago had prepared them for more extended service. They worked in perfect harmony with ministers of all the evangelical denominations and linked their efforts directly to the churches. They were endowed with great common-sense and they were eminently human. The message they spoke and sang touched the deepest chords in the lives of men and women struggling with a sense of sin and guilt. They put the great evangelical remedies in the foreground, and above all, they spoke and sang as men who themselves were fully persuaded in their own minds of the truth they conveyed. They were obviously sincere and in earnest and had themselves achieved peace through the gospel they pressed on others.

But above all else, Mr. Moody himself was a man most unusually anointed for the very work in which he was engaged. "Mr. Moody knew he had 'the baptism with the Holy Ghost.' He had no doubt about it. In his early days he was a great hustler, he had a tremendous desire to do something, but he had no real power. He worked very largely in the energy of the flesh. But there were two humble Free Methodist women who used to come over to his meetings in the Y. M. C. A. One was 'Auntie Cook' and the other Mrs. Snow. These two women would come to Mr. Moody at the close of his meetings and say: 'We are praying for you.' Finally, Mr. Moody became somewhat nettled and said to them one night: 'Why are you praying for me? Why don't you pray for the unsaved?' They replied: 'We are praying that you may get the power.' Mr. Moody did not know what they meant, but he got to thinking about it, and then went to these women and said: 'I wish you would tell me what you mean,' and they told him about the definite baptism with the Holy Ghost. Then he asked that he might pray with them and not they merely pray for him.

Moody and Sankey

"Auntie Cook once told me of the intense fervor with which Mr. Moody prayed on that occasion. She told me in words that I scarcely dare repeat, though I have never forgotten them. And he not only prayed with them, but he also prayed alone. Not long after, one day on his way to England, he was walking up Wall Street in New York (Mr. Moody very seldom told this and I almost hesitate to tell it) and in the midst of the bustle and hurry of that city his prayer was answered; the power of God fell upon him as he walked up the street and he had to hurry off to the house of a friend and ask that he might have a room by himself, and in that room he stayed alone for hours; and the Holy Ghost came upon him filling his soul with such joy that at last he had to ask God to withhold His hand, lest he die on the spot from very joy. He went out from that place with the power of the Holy Ghost upon him, and when he got to London (partly through the prayers of a bedridden saint in Mr. Lessey's church) the power of God wrought through him mightily in North London and hundreds were added to the churches, and that was what led to his being invited over to the wonderful campaign that followed in later years."[2]

All ranks of society were reached. In this respect, Edinburgh was typical of the whole country. Of the work there, it was written that "all classes without exception have been represented in the enquiry meetings. Ladies and gentlemen moving in the highest circles of society and poor ragged men and women from the Grassmarket and the Cowgate; the highly educated and cultivated and the very ignorant; students at the University and working men; old men and women and boys and girls from school; respectable church-going people and even church members; and skeptics, scoffers, drunkards, libertines and prodigals—all have come to the enquiry meeting asking

---

[2] R. A. Torrey, *Why God Used D. L. Moody*, 1923, pp.51-54.

with every indication of deep feeling, 'What must I do to be saved?'" More than one observer noticed the frequency with which those trained in Christian homes professed to be converted to Christ. At the concluding meeting for converts in Edinburgh, "not fewer that 1,700 were present, young men and women of all social grades, but mainly belonging, it has been ascertained, to the families of Christian professors."

The permanent effects of the movement, in addition to individual conversions, were very great. Something was done by it to brighten the ordinary services of the sanctuary and part of the present-day desire for improvement in the conduct of public worship can be traced to it. It gave a new impetus to congregational and religious activities over the whole land, every denomination sharing in the advance. It provided a new army of Christian workers, many of whom are still actively engaged in service. The age of many converts made it possible that two generations would not exhaust the direct influence thus exerted on the Christian life of the community. This revival deepened the impression left by that of 1859-60, that the laity as well as the ordained ministry had a religious responsibility toward their fellows, and that it was the duty of all followers of Christ to spread His Kingdom to the utmost of their ability.

One of the most satisfactory results was the place given to the Bible in the minds and hearts of the converts. A new zeal for its study was created and a higher place than ever assigned to it as an indispensable means of spiritual growth. Moody's afternoon "Bible Readings" showed what could be done by systematic and prayerful consideration of its pages. "The revival," wrote Principal Cairns, "made very hopeful the whole future of the Bible class in Scotland."

The Awakening of 1859-1860 had definitely turned men's minds toward the social needs of their brethren; the movement of 1873-1874 went far to confirm the impression then made on

Moody and Sankey

the public conscience. In Glasgow, where the need was sore, missions were started to the criminal classes and the friendless. "The lodging-houses were visited and every haunt of vagrants. Temperance work was organized. New interest was roused in industrial schools and on the advice of Sheriff Watson, a veteran in this line of education, an industrial feeding-school was established for ill-fed or ill-clad children. At Saltcoats a house was bought and furnished for orphans; new impulses were given to the Orphan Homes of Scotland founded in 1871 by Mr. Quarrier.... A boarding-house was opened in Glasgow for young women. Mr. Moody gave great attention to Young Men's Christian Associations." New premises were procured from Carrubbers' Close Mission in Edinburgh, and over the whole country the conviction was brought home that the cause of Christ could be furthered in other ways in addition to the direct preaching of the gospel. It would be difficult to say how much of the present interest shown by the Church in social problems can be traced to the Moody and Sankey Revival.

Among what may be considered minor results was the position of influence to which the work in Scotland and elsewhere in Britain called the evangelists in their own country. Moody had left America two years before, "known only," says his son, "to a comparatively small circle of Sunday School workers and Young Men's Christian Association friends. In Chicago his name was more prominent than elsewhere, but to the general public his work was not familiar. It may be said, then, that Mr. Moody was introduced to America by Great Britain, as he, in turn, is said to have introduced several English-men to their own country." Invitations reached him from all parts of the United States to conduct evangelistic services, and he became one of the most prominent figures in the public life of America. Scotland had so frequently been indebted to the west for revival impulse, that it must be a matter of thankfulness that even in this round-about way the obligation was reversed.[3]

But perhaps not everyone is prepared to interpret the Moody-Sankey ministry in Scotland as true revival. Some may be prone to regard it merely as American mass-evangelism at a higher than normal level. The opinion, however, of no less a contemporary of Moody than Charles Haddon Spurgeon must be weighed: "The gracious visitation which has come upon Edinburgh is such as was probably never known before within the memory of man. The whole place seems to be moved from end to end. When we hear of many thousands coming together on weekdays to quite ordinary meetings, and crying, 'What must we do to be saved?' there is, we are persuaded, the hand of God in the matter."

---

[3]Moody and Sankey returned by invitation to Scotland in 1881, but the work accomplished, although great in itself, is acknowledged to have fallen far short of the campaign of 1873-1874.

Chapter 18

Summary and Conclusion

No two revivals are ever identical. The very God who made an infinite assortment of finger prints and snowflakes has given revivals in endless varieties. Even so, a comparison of Scottish revivals with those that have taken place elsewhere shows that there is no material difference between them. The essential elements of revival are always present. As Principal Lindsay says, "The revival is always the same. Space and time, so potent over all other things, seem powerless to change it. What it was in Achaia in the first century, or in Italy in the thirteenth, or in the Rhineland in the fourteenth, or in England in the eighteenth, it is in Wales to-day." The natural characteristics of the Scotch people could not of necessity be suppressed. National traits may be seen in the reserved attitude with which the beginnings of revival movements were received as well as in the ardent enthusiasm with which they were accepted. That they should have happened at all is surely the most astonishing thing about them. The reticent Scottish temperament that refuses to make common show of religious feeling and emotion and tries to hide the deeper secrets of the inner life seems to forbid them altogether. Yet they have happened, and there is no spiritual benefit or physical phenomenon that appeared in England and America that cannot be duplicated in events at Shotts, Cambuslang, and Skye. The critical ingredients are always present in revivals: prayer, brokenness, repentance, confession, restoration from backsliding and radical conversions. "We do not want anything new in revivals," wrote Prof. Henry Drummond in reference to what was happening in his day. "We want always the old factors—the living Spirit of God,

Scotland Saw His Glory

the living Word of God, the old Gospel. We want crowds coming to hear—crowds made up of the old elements: perishing men and women finding their way to the prayer meeting, Bible reading, enquiry room." These have always been present in every Scottish movement.

No one can read the story of revivals in Scotland without noting how closely they are associated with sacramental occasions. Communion seasons with all their solemnity seemed suitable opportunities. Minds were more open; hearts more tender; thought circled more closely around the central facts of salvation. There is no record that the moment of the actual partaking of the Supper was the occasion of any extraordinary movement,[1] but over and over again it can be read that special blessing attended the meetings held either preliminary to the dispensation of the sacrament or immediately subsequent to it. It was so at the ever memorable communion at Shotts, whose Monday thanksgiving service started the great succession. The time when reaping was apparently the greatest at Cambuslang and Kilsyth was the week following the dispensation of the sacrament. So convinced were both Robe and M'Culloch of the efficacy of the celebration in awakening consciences and in bringing men and women to decision that, contrary to the usual custom of the day, they agreed to have the Supper repeated within a few weeks. At many centers in the Highlands, the

---

[1] "George Gillespie, following John Calvin and other great evangelical reformers, argues with great convincingness that the Lord's Supper was not originally intended to be a converting ordinance. The Lord's Supper, Gillespie conclusively proves, was instituted by our Lord in order to nourish and to strengthen the life of grace where it has been already begun. But neither John Calvin nor George Gillespie ever said that the Lord's Supper is not often over-ruled to be a converting occasion. As a matter of fact it has been made a converting occasion to many in all ages of the Church." Dr. Alexander Whyte.

Summary and Conclusion

annual celebration was accompanied with showers that continued to fall for weeks after the special occasion had passed. The great gatherings that then took place did much to spread revival impulses over wide districts. This was especially the case in Breadalbane and Ross-shire at the beginning of the nineteenth century. The revival that began during the communion season at Kilsyth in July 1839 did not exhaust itself for years and extended to places far and wide. It is perhaps needless to elaborate the matter further, but the point is surely worth holding in remembrance. Revivals in Scotland are intimately associated with the most personal, loving, and evangelical rite the Reformed Church knows.

Revivals are frequently classed among movements that are due to ignorance, fanaticism, and unhealthy imitation. Some who claim a measure of culture and sanity are inclined to brush them aside as products of a disordered imagination and a false emphasis. The story of Scottish revivals, read sympathetically, should do much to remove the prejudice. From first to last, the great majority of the leaders in them were men of known scholarship, wisdom, and prudence. Not a few of them belonged to the higher ranks of society. One ought to pause long before condemning as illusionary and deceptive, movements which had the approval of statesmen like Andrew Melville and Robert Bruce; of scholars like David Dickson, Boyd of Trochrigg, and John Livingston; and of men of varied attainment like Dr. John Erskine, Brownlow North, and Prof. Drummond. Nor should revivals be classed with the irrational motions of superstition that have sometimes swept over the lower orders. The names of women who took part in them are curiously few, but those known belonged to women of culture and standing. The elders who officiated at the second Cambuslang communion could use territorial designations. In still later times, even members of the nobility have taken their

Scotland Saw His Glory

place as revival preachers. No cause can be defended simply on the ground that it has the support of a privileged or educated class, but that revivals have been aided by such men can surely be counted in their favor. If the apologetic for Scottish revivals had to rest only on the standing—social, intellectual, and spiritual—of the men who have approved of them, their position as rational and beneficent movements could be amply maintained.

As the story of the various revivals is unfolded, it is interesting to note the golden thread of connection that links them all together. Shotts became a kind of standard event to which all who either yearned for revival or were actually working in the midst of it looked back. Robe used it to justify some of the features of the movement of which he was himself the chief part and which perplexed many of his contemporaries. William Burns's recitation of what had happened on that far-off day precipitated the blessing at Kilsyth in 1839. That movement had also already been prepared for by the sermon which Burn's father preached at Robe's grave and by the references he made to his predecessor's labors. At Dundee, during the revival there in the autumn of 1839, Williams Burns systematically read sections of Robe's *Narrative* and made comments upon what he read. The work at Moulin was connected with that of Skye through the person of John Shaw. Alexander Macleod, a revival convert in Skye, was one of the leaders of the subsequent movement in Lewis. The religious concern which visited Breadalbane in 1817 was partly due to reports of the awakenings in the far north under Dr. Macdonald, and the harvest was reaped when that preacher himself came.

In fact, it is common for revivals to be greatly aided by some connection of this kind. M'Culloch of Cambuslang continually gave accounts to his people of what was going on elsewhere. He was so convinced of the propriety and excellence

Summary and Conclusion

of this course that he issued a periodical spreading the news. While a movement was in progress in one part of the country, notices of what was taking place helped to bring the blessing to other districts. This was the case in 1742 when narratives of what was happening in the south stirred up the people of Ross-shire. During 1859-1860, the spread of the movement was greatly aided by the issue of *The Wynd Journal* which reached a large circulation,[2] just as the publication of *Times of Blessing* helped on the work under Moody. In 1841, Campbell of Breadalbane wrote that "reports of revivals in other parts of the world were regularly laid before the people; and these statements were greatly blessed in stirring up the people to seek the Lord." In short, the story of the abundant supply of grace at a different time, or in another place, created a soul-hunger which in many cases led to its satisfaction.

It must not be supposed, however, that the course of Scottish revivals shows that information of this kind was a necessary preliminary in any particular place. A general knowledge of God's methods of work among other men and at other times must always have its effect in the way of mental and spiritual preparation. But the Spirit of God is without limits and bonds, and over and over again He caused revivals to come which cannot be traced to any particular source. The movement at Moulin may be called self-contained. It first arose in the heart of the parish minister and spread outward until it embraced the entire neighborhood. More than once, religious concern was at work simultaneously in different parts of the

---

[2] Much, too, was done by *The Revival*, a periodical started in London in July 1859, the title of which afterwards became *The Christian*. Its avowed object was to supply "authentic and continuous intelligence respecting the present extraordinary work of God in America and in our own land."

country, no connection between the different places being traceable. This is particularly true of certain Highland districts in the second decade of the nineteenth century. Over the whole Gaelic area a spiritual susceptibility, which found articulate expression in Arran, Skye, and Perthshire almost at the same moment, seemed abroad. The great awakening of 1859-60 was evidently hastened and encouraged by the news of events elsewhere, but many of its phenomena seemed to be independent and to have no discernible connection with contemporary transactions. "Similarly, in 1874, when Mr. Moody's work was so greatly blessed on the mainland, the isles, especially Tiree and Lewis, were experiencing a gracious awakening," the only point of contact being that they were going on at the same time.

During the course of the Revival of 1839, Hugh Miller observed that in places "where the divine fire had been kindled of old, it seems ever readiest, though often after long intervals, to ascend anew." The foregoing narratives bear ample testimony to the truth of that statement. It is well illustrated in regard to the district of Easter Ross, from whose history Miller drew his inference. MacDonald of Ferintosh found the ground prepared for him there by the response made by the inhabitants a century before to the evangelical ministrations of his predecessors. The service rendered by his labors in turn made the neighborhood ready for further blessing and it has been mercifully visited on several occasions since his day. In fact, once a name appears in the narrative of any revival, its recurrence in movements of later date is almost assured. North Ayrshire began what may be called its evangelical history with the Lollards. The valley of the Annick, with the seventeenth century revival centers of Stewarton and Irvine, lies within that part of the western country. The district was one of those that notably shared in the movement that followed Cambuslang and was among the very earliest to feel the awakening influence of 1859. Kilsyth was

Summary and Conclusion

twice made a starting point. Breadalbane, Glenlyon, and Skye each had awakening impulses at intervals, and the names of villages like Muthill and Ferryden appear in successive stories. It is almost a revival law that a place once visited by the Spirit of God will be visited again.

It is not difficult to account for this repetition. The movement created an evangelical tradition in the neighborhood which made the people less shy of what, on the first occasion, seemed so unusual and extraordinary. Seed sown long ago disappeared from sight and only required the appointed conditions to germinate. Families were nurtured on the memories of what their parents had enjoyed, and when the opportunity came, they entered into the same privilege. The son of Ingram More, for example, appears in the session records of Cambuslang as an elder carrying on the same work as his father. The son of Moulin converts became the missionary evangelist of Bengal, while the grandson of one who helped to revive the spiritual life of Skye, besides attaining to high office of state in India, was placed in the Moderator's chair of the Presbyterian Church in that land. Many of the evangelical pulpits of the Scottish Churches are today filled with the sons of those who trace their conversion to revival movements. If this continuity is true in families, it has all the chance of being true also in the district where the original movement took place. There is an evangelical succession in such experiences.

Frequent attempts have been made to describe under a single phrase the leading truth taught in each revival or, at least, that aspect of truth which seemed to affect the people most. "Justification by faith" was the watchword of the Reformation, but too little is known about the subject matter of the preaching in the earlier revivals to determine whether one particular doctrine outstripped another in the emphasis laid upon it. It is indeed said that repentance, conviction of sin, and the work of the Holy Spirit might each be described as the keynote of the Revival of 1859-60, just as in the Moody and Sankey Revival, grace, faith, and assurance of salvation are supposed to have been the most prominent ideas. But all this can only be partially true; the substance of the preaching must always have been wider than any of these phrases.

There can be no doubt, however, about the general content of the message that stirred men's hearts during these times of religious awakening. We know what effect the proclamation of the "terror of the Lord" has had, but it does not appear that fear was always the instrument used. On the contrary, it is frequently noted that the love of God was the prevailing motive and that the declaration of His grace in Christ melted the most stubborn hearts. Sometimes the addresses were frankly doctrinal, as when M'Culloch and Robe in the eighteenth century and Anderson in the nineteenth dwelt for weeks on regeneration. In revivals, no particular oratorical power is required in the preachers, and with a few exceptions, they have been men of ordinary gifts. What the people have needed and demanded were simple, direct Gospel addresses that touched the whole man: mind, emotions and will. As was succinctly stated by one of the preachers during the second Kilsyth Revival, "Ruin by the fall, redemption by Christ, and regeneration by the Holy Spirit, were the truths which we chiefly preached and which God seemed specially to bless."[3] To the preachers themselves, the effects produced had no explanation in anything they did. "Not by might nor by power, but by my Spirit, saith the Lord," was their confession.

---

[3] It has been emphasized that the Moody and Sankey Revival "arose and was maintained in connection with the preaching of the theology of the Westminster Confession." *Religious Life in Scotland,* page 279. The words might be written generally of every Scottish revival.

Summary and Conclusion

But whatever might be the nature and motive of the preaching, it had one result. The English merchant declared that David Dickson of Irvine showed him all his heart. The work of the preachers produced the same effect in hundreds of cases during each revival. Men's eyes were opened to know their own estate. Harrowing pictures can easily be drawn of the despair into which many souls were plunged and of the agonies they endured before the light of hope dawned upon them. It is easy to denounce prostrations and other mental and bodily manifestations, but however harmful and mistaken they may have been, they yet gave evidence of this—that those who came under their influence were in deadly earnest. It has been said, almost as a complaint, that the more recent movements did not awaken heart and conscience to the deep sense of sin that prevailed during 1859-60 and earlier movements. This statement certainly seems to be true; it may also supply a significant key to the decline of revivals in the English-speaking world. Surely, thinking people must be struck with the fact that Scotland itself has not had nearly as frequent or as extensive outpourings of the Holy Spirit in the twentieth century as in the preceding three hundred years. To ask why is urgent! To correctly answer may make a tremendously important difference in days to come!

The desire is sometimes expressed that the next revival should be an ethical one, and it is even prophesied by some that it is bound to be so. If this is meant to be a criticism upon past revivals, it is false to their history. Nothing can be easier than to take the Scottish revivals in succession and to show that each was in a very real sense an ethical movement. The various preachers may not have laid emphasis upon conduct, allowing right action to be the true outcome of a changed life, but that their discourses were ethical in their effects is beyond all reasonable doubt. In consequence of the open confession of wrongs done by converts to their neighbors, something of a scandal was produced at Kilsyth, and Robe had to take strong measures to bring such public unburdening of conscience to an end. Other leaders have had Robe's experience. In various places in the Highlands, revivals did much to banish the barbarous customs that prevailed. There is scarcely a narrative which does not contain statements regarding the decrease of crime, drunkenness, profanity, and idleness, both during the period each revival lasted and for some time after its more immediate manifestations had died down. Streets were declared to be quieter, property and persons safer, magistrates had less employment, and the whole community became more orderly and law-abiding.

The same story can be told of individuals who lived notoriously bad lives and were completely changed. It seems almost superfluous to cite examples, but two testimonies will suffice. A Skye minister, writing of the revival in that island in 1817, severely criticized the movement but was at the same time compelled to acknowledge that "some of both sexes, who were before of abandoned lives, came, at that time, under serious impressions of religion which have ever since remained undefaced; and to this day they continue patterns of piety, of zeal and devotedness to God." Recently the minister of that place could make the following remarkable statement: "The village of Ferryden was transformed by these revivals, chiefly the one of 1859-60. The most of the converts are now asleep, but the fruit of the work remains. We have a Deacons' Court of thirty-six, of whom thirty-one can engage in public prayer. They are nearly all either converts of these revivals or the sons of such converts." There can be no doubt about such movements being ethical.

A normal, indirect effect of revival is that the fresh and powerful awareness of God's immediate presence in seasons of

Summary and Conclusion

awakening has so affected even the unrepentant and notoriously wicked that the shame of sin has kept many, otherwise untouched by the revival, from forcibly pushing their irreligion and vice on the public. If you contrast the conduct of degenerate persons in days of moral and spiritual declension with the conduct of these same persons during seasons of spiritual awakening you have one of the strongest possible reasons for the most fervent longings and incessantly urgent prayers for revival that could ever be found.

Except in the case of the Reformation, material does not exist for estimating the effect which revival movements have had upon the general life of the community. The Reformation became a political enterprise, and its results are nothing less than the after-history of Scotland. It created a new era for almost every section of the nation and started fresh lines of thought and energy. "It found," said Dr. A. M. Fairbairn, "a people, barbarous, down-trodden, enslaved, made coarse and brutal by a long war of independence against their mighty neighbor; and, as it were by the breath of a creative word, it made that people stand up happy, free, educated and strong. Whatever success the sons of that land have achieved, they have achieved by the faith, and the political energy created of the faith, they received from the reformed religion."

Subsequent revivals do not always show such obvious results. The Covenanting struggle did much for civil and religious liberty, but it can hardly be classed among the phenomena discussed in these papers. On the other hand, the Cambuslang Revival had a powerful effect on the State Church and helped to modify and mould its history for more than a century afterwards. Not only did it win for the evangelical party within it the right to have their views expressed from the pulpits of the land, but in a very real sense it prepared for that event of national importance, the Disruption of 1843, by

Scotland Saw His Glory

making their continuance possible. On the whole, however, revival results are not likely to find their way into State documents or to be written large in definite events or movements. Their influence is more likely to resemble that of popular poetry and national song—pervasive, quiet, and unnoticed. It is curious that many Scottish historians have either assigned them no place among the forces that have molded Scottish character or have dismissed them in brief paragraphs, too often unsympathetic and sarcastic. Yet what Hugh Miller wrote of his native district could be said of many another place. Describing the effects of the revival which lingered in Easter Ross about the middle of the eighteenth century, he says they were felt "for more than eighty years after. There were few dwellings, however humble, in which regularly as the day rose and set, family worship was not kept; and in the course of an evening walk, the voice of Psalms might be heard from almost every hamlet. There was a higher tone of morals among the inhabitants than in many localities at least as generally favored; more content, too, with not less privation; no Chartism, no Socialism, no infidelity. The people in short were what the statesmen termed a 'well-conditioned people.' Effects such as these should render even the utilitarian tolerant of revivals." The whole district is called the "Garden of Ross-shire," and it would take much absurd boldness to deny that part of its beauty and productiveness is not due to its religious history.

In short, revivals in the past have done much to strengthen the Scottish character and to provide the land with those men who have carried its name for integrity and industry over the world. At the present time, as in former years, there is need for the urgent cry to go up:

"O Lord, revive Thy work in the midst of the years, in the midst of the years make known; in wrath remember mercy."

Bibliography

In this volume no attempt is made to provide an extensive bibliography of revivals in Scotland. Readers desiring the same are urged to note the extensive listings in the indexes of the following two annotated bibliographies:

Roberts, Richard Owen - Revival Literature: an Annotated Bibliography with Biographical and Historical Notices. Wheaton, Illinois: Richard Owen Roberts, Publishers, 1987. xxxii,575p. Details are provided on over 5,900 books and pamphlets, many of which deal directly with Scotland.

Roberts, Richard Owen - Whitefield in Print: a Bibliographical Record of Works By, For, and Against George Whitefield, With Annotations, Biographical and Historical Notices, and Bibliographies of His Associates and Contemporaries, the Whole Forming a Literary History of the Great Eighteenth Century Revival. Wheaton, Illinois: Richard Owen Roberts, Publishers, 1988. xlii,765p. Details on more than 8,000 books and pamphlets pertaining to the movement.

*****

Anderson, Jonathan Ranken - Days in Kirkfield: Being Discourses on a Revival Occasion in Kirkfield Chapel, Gorbals of Glasgow. From 24th November, 1839 to 5th January, 1840. London, Glasgow, and Edinburgh: Blackie & Son, 1872, vii,222p.

Anonymous - Narratives of Revivals of Religion in Scotland, Ireland, and Wales. Philadelphia: Presbyterian Board of Publication, 1842. 204p. The major portion of this little volume is devoted to Scotland, namely pp. 5-101; 122-138; and 159-204.

Anonymous - Reminiscences of the Revival of '59 and the Sixties. Aberdeen: The University Press, 1910. xix,147p.

Anonymous - Revivals of Religion. Glasgow: William Collins, nd. Thirteen parts.

Barnwell, R. Grant - Life of Moody and Sankey, the American Evangelists, Together With Scenes and Incidents of the Revival In Great Britain. Philadelphia: Printed for the Author, 1875. 32p.

Scotland Saw His Glory

Blaikie, William Garden - The Religious Awakening in Edinburgh in Connection With the Visit of Messrs. Moody and Sankey. Edinburgh: np, 1874. 8p.

Burns, Islay - Memoir of the Rev. Wm. C. Burns, M.A. Missionary to China From the English Presbyterian Church. New York: Robert Carter & Brothers, 1870. 595p.

Burns, Islay - The Pastor of Kilsyth; or, Memorials of the Life and Times of the Rev. W. H. Burns, D.D. London: T. Nelson & Sons, 1860. 288p.

Calderwood, David - The History of the Kirk of Scotland. Edited from the original manuscripts preserved in the British Museum, by the Rev. Thomas Thomson. Edinburgh: Wodrow Society, 1842-1849. 8 vols. A tremendous source of varied information on revivals and revival men.

Couper, W. J. - Scottish Revivals. Dundee: James P. Mathews & Co., Printers, 1918. 160p. This privately printed volume was limited to thirty-seven copies.

Currie, John - A New Testimony Unto, and Further Vindication of the Extraordinary Work of God at Cambuslang, Kilsyth, and Other Places in the West of Scotland. Edinburgh: Robert Smith, 1743. 63p.

Duncan, Mary [Grey] Lundie - History of Revivals of Religion in the British Isles, Especially in Scotland. Edinburgh: William Oliphant and Son, 1836. 402p. A very worthwhile volume, much of which is drawn from the pamphlets published by the Glasgow Revival Tract Society.

Fawcett, Arthur - The Cambuslang Revival: the Scottish Evangelical Revival of the Eighteenth Century. London: The Banner of Truth Trust, 1971. ix,256p. A much-needed study first written as a Ph.D. thesis for the University of Glasgow in 1952.

Fisher, James - A Review of the Preface to a Narrative of the Extraordinary Work at Kilsyth, and other Congregations in the Neighbourhood. Glasgow: John Bryce, 1742. 68p.

Fleming, Robert - The Fulfilling of the Scripture. Or an Essay, Shewing the Exact Accomplishment of the Word of God in His Works, Performed and to Be Performed, For Confirming of Believers and Convincing Atheists of the Present Time: Containing Some Rare Histories of the Works and the Servants of God in the Church of Scotland. Boston: Rogers and Fowle, 1743, xxiv,xii,522p. A work directly relating to revivals which was enlarged from "The Confirming Work of Religion."

Gillon, R. Moffat - John Davidson of Prestonpans: Reformer, Preacher and Poet in the Generation After Knox. London: James Clarke & Co.,

Bibliography

(1936). 275p. Chapter 7 (pp.147-166) is on the Revival of 1596 and is strikingly similar to Couper's chapter but with documentation and some additional material.

Glasgow Revival Tract Society - Narratives of Revivals of Religion in Scotland, Ireland, and Wales. Published under the auspices of The Glasgow Revival Tract Society. Glasgow: William Collins, 1839. 132p.

The Glasgow Weekly History Relating to the Late Progress of the Gospel at Home and Abroad; Being a Collection of Letters Partly Reprinted From the London-Weekly-History, and Partly Printed First Here at Glasgow. For the year 1741-1742. Glasgow: Printed by William Duncan, 1742,1743. 52 issues. Splendid first-hand accounts of Whitefield and the Evangelical Revival.

Haldane, Alexander - Memoirs of the lives of Robert Haldane of Airthrey and of his brother James Alexander Haldane. New York: Robert Carter & Brothers, 1853. 604p.

Hetherington, William Maxwell - History of the Church of Scotland from the Introduction of Christianity to the Period of the Disruption. Edinburgh: John Johnstone, 1848 7th ed. 2 vols.

Kennedy, John - The 'Apostle of the North.' The life and Labours of the Rev. Dr. M'Donald. Toronto: James Campbell and Son, 1866. 336p.

M'Crie, Thomas - The Story of the Scottish Church from the Reformation to the Disruption, London: Blackie & Son, 1875. xv,576p.

MacFarlan, Duncan - The Revivals of the Eighteenth Century, Particularly at Cambuslang. With Three Sermons by the Rev. George Whitefield Taken in Shorthand. Wheaton, Illinois: Richard Owen Roberts, Publishers, 1980. 263,49p. Reprinted from the 1847 Edinburgh edition.

MacGillivray, Angus - Sketches of Religion and Revivals of Religion in the North Highlands During the Last Century. Edinburgh: John Maclaren, 1859. 47p.

Macinnes, John - The Evangelical Movement in the Highlands of Scotland, 1688-1800. Aberdeen: The University Press, 1951. xii,299p.

MacKay, John - The Church in the Highlands: or the Progress of Evangelical Religion in Gaelic Scotland, 563-1843. London: Hodder & Stoughton, [1914?] 280p.

McKay, W. A. - Outpourings of the Spirit; or, a Narrative of Spiritual Awakenings in Different Ages and Countries. Philadelphia: Presbyterian Board of Publication, 1890. 141p. Chapter 4 (pp.41-55) provides but brief details on Revivals in Scotland.

Scotland Saw His Glory

MacPherson, John - Revival and Revival-Work. A Record of the Labours of D. L. Moody and Ira D. Sankey, and Other Evangelists. London: Morgan & Scott, nd. viii,314p.

MacRae, Alexander - Revivals in the Highlands and Islands of the 19th Century. Stirling: E. Mackay, 1905. 203p.

Ministers of the Church of Scotland - Lectures on the Revival of Religion. Wheaton, Illinois: Richard Owen Roberts, Publishers, 1980. xxvi,444p. Reprinted from the 1840 Glasgow edition.

Peddie, Mrs. Robert - A Consecutive Narrative of the Remarkable Awakening in Edinburgh under the Labours of Messrs. Moody and Sankey. London: S. W. Partridge & Co., 1874. 96p.

Randolph, Anson Davies Fitz - Narrative of Messrs. Moody and Sankey's Labors in Great Britain and Ireland, with Eleven Addresses and Lectures in Full. New York: A. D. F. Randolph & Co., 1875. 247p.

Reid, William - Authentic Records of Revival, Now in Progress in the United Kingdom. Wheaton, Illinois: Richard Owen Roberts, Publishers, 1980. viii,478p. First issued in London in 1860.

Robe, James - The Christian Monthly History; or, An Account of the Revival and Progress of Religion, Abroad and at Home. Edinburgh: R. Fleming and A. Allison, 1743-1746. In 2 vols.

Robe, James - A Faithful Narrative of the Extraordinary Work of the Spirit of God, at Kilsyth, and other Congregations in the Neighbourhood, near Glasgow. Glasgow: William Duncan, 1742. 224p. [For numerous other titles by Robe see the Annotated Bibliographies listed above.]

Stewart, Alexander - Account of a Late Revival of Religion in a Part of the Highlands of Scotland, in a Letter to the Rev. David Black. Edinburgh: Printed by J. Ritchie for Ogle and Aikman, 1800. 38p.

Webster, Alexander - Divine Influence the True Spring of the Extraordinary Work at Cambuslang and Other Places in the West of Scotland; Illustrated in a Letter. Edinburgh: T. Lumisden and J. Robertson, 1742. vi,54p.

Index

Abbey of Holyrood, 45
Aberdeen, 183, 238, 281-284, 291, 294, 296, 300, 303, 305, 316
Aberdeen Herald, 282-284
Aberdeen Presbytery, 281-282, 287
Aberdeenshire, 296
Aberfeldy, 213, 246, 250, 252
Abernethy, 194
Achaia, 325
Acharn, 238, 240
Adam, Mr. of Cathcart, 140
Adams, William, 9
Adderny, 114
Adrossan, 292
Aitken, Canon, 296
Allan, Alexander, 98
Alness, 182, 278, 283
America, 9, 10, 28, 126, 130, 137, 166, 167, 184, 187, 203, 219, 240, 291, 297, 308, 309, 310, 313, 323, 325
Ancrum, 282
Anderson, Dr. of Glasgow, 276, 332
Angus, 13
Annals of the Disruption, 284
Annan, 297
Annan, Robert, 295, 297
Annick, 99-101, 330
Anstruther, 94
Apostle of the North, 26
Arbroath, 316
Ardeer, 140
Ardeonaig, 238, 239, 241, 242, 243, 244, 245, 247, 286
Ardtalnaig, 238, 239
Arndilly, 295, 296
Arndilly, Grant, 296
Arran, 215-224, 264, 330
Assembly of 1596, 16
Associate Presbytery, 124, 192
Associate Synod (Burgher), 249
Assynt, 260
Atholl, Duke of, 197

Auchterarder, 179
Augustine, 35
Avoch, 182
Ayr, 17, 27, 66, 73, 74, 76, 79, 80, 81, 99, 108
Ayrshire, 170, 292, 316, 330
Ayrshire Express, 292
Ayrshire, North, 330

Back, 263
Balcalquall, Walter, 87
Baldernock, 171, 174
Balfour, Dr. of Glasgow, 221
Balfour, James, 38
Balfour, John, 180, 181
Ballanytne, Richard, 62
Ballymena, 291
Balnaguard, 287
Banff, 300
Banffshire, 300
Baptists, 213, 240
Barclay, George, 123
Bayne, Kenneth, 221
Beaton, Cardinal David, 31, 35-36, 65-69
Beaton, James Archbishop, 64, 65
Belfast, 296, 317
Bellamy, Joseph, 234
Ben Lawers, 243
Bengal, 331
Bennet, Mr., 122
Berbera, Island of, 261
Berriedale, 302
Berwick, 39, 313
Berwick-on-Tweed, 290
Berwickshire, 183, 299
Beza, 35
Black Rubric, 39
Black, David, 96, 199-202, 208
Blackburn, Peter, 87
Blackness, 78
Blaikie, William Garden, 319
Blair, Parish of, 208

341

Scotland Saw His Glory

Blair, Robert, 100, 103, 104, 105, 106, 107, 112
Blair-Atholl, 197, 202
Blairgowrie, 283
Blantyre, 140, 169
Bochim, 91, 153
Bonar of Collace, 280
Bonar, Andrew, 278
Bonar, Horatius, 278, 282
Bonner, John, 140, 143
Book of Discipline, 56
Borders, 73, 74, 297
Boston, Mass., 169
Boston, Thomas, 263
Botanical Gardens, 315
Bothkenner, 70
Bothwell, 169
Bothwell Bridge, 121
Bowman, Robert, 131, 134
Boyd of Trochrigg, 327
Boyd, Robert, 105, 107
Bracadale, 230, 232, 234
Brahan, 260
Breadalbane, 26, 27, 229, 237-254, 286-288, 327, 328, 329, 331
Bridgegate Church, 292
Britain, 30
British and Foreign Evangelical Review, 304
British Colonies, 132
Brodick, 223
Brown, Hume, 12
Brown, James, 318
Brown, John, 195-196, 249-250
Bruan, 223
Bruce of Kennet, 140
Bruce, Robert, 17, 86, 89, 113, 115, 121, 122, 327
Buchanan, Dr., 146, 290
Buchanan, Thomas, 86, 92
Buckie, 300, 301
Buckle, Dr., 55
Burgher Synod, 249
Burleigh, Lord, 50
Burns, Dr. of Paisley, 275-276
Burns, Robert, 53
Burns, William Chalmers, 273-288, 302, 328
Burns, William H., 212-213, 269-288, 328
Burnside, James of Kirkintilloch, 154, 176
Burton, Hill, 16, 92, 145, 185
Bute, 222
Butler, Bishop, 125

Cadder, 20
Cairns, Principal John, 125, 313, 318, 322
Caithness, 25, 301, 316
Calder, 122-123, 154, 173-175
Calderwood, David, 17, 83, 92, 93, 94, 97, 113
Callernish, 258, 261
Calvin, John, 39, 326
Cambridge, 65, 201, 214
Cambuslang, 9, 23-24, 109, 125-144, 145, 148, 149, 151, 153, 154, 157, 165, 166, 167, 168, 169, 170, 173, 174, 179, 183, 185-196, 207, 290, 325, 326, 327, 328, 330, 331, 335
Cameronians, 189, 191, 192
Campbell of Breadalbane, 329
Campbell, David, 244, 247, 254
Campbell, Dugald, 286
Campbell, Duncan, 254
Campbell, John, 215, 239
Campbell, Mr., 297
Campbell, Patrick, 254
Campbeltown, 316
Campsie, 154, 155, 175-176, 177
Canada, 279
Carlyle, Thomas, 12, 34, 49, 59, 60, 125
Carnock, 154
Carrick, 105
Carstairs, John, 20, 122, 123
Carswell, Bishop, 256
Cartlechan, 240
Carubbers' Close Mission, 323
Castle Park, 302
Castlelaw, William, 100, 108, 112
Cathcart, 122, 140, 169
Catholics, Roman, 43, 45
Cavers, 273
Cellardyke, 302
Cennick, John, 152

Index

Chalmers, James, 304
Chalmers, Thomas, 234
Charles I, 102
Charles II, 20, 139
Chicago, Illinois, 320
China, 279
Christian Monthly History, 146, 168
Christian, The, 329
Chrystoun, 121
Church Missionary Society, 214
Church of England, 38-39
Church of Rome, 63
Clark's Lives, 72
Cleghorn, John, 26
Clyde, Valley of, 112
Clydesdale, 120, 123
Cockenzie, 302
Coldingham, 183
College of Glasgow, 105
Colville, John of Culross, 113
Comizars, 193
Communion occasions, 24, 26, 136-142, 153-157, 168, 178, 180-181, 202, 204-206, 215, 222, 245, 247, 254, 261-263, 274-275, 280, 283, 326-328
Complaynt of Scotland, 51
Comrie, 250
Concert of Prayer, 183-184
Congregationalalist, 213, 239, 282
Continent, 30, 39
Cook, Archibald, 223
Cook, Auntie, 320-321
Cook, Finlay, 223, 264
Cooper, William, 70-72
Corn Exchange, 312
Cotter's Saturday Night, 53
County Antrim, 291
Court of High Commission, 101
Covenant, 313, 335
Covenanters, 145
Cowgate, 321
Cowper, William, 16
Crawford, Mr., 99
Crieff, 179, 303
Cromarty, 182
Cromwell, Oliver, 20
Cross, 264

Croy, 228
Cullen, 299, 300
Culross, Lady, 113-115
Cumbernauld, 114, 145, 150, 176
Cumming of Dunbarney, 278, 280
Cunningham, David, 105
Cunningham, Robert, 295, 297
Currie, Mr., 140

Dairsie, 128
Dalgleish, Nicol, 86, 87
Dauphin of France, 45
Davidson, George, 301
Davidson, John, 16, 84-98
Davidson, Thomas, 300
Davies, Howell, 126
Debatable Ground, 72
Defoe, Daniel, 22
Denny, 152, 176
Dewar, Daniel, 238
Dewar, James, 239
Dickson, David, 17, 74, 101-109, 112, 113, 120, 327, 333
Dilmaurs, 193
Dingwall, 212
Disruption of 1843, 27, 287, 335
Dissenters, 189, 190
Dixon, Dr. of Montrose, 298
Doddridge, Philip, 148
Dornoch Firth, 182
Douglas, 140
Douglas of Cavers, 273
Dreghorn, 99, 293
Drummond, Henry, 28, 317-218, 325, 327
Duff, Alexander, 214
Duff, James, 214
Duirinish, 213, 228, 234, 235
Dumbarton, 100
Dumfries, 297
Dunbar, 42, 66, 302
Dunbarney, 278
Dunbeath, 302
Duncan, Alexander, 133
Duncan, Mrs. Lundie, 223, 268
Dundee, 13, 26, 38, 65, 66, 134-135, 149, 165-166, 183, 247, 273-274, 277-279, 288, 296-297, 302, 310, 314, 316, 328

343

Dundee Psalms, 14
Dunfermline, 95, 192
Dunipace, 176
Dunkeld, 202, 208, 253
Dunkeld, Bishop, of 32
Dunoon, Walter, 182-183

East Kilbride, 169
East Lothian, 35, 290
Easter Ross, 24, 179, 283, 330, 336
Edinburgh 16, 23, 40, 42, 43, 76, 78, 81, 86, 94, 95, 98, 102, 118-119, 134, 137, 139, 140, 165, 166, 186, 199, 200, 253, 256, 257, 274, 303, 309, 310, 311-315, 317, 319, 321, 323
Edinburgh Gaelic Society, 257
Edinburgh University, 28, 86
Edmonstone, Sir Archibald, 276
Edward VI, 38, 39
Edwards, Jonathan, 10, 98, 126, 130, 167, 250
Eglintoun, Anna Countess of, 105-106
Eglintoun, Earl of, 102
Eigg, 285
Elchies, Lord, 139
Elgin, 296, 317
England, 22, 30, 38, 39, 42, 43, 44, 72, 78, 126, 127, 130, 139, 184, 279, 303, 310, 319, 321, 323, 325
Erskine, Charles, 140
Erskine, Ebenezer, 125-126
Erskine, John, 139, 195, 327
Erskine, Ralph, 188, 194-196
Established Church Presbyteries, 293
Established Church Assembly Hall, 311
Europe, 11, 12, 29, 30, 44
Ewing Place Church, 318
Eyemouth, 299, 302

Fair City, 303
Fairbairn, A. M., 335
Fairy Bridge, 285
Farquharson, John, 229-230, 237-240, 242
Fenwick, 19, 103
Ferguson, David, 95, 96
Ferguson, John, 80, 82
Ferintosh, 260-261, 278, 285

Ferryden, 27, 296, 298-299, 331, 334
Fife, 13, 22
Fife, Synod of, 95
Fifeshire, 152
Findhorn, 300
Findlater, Robert, 240-254
Findochty, 300
Finlayson, Robert, 258, 261, 264
Fintry, 178
Firth of Forth, 302
Fisher, James, 195
Five Articles of Perth, 101
Fleming, Margaret, 105-106
Fleming, Robert, 10, 18, 75-76, 82, 101, 104, 107-108, 115, 117, 120, 127
Flyster of Alness, 278
Folger, Peter, 9
Forbes, Mr., 77
Force of Truth, 200
Forfarshire, 27
Forlong, Gordon, 296
Forres, 300
Forsyth, James, 171-174
Forth, 171, 302
Fortingall, 241, 245, 250, 254, 286
Fowlis, Lady, 21
France, 11, 30, 37, 43, 44, 45, 78, 80, 81
Frankfort, 40
Fraser, Dr. of Kirkhill, 24
Free Assembly Hall, 311-313
Free Church, 285, 290, 292
Free Church Assembly, 290, 295
Free Church at Pitlochry, 214
Free Church Synod, 293
Free High Church, 312
Free Methodist, 320
Freehold, New Jersey, 126
Frith, 13
Froude, Mr., 50

Gaelic, 198, 227, 231, 245, 255, 256, 267, 316, 330
Gaelic Bible, 256 -258, 263
Gaelic School Scoiety, 256-260, 264, 284
Galashiels, 22
Gargunnock, 177
General Assembly, 44, 70, 83-98, 255-

Index

257
Geneva, 34, 39, 40, 52, 278
Gentleman in the Gorbals of Glasgow, 131
Germany, 13, 64
Gib, Adam, 195
Gilfillan, George, 250, 314
Gilfillan, Samuel, 250, 251
Gillespie, George, 326
Gillespie, Thomas, 154
Gillies, Francis, 283
Gillies, John, 22, 64, 118, 123, 140, 167-168
Gillon of Wallhouse, 140
Gilpin, Bernard, 73
Glasgow, 19, 20, 63, 100, 117, 118, 119, 130, 131, 134, 140, 150, 154, 167, 168, 213, 221, 257, 270, 272, 278, 292, 293, 296, 297, 299, 303, 305, 314-316, 318, 323
Glasgow, Bishop of, 66
Glasgow Bulletin, 292
Glasgow College, 34
Glasgow Herald, 308, 314
Glasgow Revival Tracts, 216
Glasgow University, 100, 217
Glasgow Weekly History, 146
Glen Sannox, 218
Glen Tilt, 237
Glenbriarachan, 208, 213
Glencairn, Earl of, 66
Glenlyon, 241, 243, 244, 246, 247, 248, 249, 250, 252, 253, 254, 286, 331
Glenorchy, Lady, 241, 300
Golspie, 166, 182
Gordon, Dutchess of, 302
Gordon, Frank, 318
Gordon, John, 296
Grampains, 179, 252
Grandtully, 287
Grange, 300
Grant, Hay M., 295, 296
Grant, William, 27
Grassmarket, 321
Gray, Andrew, 121
Gray of Perth, 280
Great Awakening, 10

Greenock, 170, 221, 303, 316
Greenwich, 39
Greyfriars Churchyard, 18
Grindlay, 154
Guise family, 44
Guthrie, Thomas, 292
Guthrie, William, 19, 20, 103

Haddington, 33, 34
Haddington, Presbytery of, 85, 87
Haddo's Hole, 86
Haldane, James, 25, 26, 202, 203, 215, 229, 237, 240
Haldane, Robert, 25, 26, 229, 237, 240, 278
Halley, William, 178, 179
Hallhill, 113
Hamilton, 19
Hamilton, Archbishop, 42
Hamilton, Duke of, 127
Hamilton, John of Barony, 167, 169
Hamilton of Douglas, 140
Hamilton of Glasgow, 136
Hamilton of Westburn, 139
Hamilton, Patrick, 49, 63-65, 69
Hamilton, Wm of Bothwell, 169
Hammond, Edward Payson, 297-299
Harris, Isle of, 259, 262-264, 293-294
Harris, Howell. 126
Hebrides, 290
Henderson, Alexander, 18, 113, 140
Herbert, George, 309
Heugh, Dr., 276
Hewison, King, 92
Highland Society, 198
Highlands, 25, 27, 215, 225-235, 237-256, 261, 286, 315-316, 326, 330, 334
Hog's Park, 247
Holland, 116, 142
Holyrood, 46
Holywood, Ireland, 119
Home and Foreign Missionary Magazine, 273
Home, John, 112-113
Hooker, Samuel, 9
Hunter, Mr., 154
Huntley, 294, 300, 302

345

Independents, 217, 246, 254, 276
India, 214, 331
Inverness, 223, 228, 230, 300, 317
Inverness Society for Educating the Poor, 226, 257-258
Invervar, 248
Ireland, 10, 79, 107, 115, 119, 139, 215, 279, 291, 292, 296, 299, 301, 307, 317
Irish Bible, 256
Irvine, 17, 74, 99, 101-104, 108, 109, 112-113, 120, 134, 139, 140, 170, 171, 330, 333
Irvine, Alexander, 253
Italy, 325

James II, 20
James IV, 31
James V, 44
James VI, 78, 106
Jedburgh, 283
John ab Ulmis, 52
John o' Groats, 290, 316
John o' Groat Journal, 301
Johnston, Adam, 87
Johnston, John, 87, 117
Jones, Griffith, 126

Keith, 300
Kelman, John, 310
Kelso, 278, 282
Kenmore, 241, 245
Kennedy, Hugh 79, 80
Kennedy, James of Aberfedy, 24, 213, 246-248, 250-251
Kennedy, John, 81-82
Kennedy, Quentin, 32
Kennet, 140
Kibble Palace, 315
Kilbride, 170, 220
Killearn, 178, 182
Killiecrankie, Pass of, 197, 202
Killin, 238, 240, 243, 245, 250, 256
Killing Times, 19
Kilmarnock, 111, 120, 139, 170, 171, 217, 224
Kilmaurs, 194

Kilmorie, 216, 217, 220, 224
Kilmuir, 182, 226, 228, 230, 234
Kilrenny, 95, 97
Kilsyth, 27, 140, 142, 145-163, 165, 166, 170, 171, 175, 176, 177, 179, 183, 193, 212, 213, 254, 269-288, 326, 327, 328, 331- 332, 334
Kiltearn, 24, 241, 254
King's Chaplain, 39
King's Confession, 92
Kinglassie, 140
Kippen, 178
Kirkcaldy, 302
Kirkcudbright, 73
Kirkhill, 24
Kirkintilloch, 20, 122, 152, 154, 174, 176, 270
Kirkton, Mr., 17, 19, 20
Kist o' Whistles, 309
Kneep, 261
Knock, 263-264
Knox, John, 14-17, 29-62, 66, 75, 87, 256, 313
Knox's Liturgy, 256

Lambert, 64
Lanark, 18, 19
Lanarkshire, 127, 145
Landsborough, Dr., 224
Lang, Andrew, 92
Lapsly, John, 154
Larbert, 152, 154, 176, 278
Latheron, 301
Laud, Archbishop, 101
Lauder, Priest, 67
Law, James, 87
Lawers, 245, 247, 254, 286
Lecky, William, 53
Leith, 45, 287, 310
Lewis, Isle of, 255-268, 290, 293, 294, 301, 330
Lindsay, David, 86
Lindsay, John, 65
Lindsay, Lord, 43
Lindsay, Principal, 10, 11, 28, 325
Linlithgow, 77, 154, 171
Linlithgow, Earl of, 106-107

Index

Linlithgow, Presbytery of, 145
Lionel, 293
Liverpool, 310
Livingston, John, 18, 19, 106, 107, 111-124, 145, 275, 282, 327
Livingston, Lady, 94
Loch Roag, 261, 265
Loch Tay, 238-239, 241, 242, 246-247, 253-254, 286
Lochabar, 255
Lochranza, 216, 220, 222
Lochs, 258, 264
Lochtayside, 229, 241, 245, 250
Logie, 182
Logiealmond, 250
Logierait, 287
Lollardism, 11, 330
London, 39, 77, 78
Long Dreghorn, 170
Lothian, 22, 112, 293
Love, Dr., 221, 223
Lowlands, 27, 52, 114, 249, 316
Luther, Martin, 13, 64
Lybster, 302
Lyndale, 234

M'Bride, Neil, 217-224
M'Bride, Peter, 223-224
M'Cheyne, Robert Murray, 274, 278-279, 288, 302
M'Coll, Alexander, 261
M'Cowan, Mr., 229
M'Crie, Thomas, 92, 94
M'Culloch, Rbt. of Dairsie, 128
M'Culloch, Wm., 127-144, 148, 153-154, 166, 186-188, 207, 326, 328, 332
M'Gavin, William, 213, 223, 250-252
M'Gillivray of Strathfillan, 247
M'Iver, Angus, 261
M'Kerrow, Mr., 196
M'Kinnon, William, 222
M'Kneight, Rev. of Long Dreg-horn, 170
M'Knight of Irvine, 136, 140
M'Laurin, Jn. of Ramshorn, 150
M'Leod, Roderick, 285
M'Millan, Angus, 216-224
Macalister, John, 223

MacColl, D., 292
Macdonald, John of Ferintosh, 26-27, 243-245, 247, 248-249, 251, 259, 260-263, 265, 278, 285, 328, 330
MacDonald, George, 299
Macdonald, John of Urquhart, 283
Macdonald, Lord, 233
Macdonald, Robert, 283
MacEwen, Professor, 196
Macfarlan, Duncan, 133
MacGillivray, A., 24
Macgregor of Dundee, 247
Mackay, Alexander, 217
Mackenzie, Mrs. Stuart, 260
Mackie, James of St. Ninians, 154, 177
Mackquherne, John, 87
MacLaurin, John of Glasgow, 136, 140, 154, 167, 168, 176, 196
Maclean, Peter, 261
Macleod, Alexander of Harris, 259, 260-268, 328
Macleod, John, 258
Macleod, Norman, 284
Macleod, Roderick, 234
MacPhail, John S. 226, 231
MacPherson, John, 288
Macrae, John, 261, 268
Maidenkirk, 290
Malan, Caesar, 278
Marchioness of Hamilton, 113
Marischal College, 316
Marrow Controversy, 23
Martin, Donald of Kilmuir, 228, 230
Martyn, Henry, 214
Mary Queen of Scots, 44-47
Mary, Queen Regent, 39-40, 41, 42, 43, 113
Mather, Cotton, 9
Mather, Eleazer, 9
Mather, Increase, 9
Matheson, Duncan, 295-297, 302
Mathieson, Angus, 261
Mauchline, 66
Maxwell of Rutherglen, 140
McKenzie, William, 24
McKnight, William, 109
Mearns, 170

347

Scotland Saw His Glory

Meek, James, 134, 141
Melancthon, 64
Melville, Andrew, 77, 86, 87, 89, 96, 327
Melville, James, 15, 62, 83, 86, 87, 93, 94, 95, 96, 113
Melvin, Thomas, 122, 123
Methodists, 126, 271, 276
Middle Ages, 11, 30
Miller, Hugh, 21, 283-284, 330, 336
Miller, James, 318
Milne, John, 279-280, 282
Milton of Lawers, 241
Missionary Magazine, 211
Mitchell, Professor, 13
Moderatism, 24
Moncrieff, Henry, 189
Monivaird, 154, 178, 179
Montrose, 145, 298, 303
Moody, Dwight Lyman, 27-28, 297, 307-324, 329-330, 332
Moray Firth, 255, 290, 296, 299, 305, 315, 316
Moray, Earl of, 62
Morayshire, 301
More, Ingram, 131, 134, 331
Morison, John, 259-261, 264
Morrison, Hector, 261
Moulin, 24, 25, 197-214, 222, 228, 237, 307, 328, 329, 331
Muir of Bothwell, 122
Muirkirk, 74
Munro, Donald, 230-235, 259
Musselburgh, 297
Muthill, 152, 166, 178, 179, 183, 331

Nairn, 239, 317
Naphtali, 19
Narnock, 300
National Covenant, 16-19, 92, 106, 117
Negative Confession, 92
Ness, 263
New College, 133, 317, 318
New England, 10, 98, 126
New Guinea, 304
New York City, 291, 321
Newcastle, 39, 310
Newhaven, 302

Newton, John, 203
Nicolson, James, 86, 89
Nigg, 180, 183
Nisbet, Alexander, 109
Nithsdale, 72
North Berwick, 302
North Bute, 219
North, Brownlow, 294-296, 315, 327
Nungate, 34

Oban, 239, 316
Obsdale, 21
Old Monkland, 169
Orkneys, 25
Orphan Homes of Scotland, 323
Orwell, 194
Oughterson, John, 150
Outer Islands, 268

Pabay, 265
Paisley, 19, 117, 274, 316
Paisley, John, 117
Parkhill, 296
Parliament, 41, 43, 65
Patrick, Alexander, 154
Pattison, Mark, 125
Peden's Life, 121
Persie, 212
Perth, 14, 40, 41, 70, 176, 199, 244, 279-280, 281, 303, 316
Perthshire, 25-26, 178, 202, 212, 237, 249, 330
Peterhead, 295, 317
Phillips, Philip, 309
Pitlochry, 197, 214
Pittenweem, 302
Pollock, Robert, 86, 89
Pont, Robert, 86
Port Glasgow, 292
Porteous, Mr., 154
Portessie, 300, 301
Portgordon, 300
Portlossie, 299
Portknockie, 299-300
Portree, 229-230, 234
Portsoy, 300
Prayer Book, 38-39

348

Index

Presbytery of Dingwall, 241
Presbytery of Skye, 226
Prestonpans, 84
Prince Charlie, 225
Prince, Thomas, 169
Provost of Ayr, 79
Pulteneytown, 302

Quakers, 193
Quarrier, Mr., 323

Radcliffe, Reginald, 294-296
Ramsay, Mr., 122
Ramshorn, 150, 167
Randolph, 43
Rattray, 283
Rattray, Jean, 214
Reay, 223
Reformation, 11-16, 18, 19, 29-62, 84, 91, 95, 112, 225, 255, 331, 335
Reformed Church, 13, 327
Reformed Faith, 34, 37
Reformed Presbyterian Magazine, 115
Reid, Mr. of Stevenston, 109
Relief Church, 154, 271, 276
Revival of 1596, 83-98
Revival of 1859-1860, 27, 289-305, 307, 311, 322, 330, 332, 333, 334
Revival, The, 329
Revolution, 22
Rhineland, 325
Ridge, William, 114-115
Riff, 261
Risby, James, 63
Robe, James, 117, 135, 140, 141, 142, 145-163, 165, 166, 168-172, 174, 176, 177, 178, 179, 187-188, 190, 195, 196, 269, 271-273, 326, 328, 332, 334
Robe, Michael, 145
Robertland, Lady, 105-106
Robertson of Irvine, 292
Robertson, Dr., 143, 186
Rochelle, 81
Rochester, Bishopric of, 39
Rodel, 259
Rogart, 182
Rosemarkie, 181

Ross, 23
Ross, Kenneth, 261
Ross-shire, 21, 24, 65, 211, 241, 284, 316, 327, 329
Rosskeen, 181
Rothesay, 223, 224, 316
Rowland, Daniel, 126
Royal Bounty Fund, 141
Rum, 285
Rutherford, Samuel, 103
Rutherglen, 140

Sage of Resolis, 262
Saline, 154
Saltcoats, 323
Sankey, Ira D., 27-28, 289, 297, 307-324, 332
Sannox, 216, 217
Scalpay, 262
Scaurnose, 299
Scott, Apologetical Narration, 94
Scott, Thomas, 200
Scottish Cong'l Magazine, 308
Seaforth, Earl of, 260
Seceders, 126, 190, 192, 194, 196
Secession, 23, 154, 190, 193, 195
Secession Church, 126, 189, 195
Second Confession of Faith, 92
Selkirk, 72
Sellars, Mr., 292
Service Book, 101
Sevennois, 193
Shaw, John, 213-214, 228, 234, 328
Shaw, Lachlan, 255
Sheld, Laird of, 66
Shepard, Thomas, 9
Sheriff, Mr., 200
Shisken, 216
Shorter Catechism, 242, 256
Shotts, Kirk of, 10, 17, 18, 20, 111-124, 137, 145, 193, 275, 290, 325, 326, 328
Sievewright, Dr., 180, 203
Simeon, Charles, 201-204, 214, 307
Simpson, Patrick, 86, 89, 96
Sinclair, Sir John, 203
Skye, 213-214, 225-235, 259, 284-285,

325, 328, 330, 331, 334
Sleat, 226, 285
Smith, Catharine, 265-268
Smith, George Adam, 318-319
Smith, John, 154
Smyton, David, 193, 194
Snizort, 230, 232, 285
Snow, Mrs., 320-321
Society for Propagating Christian Knowledge, 231, 241, 256, 259
Society for the Propagation of the Gospel at Home, 237
Solway, 290
Solway Moss, 44
Somerset, Protector, 13
Sommerville, A. N., 272, 278
Spain, 85, 87
Spiers, Mr., 154
Spottiswood, John, 93
Spurgeon, Charles Haddon, 324
St. Andrews, 15, 18, 36, 38, 42, 62, 64, 65, 197, 279
St. Andrews Presbytery, 95
St. Cuthberts, 86
St. Giles, 44, 45, 46, 48, 60, 62, 86, 91
St. Kilda, 259
St. Leonards, 279-280
St. Madoes, 199, 200-201
St. Ninians, 154, 176, 177
St. Peters, 274, 278, 288
Stalker, James, 318
Stark, James, 294, 305
Steinish, 293
Stevenson, Mr., 99
Stevenston, 170
Stewart of Molin, 270
Stewart, Alexander, 197-214, 222
Stewart, James, 256
Stewart, John, 73, 78-82
Stewart, Major-General of Garth, 252
Stewart, Margaret, 198
Stewarton, 10, 17, 99-109, 111-112, 124, 139, 170, 187, 193, 330
Stirling, 152, 171, 176, 282
Stirling Castle, 31
Stirling, Presbytery of, 94
Stirlingshire, 70

Stornoway, 264
Stow, 22
Strath, 285
Strathardle, 251
Strathfillan, 241, 247
Strathmartin, 167
Strathtay, 286-288
Sunderland, 310
Supreme Court, 96
Sutherland, 23
Sutherland, Earl of, 182-183
Sutherland, John, 166
Synod of Argyle, 256
Synod of Boston, 9
Synod of Fife, 84, 92
Synod of Glasgow, 189
Synod of Teviotdale, 282

Tain, 223, 283, 317
Tarbat, 283
Tarbert, 294
Tarbet, 262
Temple Patrick, 79
Thirty-Nine Articles, 39
Thomas a' Kempis, 33
Thompson, Andrew, 309
Thomson, J. H., 115
Thurso, 291
Times of Blessing, 329
Tiree, 330
Tolbooth Church, 312
Tongue, 24
Torphichen, 140, 143
Torrey, Reuben Archer, 321
Trinity Church, Cambridge, 201
Trochrigg, 105
Tulloch, Principal, 23
Turiff, 102
Turner, James, 295-296
Tweedale, 293
Tyndale, William, 13
Tyne, River, 34

Uig, 257-265, 268
Uig Bay, 229
Uig Ferry, 263
Ulster, 291

Index

Unish, 284-285
United Presbyterian, 293
University of Glasgow, 34, 101
Urquhart, 26, 283

Visible Signs of the Lord's return to Scotland, 140

Wales, 126, 325
Walker, Mr., 121
Walker, N. L., 28
Walker of Muthil, 271
Walker of Truro, 200
Walker, Patrick, 123, 124
Wallace, Mr. of Baldernock, 171
Wallhouse, 140
Warden, John of Gargunnock, 154, 177
Warden, Mr. of Calder, 174-175
Warner of Ardeer, 140
Warner, Patrick, 109
Waternish Point, 284
Watson, Sheriff, 323
Weaver, Richard, 303
Webster, Alexander, 137, 138, 140, 141, 143, 186, 193, 195
Weddeerburn, 14
Weekly History, 130
Welch, John, 108
Wellington Street United Presbyterian Church, 315
Welsh, John, 17, 72-82
Welsh, Josiah, 79
Wesley, John, 126, 187, 194
Westminster Confession, 332
Whitburn, 249
Whitefield, George, 22-24, 125-144, 152, 156, 165, 170, 176, 185-196, 307, 308, 311, 315
Whyte, Alexander, 326
Wick, 26, 301-302, 317
Wickliff, John, 63
Wigton, Countess of, 114
William and Mary, 22
Williamson, H. W., 294, 300
Willison, John, 135, 149, 165-166, 195
Wilson, Dr. J. H., 311, 318
Wishart, George, 35-36, 65-70, 73
Witness Newspaper, 214, 291
Wodrow, Robert, 17, 21, 99, 103, 104, 106, 107, 112, 117, 127, 129-130, 139
Wood, Julius, 290
Wynd Journal, 329
Wynds, 292

York, England, 310
Young Men's Christian Associations, 323
Young of Logiealmond, 250, 251
Young, James, 133

351